YOU MUST BE
THIS TALL
TO RIDE

B.J. HOLLARS

YOU MUST BE
THIS TALL
TO RIDE

CONTEMPORARY WRITERS
TAKE YOU INSIDE THE STORY

WRITER'S DIGEST BOOKS

www.writersdigest.com
Cincinnati, Ohio

For more resources for writers, visit www.writersdigest.com/books.

To receive a free weekly e-mail newsletter delivering tips and updates about writing and about Writer's Digest products, register directly at http://newsletters.fwmedia.com.

13 12 11 10 09   5 4 3 2 1

Distributed in Canada by Fraser Direct, 100 Armstrong Avenue, Georgetown, Ontario, Canada L7G 5S4, Tel: (905) 877-4411. Distributed in the U.K. and Europe by David & Charles, Brunel House, Newton Abbot, Devon, TQ12 4PU, England, Tel: (+44) 1626-323200, Fax: (+44) 1626-323319, E-mail: postmaster@davidandcharles.co.uk. Distributed in Australia by Capricorn Link, P.O. Box 704, Windsor, NSW 2756 Australia, Tel: (02) 4577-3555.

Library of Congress Cataloging-in-Publication Data

You must be this tall to ride : contemporary writers take you inside the story / [edited] by B.J. Hollars.

p. cm.

Includes index.

ISBN-10: 1-58297-574-4 (pbk. : alk. paper) -- ISBN-13: 978-1-58297-574-0 (pbk. alk. paper)

1. Short stories, American. 2. Short story--Authorship. I. Hollars, B.J.

PS648.S5Y68 2009

808.3'1--dc22

2008045568

Edited by Lauren Mosko
Designed by Claudean Wheeler
Production coordinated by Mark Griffin

DEDICATION

To my families, old and new. They'll always be for you.

ACKNOWLEDGMENTS

Thank you to Random House, Jonathan Cape, Counterpoint Press, MacAdam/Cage, Ballantine Books, Alfred A. Knopf, Graywolf Press, University of Nebraska Press, University of Georgia Press, Scribners, and the multitude of important literary magazines from which many of these stories were culled.

A thank you, also, to my friends at Knox College and to the supportive MFA crew at the University of Alabama.

A thank you to the Ragdale Foundation for their support as well.

And, of course, to my steadfast, indefatigable editor, Lauren Mosko, whose vision and voice were invaluable to the success of this project.

Table of Contents

Conjuring All the Old Ghosts

On Breconshire Drive, the street where I grew up, a ditch divided our yard from the next. There, buried in cattails, a rat-infested culvert ran directly beneath the road. If you were willing to risk dirty knees, you could peer through one end of the culvert and catch the slightest glimpse of sunlight winking fifty yards away. To my eight-year-old self, taking the even greater risk—crawling through the culvert, with its spiders, leeches, and snakes—and reaching that sunlight on the other end was a near impossibility and, therefore, the holy grail of my childhood.

One June morning, I decided to tackle the culvert. Hunkering low, I army-crawled through the sludge and the muck, all for the sweet reward of displaying my ruined Velcro shoes as proof of my accomplishment. I slid down the cattails to the creek and, once enshrouded by the tunnel, was immediately overcome by my imagination.

"Hey guys," I called up to my friends, "I think I see a Komodo dragon down here. No wait, maybe it's a Gila monster."

Regardless of the dragons and monsters lying in wait for me, my friends urged me onward, and with peer pressure on my side, I soon found myself unscathed on the other side of the street. In the coming weeks, all of my neighborhood friends overcame the challenge as well, reducing the culvert to "baby stuff." Our mothers, of course, never fully grasped the symbolic achievement stained deep into our shoes, though throughout our grade-school days and well into high school, we would keep those shoes tucked in the backs of our closets, a testament to a time when we were fearless.

Culvert or otherwise, each of us has endured some equivalent childhood obstacle, most likely ruining a perfectly good pair of shoes in the process. But having survived the ordeal, we began walking a bit taller, brandishing our scraped knees and elbows like merit badges, guiltily proud of doing what our parents told us not to.

Writing affords us this same opportunity: to test ourselves, with the hope of emerging from each story just a little braver, a little more confident. Scraping knees and wounding egos are all necessary parts of the process. Not a draft goes by when we are not encountered with difficult decisions: whether we can cut, rip, tear, and maim the words we thought we loved. And always, that inner voice whispers, *Was the salvage worth the sacrifice?*

And this is the hard truth: sometimes it's not. Sometimes, despite our best efforts, we manage to cut all the wrong phrases, expand all the wrong paragraphs, and our stories simply explode, the sky filling with our unreadable words. In these situations, we find ourselves stuck midway through the culvert, our peer-pressuring friends yammering from both ends, and yet each direction seems to lead us farther away from where we want to be. Not all our stories will be successful, though perhaps we can learn enough to write our way out of danger.

★★★

Fifteen years later, on a warm June night, I've returned to this ditch once again—not for the muddy shoes or my cheering friends, but for you, reader. I have driven here with the sole intent of crossing this culvert once more, proving that our collective transformations from childhood to adulthood have only made us stronger, wiser, and better equipped for future perils; to reassure us that we are now the final drafts of lives—no longer haphazard works in progress. But it seems as if the ditch has changed, or I have. Two feet taller now, and eighty pounds heavier, the culvert looks a bit more cramped than I remember.

It's still terrifying. Still overflowing with monsters.

And still, it maintains the same sweet allure: calling me, beckoning, double-dog daring me to give it one more go, one last crawl to the other side ....

But some rites, it seems, can only be performed once. The invincible eight-year-old has grown up, and he has also grown fearful: afraid of muddying his shoes, ruining his chinos, arriving late for dinner. It is as if maturity scolds that it's unwise, irresponsible, or even dangerous to take a single step out of the adult world and back to the one we've left behind. As I peer down into the ditch, an even more terrifying thought occurs to me: *What if, after all my allegiance, the child world won't have me back?*

★★★

Why are we, as a culture, so fascinated with coming-of-age stories?

It's simple: If we can't relive our glories on the football field, why not read about it? Nostalgia is a habit we can't quite kick, and for some, these stories offer the reader a second chance at youth, a second crack at those monsters, an opportunity to wash our faces properly before the pimple appears on prom night. These stories put one more second on the play clock, squeeze in one last dance, allow us to conjure all the old ghosts from our past.

Coming-of-age stories also offer a measure of reassurance, of encouragement. After enduring the teasing and heartbreak of adolescence, we reemerge with thicker skin and, more importantly, a shared sense of solidarity. If we can survive being wedged in a locker, tossed in a trash can, and forced to salute our boxer briefs at the top of the flagpole, then surely we can find a job, pay a mortgage, and act like respectable adults.

Undoubtedly, the motif of "the awkward adolescence" is as American as apple pie. But also, it's the great equalizer. We are each a part of a world of boogers and wedgies and falling flat on our faces, all while reaching for our diplomas. Sure, there's insecurity, but there's also laughter. Our commiseration brings us one step closer, that inner voice reassuring us once more, *Don't worry; once my voice cracked, too.*

And for writers, these stories establish an even greater bond: a bridge that closes the gap between author and audience. Of all our possible shared experiences, we know this much is true: We are all born, we will all die, and at some point, we will all fall victim to the voice-cracking, menstruating, hair-where-there-wasn't-hair-before calamity known as growing older; from childhood to adolescence and eventually—after enduring life's hazing rituals—the much sought-after adulthood.

Whether we asked for it or not.

★★★

It is my intent that this book offers guidance for mining your own experience and transforming it into rich, honest writing, and that our commonality in enduring the hardships of growing up functions as a launching point, giving us a thematic start with which to practice craft.

Included here, you'll find many of today's preeminent storytellers sharing some of their own coming-of-age tales. These stories have been culled from the best literary magazines in the country. Many of these stories have been included in *The Best American Short Stories*, *The Best American Nonrequired Reading*, and the annual *Pushcart Prize: Best of the Small Presses* anthologies. In these stories, characters lose virginity, suffer bloody noses, and dress up as Hitler for Halloween, all in attempts to strive for what we, too, once strived for: to grow a little taller.

Alongside each story, you'll find an essay and exercise that takes you inside the writing process. Each author explains the challenges, hiccups, and lessons discovered along the way, serving as a personal guide through the most difficult of tasks: writing a story that matters.

Let me be clear: This book is no answer key. As most writers can attest, there is no magic bullet to writing, no set-in-stone rule by which to abide. Quite the contrary, writing seems to flourish when rules are broken, when reality is subverted, when each tale is told through its distinct lens. You will find few answers here, but plenty of questions. It is my great hope that the resources within this book serve as a flashlight to help guide you through your own explorations, allowing you to see those dragons and monsters, that muck and sludge, for what it truly is.

May the stories and essays herein motivate you to write your own tales. And may you write tirelessly and endlessly, eventually stumbling upon the spell that convinces all the words to line up accordingly, to shout rather than stammer.

Here on Breconshire Drive, the night is only getting darker, and it looks like rain ahead. I have a culvert to crawl into, and Gila monsters to face, so to hell with these shoes. And to hell with dinner, too. Sometimes, the salvage *is* worth the sacrifice.

Meanwhile, you, dear friend, have a lot of growing up to remember.

—B.J. Hollars

Tell Me Where It Hurts

This was the year that little girl fell down a well in her backyard and lay there stuck for what seemed like months. We were driving west, creeping up on Phoenix by night, with a load of stained glass lamps in the back of the van and Jamil in the driver's seat munching on babaganoosh. "Earl," he said. "You wanna drive?"

"No shit?"

"I gotta sleep. Don't crash, right?"

Our final destination was Los Angeles, where Jamil and I would sell the lamps, which we had made. Jamil was my stepfather. He was from Lebanon, which explained the babaganoosh, as well as his loose appreciation of U.S. driving laws. I was, at the time, not quite fifteen years old.

Jamil eased onto the shoulder. "Don't tell your mother," he said.

"No way," I said. "No fucking way."

Interstate 10 was empty, straight black lanes and pink scrub fading away in all directions. I was amazed at how easily the steering wheel agreed to move the car. (The least little jerk, I was certain, would send us hurtling end over end.) When Jamil took the wheel again, outside Palm Springs, I had trouble opening my hands.

We arrived in L.A. cramped and tired and checked into this ratty hotel, the Wandering Shepherd. The big news on TV was that the girl who fell down the hole, Baby Jessica, had been rescued. The story had been front-page stuff for weeks in Fort Worth, and now all three channels showed a fireman, dark and powerful, lifting Jessica gingerly into the world again. She looked like an old doll, scuffed and pale. "What kind of father lets a child fall into a hole?" Jamil muttered.

The next day, he took me to meet his distributor, George, who was also Lebanese. They sat around drinking coffee from little glasses and spoke Arabic, a language that sounded to me like sandpaper poetry. George kept looking my way and laughing. Jamil must have noticed my expression, because he said something and George shut up. Back at the hotel, Jamil told me he needed to run an errand and suggested I clean up. I took a shower and put on my pajamas. Jamil was back half an hour later, with a visitor.

"Earl," he said. "This woman here wants to sleep with you." He turned and walked out of the room.

★★★

Jamil had showed up in Fort Worth five years before all this, and moved in with his cousin Michel. Michel had managed to marry Judy, our next-door neighbor, within a couple months of his arrival. Judy was not an attractive woman. She was maybe forty and chain-smoked and had a few whiskers when you looked close.

The kids in our complex said Michel had married Judy to get his green card. I wasn't sure what this meant at first; I imagined a green card to be a sort of magical version of American Express that allowed Michel to withdraw money from the U.S. Treasury. Then Tommy Bibb, the one kid that spoke to me most often, explained that a green card was like a citizenship thing and meant Michel could work without being arrested.

Jamil started dating my mom pretty soon after he moved in with Michel and Judy. He was a handsome guy, what you would call swarthy, with hair all over his body, including his back. This confirmed my vague notions of what an Arab should look like. (I was, at this time, ten.) Soon, he was spending the night, which I figured out because his hairs showed up in the shower, though my mom and him snuck around for weeks, thinking they were real sly dogs for keeping me in the dark.

One morning, my mom came into the kitchen and sat down across from me. I was eating breakfast and trying to piece together some dorky jigsaw puzzle of these red clay roads they have around East Texas.

"Earl, honey," she said. "I have something to tell you."

She waited for me to say something like "Yes?" or "What?" but I knew what was coming.

"Jamil and I are getting married. He's coming to live with us."

I stared at my stupid, half-finished puzzle. "Okay," I said. It wasn't as if I had veto power. Then out came Jamil, on cue, and he walked around the table and put his hands on my shoulders and kind of bit his lip. "Congratulations, Jamil," I said. "This should make getting your green card a cinch."

★★★

The girl was wearing a denim jumpsuit. She looked like she had stepped right out of one of my jack-off fantasies. "I'm Kim," she said.

I was too freaked to say anything. I looked at her sandals, her brightly painted toenails. Even the little blond hairs on her calves shined. "Aren't you going to show me around?" she said, in this wispy voice.

So I gave her this little tour of the room: "Here's the TV, and here's the bathroom, and, uh, here's the bed."

She smiled, like I had done a real great job, and walked over to the ice bucket on the table next to the TV and put ice in two plastic cups and pulled this little flask out from somewhere and poured us drinks. She brought me mine and sat on the bed and patted the spot next to her. The ice in my cup knocked around.

"Are you cold?" she said.

"Yeah," I said. "I guess."

"Maybe we should get under the covers," she said.

"Yeah," I said. "Okay."

She stood up and unzipped her outfit and stepped out of it. Her breasts were there, swaying. Her skin went on forever. The smell of coconut lotion filled the room. "I'm gonna turn off the lights, okay?" she said. "Are you going to take your pajamas off?"

This was all happening very fast and between the drink and her body and that warm, too-close room, I started breathing a little too deeply.

"Listen," Kim said, "I'm going to go to the little girl's room for a second, okay? You just go ahead and get under the covers when you're ready."

"Yeah," I said. "Cool. No problem." I pulled off my tops and bottoms and thought about her, there in the bathroom, her skin, and my boner nodded, like it knew the answer to a very simple question. "Okay," I said. "Ready."

I had seen what came next, but I wasn't sure how to make it happen. I just sort of hovered above her, unsure where to place my hands, afraid to handle her breasts. Kim looked at me and smiled a small, sweet smile. Then she reached down and took hold of me. "Tell me when you're going to come," she said, as she guided me inside. Her words were soft but kindly, like when the doctor tells the patient, *Tell me where it hurts*.

★★★

News of the marriage spread pretty fast around the complex and my position in the pecking order, which was at the level of tolerated geek, slipped to untouchable, like the Mexicans. I wasn't so upset about that. I was used to being ignored. I wasn't upset about my dad being replaced, either, because I'd never met him. All I knew from my mom was that he'd been shot in some supposed hunting accident before I was born. What really got to me was that my mom would choose to live with another man, especially *Jamil the Camel*, which is what the other kids took to calling him. That wasn't such a bad name compared to what they called me: *Earl the Girl*.

I'd grown up with just my mom, which I suppose was pretty clear to the kids in school, who used to tease me because I carried my books clutched to my chest in front of me. I stood like a girl, too, with one foot pointing straight ahead and the other at 90 degrees, and moved a bit too lightly. When I sat down in class, the guys behind me, the burnouts, would meow. This meant that I was a pussy. Sometimes they called me *queebo*. Mostly, though, it was *Earl the Girl*.

This hurt, this nickname, because I was going through all kinds of hell on the sexual identity front. I was totally preoccupied with sex, with finding a girl who would agree to take part in anything remotely physical with me. It didn't help that I was as thin as a refugee, or that I had this shaggy blond hair that I never combed, or that I didn't bathe a lot. Performing any of these actions would have signified that I was trying, I guess, and confirmed my sense of failure.

I whacked off. Three or four times a day was not uncommon. With Tommy Bibb's help, I came into some half decent pornography. But even this was kind of disturbing, because I found myself staring not just at the women, but at the men, these greased up guys with huge pricks. Most of the time you couldn't even see their faces. But I admired them. And if I admired them, did that mean that I wanted to be like them or could it be that I secretly wanted *them*? This had me worried.

I was pretty sure it was girls I wanted. But then, I wasn't into any of the standard guy things: sports, cars, loud music. The stuff I enjoyed, such as cooking, I had done with my mother, and these were not passions I made public.

Jamil himself was an excellent cook. After he moved in, we used to eat all kinds of Arab food, kibbe and shish kafta and hummus with homemade pita. I liked to watch Jamil cook, liked the way he handled the knives and pinched out just the right amount of cumin. There was nothing girlish about the way he cooked.

He also liked to hunt, something that drove my mother crazy, and made it instantly attractive to me. For my twelfth birthday, Jamil proposed that he take me with him on a trip. I could hear the argument from my room.

"He's a big boy, Janie. He wants to go."

"I won't have him handling guns."

"I'll be careful, Janie. Real careful."

"No hunting."

"He'll just watch."

"I said *no*." My mother was shrieking now. "He's *my* son and I say *no*."

There was a long silence. Then Jamil said, "I know he is your son. But lemme tell you something, Janie: I live here too. Don't forget."

I didn't speak to my mother all day and ran out to meet Jamil when he got home. He was holding an old shotgun in one hand and a blood-stained bag in the other. He had killed seven doves, which he insisted on cooking right then, while they were fresh, over the hibachi. He cut their heads off with a kitchen knife.

"Look at their little necks," my mom said. "That's disgusting."

Jamil had me plucking the feathers, there on our little concrete porch. "It's better to shoot birds than peoples," he said. "Remember that, right?" He rolled the doves in a garlic-butter marinade and set them on the grill.

Jamil had learned to hunt in Lebanon, he said, before the war started up again. The war had pretty much ruined his childhood, was what it sounded like. He told me he used to have to stay home from school some days, because there was a battle zone in his neighborhood. Once he got caught in the middle of a firefight and had to jump into some abandoned butcher shop and stay there until the shooting stopped. It sounds terrible to admit, but listening to him, I sort of wished I'd grown up in Lebanon. I thought of it as heroic, not the kind of place where you'd get teased all the time because of the way you held your schoolbooks.

"Beirut was beautiful city before war, but today it's crazy people and blood," he told me. "You don't want no part of Lebanon, Earl."

That was another nice thing about Jamil. He didn't talk to me like I was a kid. Occasionally, he'd give me advice, and later on he taught me how to make lamps. But he didn't assume this phony paternal attitude, like we had some deep emotional bond, when really it was just circumstance that had shoved us under the same roof.

★★★

I knew that this was supposed to be a big deal, losing my virginity, but I was so keyed up or drunk or something that the whole scene played itself out like a movie. It felt like the thing that was happening, my dick moving in and out of an actual pussy, was happening not to me, but to a vague, slightly dizzy character being played by me.

This is probably the only reason I didn't come after four seconds.

When I finally did start coming, I forgot all about telling Kim. I didn't even recognize what was happening as an orgasm. It was more like a tremendous burst of relief, like the air being let out of an over-inflated tire. Kim picked up on it, though. I thought she was going to be mad, but all she said was, "You came, didn't you?" and slipped out of bed and into the bathroom.

I lay there for a while, with my head in this not-unpleasant fog. Then Jamil walked in. "Where's your friend?" he asked.

I pulled the covers up and pointed to the bathroom and he walked right in there. I heard them talk a little, and him laugh, and someone turned on the faucet, as if to run a bath. They were in there for a few minutes. Then Jamil came out, with his shirt untucked from his slacks.

"I'm going again," he announced, and did.

Kim stepped out of the bathroom wrapped in a towel. She came and sat on the foot of the bed. "Do you want me to kiss you?" she asked.

I had never actually made out with a girl, let alone a beautiful woman. I figured this was my chance to learn something useful, something I might be able to apply when I got back home. But, as it turned out, kissing my lips was not what Kim had in mind at all.

Afterwards we lay on the bed together. It had gotten dark outside, but the bathroom light was still on. I could see the outline of her body next to mine. She was smaller than she'd seemed at first; her hip bones looked like delicate rails.

"Did you enjoy that?" she asked.

"I sure did," I said.

For a time, all you could hear were cars on the highway. "That was really neat that your father did this for you," Kim said.

"He's my stepdad, actually."

"I kind of wish someone had done that for me."

The way Kim said this, the way her voice might have cracked, made me want to look at her. But she turned away, reached for the remote control. There was Baby Jessica, in a flood of camera lights, her arm like a broken wing.

★★★

God only knows how Jamil got into stained glass. Maybe he stole the idea off a book of matches. Maybe it came to him in a dream. Whatever the case, he borrowed some money from my mom and opened his own studio, which was really just a tiny garage in the same shitty part of town where we lived. My mom dragged me there, of course.

She was trying to be all enthusiastic about everything, nodding like crazy as Jamil showed us around. But you could see she was nervous as hell about tripping. There were these rusty tools and broken glass all over the floor. "Don't you want to see what your stepdad does all day?" she asked. I shook my head and went outside and threw rocks at the junkyard dog next door.

It was another couple of summers before I went to work for Jamil. Better to work for him, I reasoned, than to sit around sweating up the stairwells of our complex.

Jamil wasn't one of those bosses who makes you do all the grunt work. He taught me the whole process; how you have to score the glass with a carbide blade, then wrap the pieces in copper foil. This was nasty work because the copper had to be smashed onto the edges of the glass and grew jagged around corners and slashed the hell out of our hands. The coppered pieces were then laid onto a wooden stand shaped like a lampshade, slipping into place until the design was complete.

Soldering was the worst part. See, the solder didn't take to copper. It beaded up, like raindrops on a waxed car. To deal with this problem, Jamil bought this stuff called flux, which was some kind of acid that made the solder bond to the copper. The problem was, when you squirted this stuff on the solder, it produced this intense chemical reaction and a cloud of nasty white smoke, which chafed the skin around our eyes. The flux also made the cuts on our hands sting like a bitch, and they took forever to heal. It amazes me when I think about it now—that I was twelve years old and working with all this shit.

But I liked those cuts. They made me feel like I was doing something useful and dangerous. I used to stare at my hands during school, during the classes and lunch periods that slipped past like distant traffic.

And I loved the glass, spent hours staring at the pureness of the colors, at the red redder than blood.

"They mix gold into that red glass," Jamil told me one time.

"Bullshit," I said.

"No bullshit," he said.

Mostly, we knocked out set pieces, those cheesy pear-and-grape numbers that hang in fern bars. But at the end of the day, while I swept up, Jamil spent a half hour or so working on what he called his *magic lamp*, a piece he crafted from leftover scraps of glass. "Waste is no good," he said.

You could tell it was more than that, though, some kind of passion. The lamp grew under his hand as a Van Gogh might, the shards like brush strokes, some no larger than a fingernail. He lay them together with a sense of reverence, proportion, nodding his head and murmuring to himself. He bent the copper foil with his bloody fingers and they bled anew. A lot of his blood went into that lamp.

★★★

"That's so sad," Kim said. "That poor little girl." She was talking about Baby Jessica, practically talking *to* Baby Jessica it sounded like, and watching the screen intently. I was watching Kim, noticing for the first time how young she was, probably no more than a few years older than me.

"You were saying something," I said. "About how you wished someone had done something for you."

"Never mind about that," she said. She made a playful grab for my cock, but I rolled toward her and reached for her face, which was smudged around the eyes. She pushed my hand away.

"I'm sorry," I said.

Kim seized up and for a second I thought she was going to get up and leave. Then she seemed to relax. "Don't be sorry," she said softly. "There's nothing to be sorry about. Shit, I'm *happy*." As if to prove her point, she smiled, and when this didn't work, she grabbed my hands. "What's with all these cuts?"

"Those are from making lamps."

"Your dad has the same thing."

"Yeah. My stepdad; he makes lamps too."

"That's beautiful," Kim said. "Maybe someday you can teach your kid, huh?" Right at that moment, I wanted to tell her something, that I would never forget her, that I loved her, that we could run off to some place with lawns and a lake, somewhere where no one knew either of us. But before I could say any of that, before my mind could feed my mouth such tender, far-fetched words, she slipped away from me and into the bathroom.

When she came out she was all made up again, her eyelids stained purple, her jumpsuit back in place. She flicked off the light and the TV, and leaned over and gave me a kiss on the forehead, like she was checking for a temperature. "You were great," she whispered.

Her footsteps grew faint in the hallway and I moved to the window to watch her cross the parking lot. Jamil always got a room facing the lot, so he could keep an eye on his van. She stopped when she got to the van and knocked on the driver's side window. Jamil popped out and the two of them went around to the rear door and he climbed in. I couldn't imagine what he was doing in there, because the van was still half full of merchandise.

A minute later he reappeared, holding the magic lamp. He handed it to Kim and she held it up to the streetlight. The glow from above shone through the glass and left patterns on her skin, patches of red and green and blue. She lowered the lamp and nodded to him, then walked off toward the interstate, carrying that gorgeous piece in front of her, with both hands, like an offering.

★★★

Jamil had told me he thought he could get as much as five hundred dollars for that lamp, and I alone knew how hard he'd worked on it, because I had watched him most of those late nights, hunched over a workbench,

15

his soldering iron dribbling smoke as dusk filtered though the room, settling onto work tables blackened by pig iron.

"It's like a puzzle," I told him. "You just have to find the right pieces is all."

"No, Earl," he said gently. He stood and ran his hand through his hair and smiled at me, perched on my bucket of flux. "See, I don't got no control over the pieces. They could be smooth or rough like, purple or green." He gestured the iron like a pointer. "That's what skill requires, right? You got to fit them together good as you can, son, and also to handle the solder real careful; and then, never forget: throw a little light behind to see what you made."

Inside "Tell Me Where It Hurts": Writing What Matters

Near as I can reckon, I started writing "Tell Me Where It Hurts" in 1994, the year before I shipped off to grad school. I spent another five years revising the story before it was accepted for publication. I'm not sure exactly how many rewrites I did. A million or so. Reading the story now is sort of painful. Many of the moves are deeply sentimental. The best scenes feel rushed. The symbols are clobbering. You can't read a line like "He smiled at me, perched on my bucket of flux" without seeing the young author smirking at his own wordplay. But I felt it was important not to rewrite the thing (yet again), not to erase the worst of my decisions, or pretend the story was any better than it was. It's an account of adolescence written by an adolescent writer.

If I were a different sort of writer—less needy, more resilient—such a story would never exist, at least not in the public record. I'd have shown the patience and humility to make better decisions before I sent my work into the world. But I'm long past trying to correct what I can't correct. In any case, it's instructive to look at your old work, to see what you were up to before you knew any better.

As it turns out, "Tell Me Where It Hurts" fits pretty neatly into what I suppose I'll have to call the "arch of my career." It includes a lot of sex and masculine insecurity and sadness. It's embarrassingly tenderhearted. The story announces its intentions right at the start. *We've got a fragile, half-broken kid on our hands*, it says to the reader, *let's see if we can get the guy fixed up*. For better or worse, that's a lot of who I am as a writer—an overt emotionalist. My central desire is to get my characters into dangerous situations, and to see them through that danger. That's how people get fixed up, in my view. I'm sure that sounds too psychotherapeutic for some folks, not subtle enough, too ready to privilege motive over language. But the only books and stories I'm interested in are the ones in which the author clearly loves his or her characters. If I get the sense, even for a moment, that an author is teasing them, or using them as a narcissistic pretext, I give up. That's not literature anymore. It's masturbation. And I already know enough about that.

This is why most of my stories come from stories I've lived through in some manner, or that my friends have. I need to feel that empathy. I suspect this reflects poorly on my imaginative capacities, but it's how I work. I'm very rarely writing about anybody other than myself. Whatever fictional disguise I might choose, the preoccupations, the sources of sorrow and hope, all come from within. They are not "created" by the act of writing, they are merely identified and articulated. Most writers are the same way, though it would pain them to admit it.

And so, to return to this story and its origins: it's based on a story told to me by one of my best friends, a guy I'll call Johnny. Johnny didn't give me a lot of details initially. He just mentioned at some point, probably after some beers, that he had lost his virginity after his stepdad bought him a hooker. I'm almost positive I asked him to elaborate, and he explained that his stepdad was Arabic and that hooker-buying-to-lose-virginity was a traditional practice, for male offspring anyway.

Johnny told me this story long before I was writing short stories myself. But it stayed with me. It got stuck in my craw, undoubtedly because it combined two of my central preoccupations: sex and how sons connect to their fathers. A few years later, after I decided I wanted to write the story, I asked Johnny for more details, and he told me about the stained-glass lamps and how they got made and maybe a little something about how he'd felt growing up. He gave me the basic plot, and some of the imagery, though I'm afraid the cheesiest symbolic details (the wandering shepherd, the magic lamp) were my own.

I'm not suggesting that I just took dictation on the story, though. At a certain point, I had to bring my own imagination and concerns to the party. It would have felt lifeless, or imitative, if I hadn't. I didn't write with some grand scheme in mind. On the contrary, most of the best writing comes from letting the artistic unconscious call the shots. It generally makes a lot better decisions.

The introduction of Baby Jessica as a motif, for instance. The story Johnny told me took place years before Baby Jessica fell down her well. In fact, Johnny had covered the story as an AP reporter. And so when I started working on this story about Johnny's life, I got to thinking about that little girl, and the opening line popped into my head: "This was the year that little girl fell down a well in her backyard and lay there stuck for what seemed like months." It presented itself and insisted on being included.

This is what I mean by the *artistic unconscious*. Though I didn't realize it at the time, the Baby Jessica story and Johnny's story were part of the same broader story, the central story of every childhood, which is the yearning for parents who will nurture and protect you. It took years before it occurred to me how Jessica fit in, that her peril made perfect psychological sense.

The Baby Jessica story also provided a certain perspective on Kim, the young prostitute. As I revised the story, she became a more complex character, a kind of moral instructor whose ultimate purpose is not to facilitate Earl's sexual initiation, but to allow him to see that his stepdad is trying to take care of him. In the end, it's a love story between a son and a father.

Again, this isn't something that I consciously "planned." All I knew going in was that Earl was going to lose his virginity, under strange circumstances. But when you're writing a short story about a kid who never knew his biological father, who doubts his masculinity, who feels alone and bereft much of the time, it's not enough just to get him laid. Not nearly. He has deeper fears and needs, which the story must honor. That's your job as an author: to identify your characters' deepest feelings and to construct a plot that gets at them somehow, forces them into the open. That's most of what writing is about for me: exposure.

This is why there's a lot of sex in my stories. It's not just because I'm a pervert, or because I'm trying to titillate the reader. The readers who focus on that stuff are forever missing the point. Or, actually, most of the time they're too embarrassed to see the point, which is that sex exposes people emotionally, forces them up against the hard truths of themselves.

"Tell Me Where It Hurts" was one of the first stories where I dared to write about sex, and where the sex became about something else, something larger, the feelings that reflect my own private anxieties and hopes. I hope it won't come as a shock that I felt a lot like Earl as a teenager, that I was insecure and lonely and aching for a father who could soothe these feelings. That's why Johnny's story stuck with me for so long—because it was my story, too.

We never outgrow who we were in adolescence. We find ways to polish up our act. We acquire business cards and spouses and hobbies. But the basic doubts and fears and wants remain inside of us, waiting to be activated. When we write, we return to those feeling states. At least when we're being honest.

I can't very well see "Tell Me Where It Hurts" as a literary masterpiece, or even an especially good short story. But it did serve as a kind of breakthrough. For all the symbolic strong-arming and earnest prose, there was an integrity of intent. I was trying to write about the things that matter to me most deeply. That's all we can ask of ourselves. It's an unthinkable task in the midst of adolescence. It's also the only sure path I know toward literary redemption.

WRITING EXERCISE

It's certainly never a bad idea to look over your old stories. But for less experienced writers, there may not be many of them. So I'm going to suggest an exercise my students have always found useful. It involves exposure and reflection.

I want you to think about a moment of extreme emotion from your youth or adolescence. It could be a first kiss, or the first time you were caught doing something wrong, or a terrifying moment at summer camp—a memory searing enough to remain vivid in your mind. Here's what you need to do:

1. **Write about the event itself.** Move moment to moment through the physical and emotional particulars of what happened. Ideally, this means you're writing about a very short period of time, anywhere from five seconds to a minute. Don't worry about making it pretty or poetic. Just get us to what it felt like. (Hint: Sensual details will help.) In the case of "Tell Me Where It Hurts," this might consist of the precious moments Earl spends with Kim.

2. **Write about who you were at the time.** Step back from the episode itself and tell us about yourself at the time this was happening. Here's where you get a chance to interrogate yourself, to explore the deeper fears and needs that will allow you (and hopefully us) to understand why this event hit you so hard. In Earl's case, most of the story is an attempt to document the relevant context: the death of his father, his uncertain passage into manhood, his stepfather's unorthodox benevolence.

3. **Now the hard part. Yes, it's time to integrate.** A good short story— or even a scene—requires this weaving of passion and perspective. Remember, the key resides in offering the reader everything you know: both what's happening at the white-hot moment in question and why it matters in the broader history of your character.

AIMEE BENDER

Tiger Mending

My sister got the job. She's the overachiever, and she went to med school for two years before she decided she wanted to be a gifted seamstress. (What? they said, on the day she left. A surgeon! they told her. You could be a tremendous surgeon! But she said she didn't like the late hours, she got too tired around midnight.) She has small-motor skills better than a machine; she'll fix your handkerchief so well you can't even see the stitches, like she became one with the handkerchief. I once split my lip, jumping from the tree, and she sewed it up, with ice and a needle she'd run through the fire. I never even had a scar, just the thinnest white line.

So of course, when the two women came through the sewing school, they spotted her first. She was working on her final exam, a lime-colored ball gown with tiny diamonds sewn into the collar, and she was fully absorbed in it, constructing infinitesimal loops, while they hovered with their severe hair and heady tree smell—like bamboo, my sister said—watching her work. My sister's so steady she didn't even flinch, but everyone else in class seized upon the distraction, staring at the two Amazonian women, both six feet tall and strikingly beautiful. When I met them later I felt like I'd landed straight inside a magazine ad. At the time, I was working at Burger King, as block manager (there were two on the block), and I took any distraction offered me and used it to its hilt. Once a guy came in and ordered a Big Mac, and I spent two days

21

telling that story to every customer, and it's not a good story. There's so rarely any intrigue in this shabberdash world of burger warming; you take what you can get.

But my sister was born with supernatural focus, and the two women watched her and her alone. Who can compete? My sister's won all the contests she's ever been in, not because she's such an outrageous competitor, but because she's so focused in this gentle way. Why *not* win? Sometimes it's all you need to run the fastest, or to play the clearest piano, or to ace the standardized test, pausing at each question until it has slid through your mind, to exit as a penciled-in circle.

In low, sweet voices, they asked if she'd like to see Asia. She finally looked up from her work. Is there a sewing job there? They nodded. She said she'd love to see Asia, she'd never left America. They said, Well, it's a highly unusual job. May I bring my sister? she asked. She's never traveled either.

The two women glanced at each other. What does your sister do?

She's manager of the Burger Kings, down on Fourth.

Their disapproval was faint but palpable, especially in the upper lip.

She would simply keep you company?

What we are offering you is a position of tremendous privilege. Aren't you interested in hearing about it first?

My sister nodded, lightly. It sounds very interesting, she said. But I cannot travel without my sister.

This is true. My sister, the one with that incredible focus, has a terrible fear of airplanes. Terrible. Incapacitating. The only way she can relax on a flight is if I am there, because I am always, always having some kind of crisis, and she focuses in and fixes me and forgets her own concerns. I become her ripped hemline. In general, I call her every night, and we talk for an hour, which is forty-five minutes of me, and fifteen minutes of her stirring her tea, which she steeps with the kind of Zen patience that would make Buddhists sit up in envy and then breathe through their envy and then move past their envy. I'm really really lucky she's my sister. Otherwise, no one like her would give someone like me the time of day.

The two Amazonian women, lousy with confidence, with their ridiculous cheekbones, in these long yellow print dresses (I met them later) said OK. They observed my sister's hands, quiet in her lap.

Do you get along with animals? they asked, and she said, Yes. She loved all animals, without exception. Do you have allergies to cats? they asked, and she said, No. She was only allergic to pine nuts. The slightly taller one reached into her dress pocket, a pocket so well hidden inside the fabric it was like she was reaching into the ether of space, and from it, her hand returned with an airplane ticket.

We are very happy to have found you, they said. The additional ticket will arrive tomorrow.

My sister smiled. I know her; she was probably terrified to see that ticket, and also she really wanted to return to the diamond loops. She probably wasn't even that curious about the new job yet; she was and is stubbornly, mind-numbingly interested in the present moment.

When we were kids, I used to come home, and she'd be at the living room window. It was the best window in the apartment, and looked out, in the far distance, on the tip of a mountain. For years, I'd try to get her to play with me, but she was unplayable. She stared out that window, never moving, for over three hours. By night, when she'd returned, I'd usually injured myself in some way or other, and I asked her about it as she tended to me; she said the reason she could pay acute attention now was because of the window. It empties me out, she said, which scared me. No, she said, to my frightened face, and she sat on the edge of my bed and ran a washcloth over my forehead. It's good, she said. It makes room for other things.

Me? I asked, with hope, and she nodded. You.

We had no parents, by that point. They'd died at the hands of surgeons, which is the real reason my sister stopped medical school.

That night, she called me up and told me to quit my job, which was what I'd been praying for for months—that somehow I'd get a magical phone call telling me to quit my job because I was going on an exciting vacation. I threw down my BK apron, packed, and prepared as long an account of my life complaints as I could. On the plane, I asked my sister what we were doing, what her job was, but she refolded her tray table and said nothing. Asia, I said. What country? She stared out the porthole. It was the airplane that told us, as we buckled our seat belts; we were heading to Kuala Lumpur, straight into the heart of Malaysia.

Wait, where's Malaysia again? I whispered, and my sister drew a map on the napkin beneath her ginger ale.

During the flight, I drank Bloody Marys while my sister embroidered a doily. Even watching her work seemed to soothe the other passengers. I whispered all my problems into her ear and she returned them back to me in slow sentences that did the work of a lullaby. My eyes grew heavy. During the descent, she gave the doily to the man across the aisle, worried about his ailing son, and the needlework was so elegant it made him feel better just holding it. That's the thing with handmade items. They still have the person's (maker's) mark on them, and when you hold them, you feel less alone. This is why everyone who eats a Whopper leaves a little more depressed than they were when they came in. (Nobody cooked that burger.)

When we arrived, a friendly driver took us to a cheerful green hotel, where we found a note on the bed, telling her to be ready at 6 A.M. sharp. It didn't say I could come, but bright and early, scrubbed and fed, we faced the two Amazons in the lobby, who looked scornfully at me and my unsteady hands—I sort of pick at my hair a lot—and asked my sister why I was there. Can't she watch? she asked, and they said they weren't sure. She, they said, might be too anxious.

I swear I won't touch anything, I said.

This is a private operation, they said.

My sister breathed. I work best when she's nearby, she said. Please.

And like usual, it was the way she said it. In that gentle voice, that had a back to it. They opened the car door.

Thank you, my sister said.

They blindfolded us, for privacy's sake, and we drove for over an hour, through winding, screeching roads, parking finally in a place that smelled like garlic and fruit. In front of a stone mansion, two more women dressed in printed robes waved as we removed our blindfolds. These two were short. Delicate. Calm. They led us into the living room, and we hadn't been there for ten minutes when we heard the moaning.

A bad moaning sound. A real bad, real mournful moaning, coming from the north, outside, that reminded me of the worst loneliness, the worst long lonely night. The Amazonian with the short shining cap of hair nodded.

Those are the tigers, she said.

What tigers? I said.

Sssh, she said. I will call her Sloane, for no reason, except that it's a good name for an intimidating person.

Sloane said, Sssh. Quiet now. She took my sister by the shoulders, and led her to the wide window that looked out on the land. As if she knew, instinctively, how wise it was to place my sister at a window.

Watch, Sloane whispered.

I stood behind. The two women from the front walked into our view and settled on the ground, near some clumps of ferns. They waited. They were very still-minded, like my sister, that stillness of mind. That ability I will never have, to sit still. That ability to have the hands forget they are hands. They closed their eyes, and the moaning I'd heard before got louder, and then in the distance, I mean waaaay off, the moaning grew louder, almost unbearable to hear, and limping from the side lumbered two enormous tigers. Wailing, as if they were dying. As they got closer, you could see that their backs were split open, sort of peeled, as if someone had torn them in two. The fur was matted, and the stripes hung loose, like packing tape, ripped off their bodies. The women did not seem to move, but two glittering needles worked their way out of their knuckles, climbing up out of their hands, and one of the tigers stepped closer. I thought I'd lose it; he was easily four times her size, and she was small, a tiger's snack, but he limped over, in his giantness, and fell into her lap. Let his heavy striped head sink to the ground. She smoothed the stripe back over, and the first moment she pierced his fur with the needle, those big cat eyes dripped over with tears.

It was very powerful. It brought me to tears, too. Those expert hands, as steady as if he were a pair of pants, while the tiger's enormous head hung to the ground. My sister didn't move, but I cried and cried, seeing those giant broken animals resting in the laps of the small precise women. It is so often surprising, who rescues you at your lowest moment. When our parents died in surgery, the jerk at the liquor store suddenly became the nicest man alive, and gave us free cranberry juice for a year.

What happened to them? I asked Sloane. Why are they like that?

She lifted her chin slightly. We do not know, but they emerge from the forests, unpeeling. More and more of them. Always torn at the central stripe.

Do they ever eat people?

Not so far, she said. But they do not respond well to fidgeting, she said, watching me clear out my thumbnail with my other thumbnail.

Well, I'm not doing it.

You have not been asked.

They are so sad, said my sister.

Well, wouldn't you be? If you were a tiger, unpeeling?

Sloane put a hand on my sister's shoulder. When the mending was done, all four—women and beasts—sat in the sun for at least half an hour, tiger's chest heaving, woman's hands clutched in its fur. The day grew warm. In the distance, the moaning began again, and two more tigers limped up while the first two stretched out and slept on the ground. The women sewed the next two, and the next. One had a bloody rip across its white belly.

After a few hours of work, the women put their needles away, the tigers raised themselves up, and without any lick or acknowledgment, walked off, deep into that place where tigers lived. The women returned to the house. Inside, they smelled so deeply and earthily of cat that they were almost unrecognizable. They also seemed lighter, nearly giddy. It was lunchtime. They joined us at the table, where Sloane served an amazing soup of curry and prawns.

It is an honor, said Sloane, to mend the tigers.

I see, said my sister.

You will need very little training, since your skill level is already so high.

But my sister seemed frightened, in a way I hadn't seen before. She didn't eat much of her soup, and she returned her eyes to the window, to the tangles of fluttering leaves.

I would have to go find out, she said finally, when the chef entered with a tray of mango tartlets.

Find out what?

Why they unpeel, she said. She hung her head, as if she was ashamed of her interest.

You are a mender, said Sloane, gently. Not a zoologist.

I support my sister's interest in the source, I said.

Sloane flinched, every time I opened my mouth.

The source, my sister echoed.

The world has changed, said Sloane, passing a mango tartlet to me, reluctantly, which I ate, pronto.

It was unlike my sister, to need the cause. She was fine, usually, with just how things were. But she whispered to me, as we roamed outside, looking for clues of which we found none, she whispered that she felt something dangerous in the unpeeling, and she felt she would have to know about it in order to sew the tiger suitably. I am not worried about the sewing, she said. I am worried about the gesture I place inside the thread.

I nodded. I am a good fighter, is all. I don't care about thread gestures, but I am willing to throw a punch at some tiger asshole if need be.

We spent the rest of the day outside, but there were no tigers to be seen—where they lived was somewhere far, far off, and the journey they took to arrive here must have been the worst time of their lives, ripped open like that, suddenly prey to vultures or other predators, when they were usually the ones to instill fear.

We slept that night at the mansion, in feather beds so soft I found them impossible to sleep in. Come morning, they had my sister join the two outside, and I cried again, watching the big tiger head at her feet while she sewed with her usual stillness. The three together were

27

unusually productive, and sewn tigers piled up around them. But instead of that giddiness that showed up in the other women, my sister grew heavier that afternoon, and said she was sure she was doing something wrong. Oh no, said Sloane, serving us tea. You were remarkable.

I am missing something, said my sister. I am missing something important.

Sloane retired for a nap, but I snuck out. I had been warned, but really, they were treating me like shit anyway. I walked a long distance, but I'm a sturdy walker, and I trusted where my feet went, and I did not like the sight of my sister, staring into her teacup. I did not like the feeling it gave me, of worrying. Before I left, I sat her in front of the window and told her to empty herself, and her eyes were grateful in a way I was used to feeling in my own face but was not accustomed to seeing in hers.

I walked for hours, and the wet air clung to my shirt and hair. I took a nap inside some ferns. The sun was setting, and I would've walked all night, but when I reached a cluster of trees, something felt different. There was no wailing yet, but I could feel the stirring before the wailing, which is almost worse. I swear I could hear the dread. I climbed up a tree and waited.

I don't know what I expected—people, I guess. People, with knives, cutting in. I did not expect to see the tigers themselves, jumpy, agitated, yawning their mouths beyond wide, the wildness to their eyes, and finally the yawning so large and insistent that they split their own back in two. They all did it, one after the other—as if they wanted to peel their own fur off their backs, and then, amazed at what they'd done, the wailing began.

One by one, they left the trees and began their slow journey to be mended. It left me with the oddest, most unsettled feeling.

I walked back when it was night, under a half moon, and I found my sister still at the window.

They do it to themselves, I whispered to her, and she took my hand. Her face lightened. Thank you, she said. She tried to hug me, but I pulled away. No, I said, and in the morning, I left for the airport.

Inside "Tiger Mending": One Question Leads to Another

This story came from looking at a painting. The artist, Amy Cutler, and I had been wanting to collaborate on something for a few years. We share some similar preoccupations: animal/human/object merges, fancy dresses, women who live in the world of the fantastic bumping up against daily routines, as she's shown by her elegant ladies with antler-chairs worn on their heads, bucking against each other. In 2005, *Black Book* magazine decided to have a few writers team up with painters, and fortuitously, they paired me with Amy. I could pick one of her paintings out of several choices, and I had a great time looking at her work, imagining the stories behind the scenes. I started several stories based on other paintings—five women all sharing the same bed, underneath which was a pig. Or the women in long black gowns who were building a brick wall up against nothing, with kites soaring in the sky. But the one I kept returning to was the painting called "Tiger Mending," of three women, with severe buns, holding the torn bodies of tigers in their laps, and sewing up the stripes with long threads. Her title was perfect for the image, and it was so evocative, to think of these tigers having some kind of problem with their stripes, the very thing that defined them as tigers. And that the ones who could help these tigers were these small and careful-looking women. You could clearly see the parts in the women's hair, as if they spent good, focused time in the bathroom, briskly getting ready, efficient with comb and brush and then thread.

The first route I took was to think of the job description. Who would get this job, to mend tigers? Who would possibly be equipped to do such a thing? The initial incarnation of the story was a job interview application, just a back and forth Q&A between a form and its applicant, and the applicant wanted to be a tiger mender more than anything. She, the applicant, had witnessed a tiger mending at the zoo, accidentally. They're supposed to be private, but she somehow came across one, as the zoo was about to close; the tiger split its stripe, and a woman emerged from behind the rock structure to sew him up. It was a beautiful thing to watch, and as soon as this applicant saw it, it's what she wanted to be.

The voice of the applicant turned out to be the same one who told the actual story here, a kind of chatty, nervous, friendly narrator, but at that time she was planning to be the tiger mender herself. The key switch in the story for me was that it turned out she was *not* going to be the tiger mender—that she would be the one closest to the tiger mender, but unable to do the work herself. It just seemed like such a tough job, and I wasn't sure my narrator would be up for those particular demands. She could do other jobs, but the steadiness of hands one would need to sew up a tiger might be too much for most. Truth is, I can't really relate, myself, to that level of efficiency with hands, and I wasn't sure just how proficient a person might have to be in order to get a tiger to sit still and be sewed. After all, a tiger would certainly eat the mender if anything were wrong in the mending.

The roles of both sisters interested me: the one who can observe, the one who can do. The limits and advantages to both roles.

Also in that job application, I was thinking about the tiger's position. If you are in someone's lap, being mended, when you are usually roaming the plains for prey, how would you feel? Likely humiliated. And also cared for, at the same time. A little tiger care, which for a tiger would be a mixed bag. Something's wrong, in Cutler's painting, with the order of things, and I think that's why it's such a great and disturbing image. It was a real pleasure to think about these questions of point of view, based on the contradictions and questions embedded in her painting.

So, once the two sisters were in place, and the story was rolling along, the next question for me became about the splitting of the tigers in the first place. Why was it happening? What did it mean? How did it take place? The course of writing the story was engaging these questions. The narrator had to watch the mending happen, and then investigate the cause. And since I didn't know why they split, as I wrote it, her investigation was mine as well. I don't usually plan my stories, so the process of walking to see the tigers was the same for me as it is for a reader. It's just like Frost's famous and wise quote: "no surprise in the writer, no surprise in the reader."

In the act of closing in on an ending, or revealing a plot movement that I myself don't know in advance, I will try out various possibilities and see how they feel. I considered the idea that someone was doing something *to* the tigers, but it just didn't feel right; it felt too easy. It was in these wonderings that I hit upon what happens, with the tigers yawning and breaking the stripes on their own. It really bothered me, to think of tigers doing such a thing. Why would they do it? It seems so off in the order of things, so against the nature of a tiger, but so does the painting, so does the idea of tigers in laps as if they are domestic cats. Yes, they are related to domestic cats, but my long-held wish of going into the zoo cage and petting a soft-looking tiger or lion like a big kitty cat is a wildly distorted human fantasy about the food chain. And in this strange flip of power—tigers in laps—it seemed like a disturbing and mysterious symptom of something larger. It changes things, to see that happening with tigers, who you think are going to behave a little differently.

Do I know what happens to the narrator at the end? Kind of, but mostly I just know that leaving was the right thing for her to do. That she'd witnessed something startling, and complicated, and she could not return to her role in the same way afterward.

How do we help each other? What is actually helpful? When does help become harmful? Who helps whom? The story, in its roundabout way, is trying to ask those questions, too, and to leave the reader with a level of ambiguity about the answers, since I think they are not easy questions to answer.

WRITING EXERCISE

Reverse something in nature, something in the order of things. Make a central change, as Cutler did, by putting wild tigers into the laps of small women. If it's too broad a topic, have someone write down an element of nature for you—waterfalls, cyclones, antelope, beetles, dirt—and then change something about this element. Make it a change that matters. Draw it. Make sure it's drawable, that you've picked a change that is tangible enough to capture with a visual image. And then write a couple pages from the point of view of someone who is affected by this change. It doesn't matter who; just jump into a few voices and see who grabs you.

KATE BERNHEIMER

A Tulip's Tale

I was but a smallish bulb—a bulbette, really—sleeping cozily beside my mother, when quite to my horror I was wrestled from that safe underground home and yanked into the face of an unblinking sun.

The shock of blue sky wide above frightened me, and I never grew to my fullest size. Too young for such solitude, I became forever sad.

No longer could I root happily into my mother's company and find comfort in her rounded shape. There was no one to tell me the facts. How much nutrition to pull from the dirt? Would the beetles bring harm? And what of the worms? Friends, foe, or nevermind?

Is it any wonder I was always so silent? Always so small?

No, I was *not* ready to leave her at all. I was but a tiny bulb, a bulbette, really, quite at home beside my mother, when those wretched hands dug me out of my peaceful slumber and moved me into that cold plot of land. There, I had no playmates to speak of, no playmates for miles. It was a bewildering journey for me from the very beginning.

I cannot say that I have appreciated it at all. No, not at all.

Then one day, nearly a hundred years after the trauma, I became blessed with a friend. She happened upon me and pulled me out of the ground. To me she whispered thoughts of great feeling: "Poor little thing, poor ugly thing," she said. How these words brought me comfort!

She said she could see I had a difficult life, never allowed to see the sun. With my best effort, I communicated agreement. This was not easy because my skin was tough and quite immobile.

She continued, "And we will *not* pretend to ignore that you are misshapen. Just as my mother taught me when I was young to accept my homeliness, so must you accept yours. My mother and father love me despite the plain features on my face. But none has a plainer face than you! Oh my dearest and ugliest friend!"

When my friend found me, she covered her heart with one hand and rested the other tenderly against my hard little body. She told me that her childhood memories were like those little boxes containing dried nuts, or fruit, that her mother sometimes received from guests she did not seem particularly eager to greet. The guests were men in black garments, clutching tiny books. This was an elaborate narration which she ended simply by trailing off her words, and stroking my spindly roots.

And then, my pretty friend put me in such a box, for her to keep. At times she opened the box and licked me. Why, she loved the taste of my dirty skin! And I liked my little box, that wooden box lined with pink paper. It fit in her apron pocket. Unlike heated potatoes—surly relatives of mine—I did not keep her warm.

She kept me from missing my mother too much.

This was all in the town of Sneek, near the Wadden Zee, just north of the Zuder Zee.

Her father was a fishmonger, her mother a fishwife. Though her father's family trade had been in diamonds, the family was of the Jewish kind. The Fishmonger's Guild did not restrict, so he made the switch. From glinting stone to lively flounder!

There is more life in fish than in jewels, though diamonds do glint.

And indeed, her father loved everything alive. It was this love that eventually brought him to ruin, but through no fault of his own. And she, the girl who suffered most badly for his tender spirit, never blamed him. Yes, he and her mother had provided well for the girl from north of the Zuder Zee a pleasant life which they designed in the meticulous manner of the era.

The mother kept the home as clean as perfection itself. The mother also labored long and hard as a bleaching maid.

(The smell of bleach and fish made the girl swoon for all her days, and still it would if she were living.)

When first she found me, my friend and I and her sisters slept in a drawer. The drawer pulled out from underneath the parents' small bed. Together the sisters huddled through hard winter nights, and the sister clutched me in her hand. And the mother, so rosy-cheeked and kind! She kept the drawer warm by piling hot potatoes inside. The potatoes she would remove just before bed. Then, the girls would clamber into the drawer and whisper stories and poems.

When you hear the Cuckoo shout, 'tis time to plant your tatties out.

While they slumbered, their parents sat by the fire and ate.

As her sisters and mother and father slept, she would open the lid of the wooden box just a crack and whisper to me. Her hot breath against the pink tissue paper moved it a bit, making a nice, wrinkling sound that made me swoon.

We shall discuss your amusement in time. It interests me because otherwise you appear so small-headed, as I appeared as a child.

My friend had several friends who had to sleep in the oven. Yes, the oven! Poor little Anneke K——, whose mother forgot she was in there when she fired it up in the morning! But they all rather *liked* her singed hair. It has the most unusual crimps and curls!

And just because poor little Anneke K—— slept in the oven does not mean her life was bad. Oh no, her life was good, my friend related. Her family lived well, and had kept their wooden floors clean and their tiny homes scrubbed and finely sparkling. At night there was much drinking of wine, much cheer all around in poor little Anneke K——'s fine house.

Just like my friend, Anneke K—— eventually was auctioned. This took place at midnight, in the town square. My friend came home for the very last time and she told me.

"There was little interest in me," she said sadly. "I am dried up like a prune at thirteen; they said my face was sour, though inside I feel fine."

"In the end, I was taken for a moderate fee," she told me. "Now I'll be taken to my new home, and to this man whom I fear will beat me."

And then she left me.

So now I feel death coming closer each day—'*tis time*, I almost can hear him say. But I am here for your comfort. I am here to make sure that you grow. I was surprised to see you sprout from my withered body, but sprout from me you did.

Lying beneath a man—I don't mean to shock with that phrase, it was common in the time to lie with men, you are so sensitive for such a rough one!—I believe she must have often thought of her parents' house. And of me?

The home in which you reside is not forever.

That swept front stoop. That waxed oak door. Even the mother's feet had brushes upon them, on their soles! This pursuit of cleanliness was performed by all of the husbands and all of the wives in all of the homes on that small and oak-lined street.

From the time my friend was five, she created a ruckus. Her poor mother, trying to clean off the door! Always, my friend insisted upon rushing outside, shoving aside her poor mother. And upon her return she always forgot to remove the straw covers upon her shoes. The filth. What reprimands she received. And deserved.

She cared not so much about cleanliness. I believe this was part of her attraction to me—indeed part of her country's fascination with my type.

It is a pity they auctioned her off so young. But it was a pity for her parents, most of all. The Jewish fishmongers. They were not allowed in many trades. They could have made a bundle in tulips, but how could they know?

But they had no idea of our worth, nor of hers.

It has been a long, cold winter. Will the spring never arrive? My dear Jewess, my beautiful friend!

Come back.

Come back.

Come back.

Inside "A Tulip's Tale":
Lead With Your Obsessions

Once upon a time, I was writing a trio of novellas about tulips. Together, they would comprise a novel. Each novella was about a different main character living in a different time in history: during Tulipomania in seaside Holland, during World War II in Dachau, Germany, and in mid-twenty-first century Manhattan, New York. The first character was a tulip bulb, the second was a young girl, the daughter of a fishmonger, and the third was an Alexander Dumas scholar who cultivated tulip bulbs, seeking to produce the ever-elusive Black Tulip.

Obsessed with tulips and with tulip history, I read book after book after book about tulips. Friends often sent me postcards of tulips. Or books about tulips. My parents took a trip to Amsterdam and brought me back catalogs from tulip museums. In not one, not two, but three consecutive gardens—for this book was in progress over a decade during which I relocated three times—I planted tulips.

TULIP GARDEN ONE
Tulsa, Oklahoma
Red tulip picture on the bag of bulbs. Purchased at Home Depot at the edge of downtown. I biked there. Planted alongside the driveway after an argument with my boyfriend. Thought, *Now the tulips will remind him of me forever.* One spring later, we're still together. (And fifteen years later, too.) They came up red with yellow inside, and still grow there. We go back to see them every time we visit his mother in nearby Sapulpa.

TULIP GARDEN TWO
Portland, Oregon
Queen of the Night tulips, the darkest that you can get. Deep, dark purple on bag. Purchased on Stark, at the beautiful nursery, on a

rainy day. Planted beside the brick patio that was always full of weeds. Never bloomed. Too wet. Not enough sun. Should have known.

TULIP GARDEN THREE

In Massachusetts, pink tulips in bag, bought down the hill at the grocery store that mainly sells bologna sandwiches, eggs. Tulips grow and bloom the first season. They came up pink, beautiful pale pink. At last, success! But hired to teach in Alabama. Many tears. Goodbye, pink tulips. Goodbye.

Meanwhile, books about tulips are boxed up and packed, and I would tell people, whenever asked what I was working on, "A trio of novellas about tulips." And I was. I was working on it, reading about it, thinking about it, hard. Yet the words! Those pesky materials of the writer! They would not come except in tiny, teeny, miniscule installments. And so while I worked on "the tulip novel," I wrote other things. Two novels, a children's book, a series of essays on fairy tales, some other short stories, some (terrible, unpublished) poems.

And yet, and yet. I kept that tulip novel in progress, there on my desk. Until one day, it was done. And here it is, in its entirety. Yes, this is a novel that is *five pages long*. It is the coming-of-age novel of a tulip bulb, a sad tulip bulb indeed.

Okay. By most standards, "A Tulip's Tale" would be considered a very, very short story. To me, it's that trio of novellas; it is even, in my imagination, a novel in its entirety, contained within its 1,200 or so words. But a novel cannot be measured by words! A novel may only be known by the form in which it happens to live, or to die, on the page.

I think that the only difference between a poem and a story is the line breaks; I think that the only difference between a story and a novella is the number of pages. And so on through the forms.

Setting aside the potential veracity of the opinion that "you can't write a novel narrated by a tulip bulb," which I am frequently offered, can this be a novel? I set out to write a novel, and I feel that I did. In a sense, I came of age as a novelist-in-trying, and by outside definitions of form failing, to write this novel.

I've been lucky, however; though my tulip novel has never been published the way I would like it to be, with one sentence per page, a generous editor at a literary journal did publish it with normal paragraph breaks, and once a book artist made it into a lovely, delicate chapbook. But if I had my way, it would be novel-length! And have pictures of bulbs, too, on some pages. The closest I have come to persuading anyone to publish it as such is in a short-story collection I have, where it appears with a paragraph per page. That makes forty-four pages.

The Dumas scholar is absent. She never spoke, much as I tried to get her to speak, night after night as I read Dumas novels, bored to tears on her behalf, though I wanted to love Dumas and I needed him desperately—needed her, too—no, she would not obey. She sat sullenly in her apartment window, staring out at the rain-soaked streets of the future Manhattan as I pictured them (more apocalyptic, more old at the same time). Perhaps if she speaks to me later—for I'm still writing this book, as all of the books I ever write live in me always, telling me how I have failed them—then perhaps, with her in there, too, others will see the lunacy at last in the right light.

"Ah, now *this* is a novel," they'll say to me then. And I will be considered a grown-up.

But not now, not just with the bulb talking and rooting around for her mother. No, that's just insane.

TULIP GARDEN FOUR
Tuscaloosa, Alabama
Not yet planted.

WRITING EXERCISE

This assignment is very simple. Write a short story from the point of view of a young flower or other plant with which you empathize. It can be very liberating to write from a non-human perspective. Also, humans are not the only species on Earth with stories to tell. We are not the only witnesses to history and loss.

Consider these strategies while you look for your story:

- Research a plant and the sorts of people who like to grow it. Write from the point of view of a plant whose owner has problems, or neglects it.

- Research a plant that has gone extinct, and write from the point of view of the last known example of its species.

- Research a plant that is unpleasant—that offers a terrible odor, or bites, or both. Your story will be narrated by an unpleasant voice.

- Narrate a story from the point of view of a plant that does not exist—a mythic plant that has special powers, perhaps.

- Consider writing a story from the point of view of a flower with an inferiority complex—for example, a dull, endangered, unflowering vine that has no society devoted to its protection, unlike its exotic neighbor, popular with hummingbirds and humans.

RYAN BOUDINOT

The Littlest Hitler

Then there's the time I went as Hitler for Halloween. I had gotten the idea after watching WWII week on PBS, but my dad helped me make the costume. I wore tan polyester pants and one of my dad's khaki shirts, with sleeves so long they dragged on the floor unless I rolled them up. With some paints left over from when we made the pinewood derby car for YMCA Indian Guides, he painted a black swastika in a white circle on a red bandanna and tied it around my left arm. Using the Dippity Doo he put in his hair every morning, he gave my own hair that plastered, parted style that had made Hitler look like he was always sweating. We clipped the sides off a fifty-cent mustache and adhered it to my upper lip with liquid latex. I tucked my pants into the black rubber boots I had to wear whenever I played outside and stood in front of the mirror. My dad laughed and said, "I guarantee it, Davy. You're going to be the scariest kid in fourth grade."

My school had discouraged trick-or-treating since the razor blade and thumbtack incidents of 1982. Instead, they held a Harvest Carnival, not officially called "Halloween" so as not to upset the churchy types. Everyone at school knew the carnival was for wimps. All week before Halloween the kids had been separating themselves into two camps, those who got to go trick-or-treating, and those who didn't. My dad was going to take me to the carnival, since I, like everybody else, secretly wanted to go. Then we'd go trick-or-treating afterward.

There were problems with my costume as soon as I got on the bus that morning. "Heil Hitlah!" the big kids in the back chanted until Mrs. Reese pulled over to reprimand them. We knew it was serious when she pulled over, being that the last pulling-over incident occurred when Carl Worthington cut off one of Ginger Lopez's pigtails with a pair of scissors stolen from the library.

"That isn't polite language appropriate for riding the bus!" Mrs. Reese said, "Do you talk like that around the dinner table? I want you both in the front seats and as soon as we get to school I'm marching you to Mr. Warneke's office."

"But I didn't do anything!"

I felt somewhat vindicated but guilty at the same time for causing this ruckus. Everybody was looking at me with these grim expressions. It's important, I suppose, to note that there wasn't a single Jewish person on the bus. Or in our school, for that matter. In fact, there was only one Jewish family in our town, the Friedlanders, and their kids didn't go to West Century Elementary because they were home-schooled freaks.

When I got to school Mrs. Thompson considered me for a moment in the doorway and seemed torn, both amused and disturbed at the implications of a fourth-grade Hitler. When she called roll I stood up sharply from my desk, did the seig heil salute I'd been practicing in front of the TV, and shouted, "Here!" Some people laughed.

After roll was taken we took out our spelling books but Mrs. Thompson had other ideas. "Some of you might have noticed we have a historical figure in our class today. While the rest of you dressed up as goblins and fairies and witches, it looks like Davy is the only one who chose to come as a real-life person."

"I'm a real-life person, too, Mrs. Thompson."

"And who would you be, Lisette?"

"I'm Anne Frank."

Mrs. Thompson put a hand to her lips. Clearly she didn't know how to handle this. I'd never paid much attention to Lisette before. She'd always been one of the smart, pretty girls whom everyone likes. When

I saw her rise from her desk with a lopsided Star of David made of yellow construction paper pinned to her Austrian-looking frock or whatever you call it, I felt the heat of her nine-year-old loathing pounding me in the face.

"This is quite interesting," Mrs. Thompson said, "being that you both came as figures from World War II. Maybe you can educate us about what you did. Davy, if you could tell us what you know about Hitler."

I cleared my throat. "He was a really, really mean guy."

"What made him so mean?"

"Well, he made a war and killed a bunch of people and made everybody think like him. He only ate vegetables and his wife was his niece. He kept his blood in jars. Somebody tried to kill him with a suitcase and then he took some poison and died."

"What people did he kill?"

"Everybody. He didn't like Jesse Owens because he was Afro-American."

"Yes, but mostly what kind of people did he have problems with?"

"He killed all the Jews."

"Not all Jews, fortunately, but millions of them. Including Anne Frank."

The classroom was riveted. I didn't know whether I was in trouble or what. Lisette smirked at me when Mrs. Thompson said her character's name, then walked to the front of the class to tell us about her.

"Anne Frank lived in Holland during World War II. And when the Nazis invaded she lived in someone's attic with her family and some other people. She wrote in her diary every day and liked movie stars. She wanted to grow up to write stories for a newspaper, but the Nazis got her and her family and made them go to a concentration camp and killed them. A concentration camp is a place where they burn people in ovens. Then somebody found her diary and everybody liked it."

When Lisette was done everybody clapped. George Ford, who sat in front of me and was dressed as Mr. T, turned around, lowered his eyes, and shook his fist at me. "I pity the foo who kills all the Jews."

★★★

Recess was a nightmare.

I was followed around the playground by Lisette's friends, who were playing horse with a jump rope, berating me for Anne Frank's death.

"How would you like it if you had to live in an attic and pee in a bucket and couldn't walk around or talk all day and didn't have much food to eat?"

It didn't take long for them to make me cry. The rule about recess was you couldn't go back into the building until the bell, so I had to wait before I could get out of my costume. I got knots in my stomach thinking about the parade at the end of the day. Everybody else seemed so happy in their costumes. And then Lisette started passing around a piece of notebook paper that said "We're on Anne Frank's Side" and all these people signed it. When my friend Charlie got the paper he tore it up and said to the girls, "Leave Davy alone! He just wanted to be a scary bad guy for Halloween and he *didn't really kill anybody!*"

"I should just go as someone else," I said, sitting beneath the slide while some kids pelted it with pea gravel. This was Charlie's and my fort for when we played GI Joe.

"They can kiss my grits," Charlie said. He was dressed as a deadly galactic robot with silver spray-painted cardboard tubes for arms and a pair of new wave sunglasses. "This is a free country, ain't it? Hey! Stop throwing those son-of-a-bitching rocks!"

"Charlie!"

"Oops. Playground monitor. Time for warp speed." Charlie pulled on his thumb, made a clicking sound, and disappeared under the tire tunnel.

Despite Charlie's moral support, I peeled my mustache off and untied my arm band as soon as I made it to the boys' room. There were three fifth-graders crammed into a stall, going, "Oh, *man!* There's *corn* in it!" None of them seemed to notice me whimpering by the sink.

Mrs. Thompson gave me her gray-haired wig to wear for the parade.

"Here, Davy. You can be an old man. An old man who likes to wear khaki."

I knew Mrs. Thompson was trying to humor me and I resented her for it. Lisette, for whatever reason, maybe because her popularity in our classroom bordered on totalitarian, got to lead the parade. I was stuck between Becky Lewis and her pathetic cat outfit and Doug Becker, dressed as a garden. His mom and dad were artists. Each carrot, radish, and potato had been crafted in meticulous papier-mâché, painted, lacquered, and halfway embedded in a wooden platform he wore around his waist. The platform represented a cross section, with brown corduroys painted with rocks and earthworms symbolizing dirt, and his fake leaf-covered shirt playing the part of a trellis. For the third year in a row Doug ended up winning the costume contest.

By the time our parade made it to the middle school I was thoroughly demoralized. I had grown so weary of being asked, "What *are* you?" that I had taken to wearing the wig over my face and angrily answering, "I'm *lint*! I'm *lint*!"

★★★

My dad made wood stoves for a living. When my mom left he converted our living room into a shop, which was embarrassing when my friends came over because the inside of our house was always at least ninety degrees. My dad was genuinely disappointed when he learned of my classmates' reactions.

"But everyone knows you're not prejudiced. It's Halloween for crying out loud." He folded the bandanna, looking sad and guilty. "I'm sorry, Davy. We didn't mean for it to turn out like this, did we? Tell you what. Let's go to Sprouse Reitz and buy you the best goddamn costume they got."

We drove into town in the blue pickup we called Fleetwood Mack. Smooth like a Cadillac, built like a Mack truck. The Halloween aisle at 6:30 P.M. on October 31st is pretty slim pickings. There was a little girl with her mom fussing over a ballerina outfit—last-minute shoppers like us. I basically had a choice between a pig mask, some cruddy do-it-yourself face paint deals, and a discounted Frankenstein mask with a torn jaw.

"Hey! Lookit! Frankenstein!" my dad said, trying to invest some enthusiasm in the ordeal. "Don't worry about the jaw, we'll just duct tape it from the inside. Nobody'll even notice."

"I want a mask with real hair. Not fake plastic lumpy hair," I said.

"You don't really have a choice here, Davy. Unless you want the pig mask."

"Fine. I'll go as stupid Frankenstein."

My dad grabbed me by the elbow and spun me around. "Do you want a Halloween this year or not? You can't go trick-or-treating without a costume and this is about your only option. Otherwise it's just you and me sitting on our asses in front of the television tonight."

That night the grade-school gym floor was covered with the same smelly red tarp they used every year for the PTA Ham Dinner. Teachers and high-school students worked in booths like the Ring Toss, Goin' Fishin', and the Haunted Maze, a complex of cardboard duct-taped together. All the parents were nervously eyeing Cyndy Dartmouth, who'd come as a hooker. She was the same seventh grader who'd shocked everybody by actually dyeing her hair blonde for her famous-person report on Marilyn Monroe. Her parents ran the baseball card shop in town and every middle-school guy in West Century wanted to get into her pants. She seemed womanly and incredibly sophisticated to me as we stood in line together for the maze. I liked her because she stuck up for me on the bus and one time told me what a tampon was.

They let you into the maze two at a time, and Cyndy and I ended up going in together.

"You go first," I said as we entered the gaping cardboard dragon's mouth. She got on her hands and knees in front of me, and for an incredible moment I saw her panties under her black leather skirt.

The maze took a sharp right turn and the light disappeared. Cyndy reached back and grabbed my arm. I screamed. She laughed and I tried to pretend I wasn't scared. The eighth-graders had done a really good job building this place. There were glow-in-the-dark eyes on both walls and a speaker up ahead playing a spooky sound effects album. I held onto her fishnet ankle and begged her to let us go back. We passed a sign reading "Watch Out For Bears!!!" and entered a tunnel covered in fake fur. I started crying. Cyndy held me, whispering it was all just made up, none of it was real, it was just cardboard stuck together with tape, holding my face in that magical place between her breasts that smelled like perfume from the mall.

Suddenly light streamed in on us. One of the high-school volunteers had heard me crying and opened a panel in the ceiling.

"Ross! Mike! Check it out! They're totally doing it in here!" the guy laughed. I looked up to see four heads crowding around the opening.

"Leave us alone, you fuckers!" Cyndy said, and it seemed a miraculous act of generosity that she didn't tell them the real reason for our embrace.

We quickly crawled through the rest of the maze. When we emerged a group of kids was waiting for us.

"Hey Cyndy, why don't you crawl through the tunnel with a guy who's actually got pubes?"

I panicked, hoping my dad wouldn't hear. I didn't want Cyndy to get picked on, but I kind of liked the idea that the other kids thought I'd done something naughty with her in the maze. When Ross Roberts asked me if I'd gotten any, I sort of shrugged, as if to suggest that I had, although I didn't completely understand what it was I could have gotten.

Cyndy bit her bottom lip and disappeared into the girls' room with three other girls who would end up sending me hate notes on her behalf the next day at school. The rest of the carnival was awful after that. I carried my Frankenstein mask upside down because I'd forgotten to bring a candy bag. Most of the candy at the carnival was that sugarless diabetic crap, handed out simply because one kid in sixth grade had diabetes and we all had to be fair to him. My dad walked around the perimeter of the gym, pretending to be interested in each grade's autumn crafts project, not really mingling with any of the other adults, even though he'd sold wood stoves to a few of them. I could tell he didn't want to be here and when I told him I wanted to leave he nodded and said it was time to do some serious trick-or-treating.

I liked my dad because he didn't seem to follow a lot of the rules
other grown-ups seemed obligated to follow. He let me watch R-rated
movies, showed me how to roll joints, and told me how to sneak into
movie theaters. We bought our Fourth of July fireworks from the Indian
reservation and used them to blow up slugs. The only times I felt like he
was a real grown-up were when he was figuring out the bills or being
sad about my mom. But tonight we were the closest of co-conspirators.
In Fleetwood Mack we sang along to the Steve Miller *Greatest Hits* tape
and picked the richest-looking neighborhoods to trick-or-treat in. With
a greasy Burger King bag salvaged from the floor of the truck, we went
door to door, my dad hanging out behind me, waving politely. Somebody even tossed him a can of beer.

I didn't know we were at the Friedlanders' house until Mrs. Friedlander opened the door. Word had it they were among the parents
who didn't let their kids go trick-or-treating since the razor blade and
thumbtack scare of 1982. Hannah Friedlander sat on the steps up to
the second story of their split-level house, leaning over in her sorcer-
ess costume to see who it was. Mike, her brother, came up the stairs
from the rec room and joined her, breathing dramatically in his Darth
Vader mask. I wanted to do something nice for them, wanted to just
hand them my whole bag, but I couldn't bring myself to do it. I'd be
too embarrassed, I'd make my father angry, I'd call too much attention
to the fact they couldn't go trick-or-treating. So I chose to do nothing but accept Mrs. Friedlander's individually wrapped Swiss chocolate
balls and thanked her, then walked back to Fleetwood Mack with my
dad and drove home, looking at all the Halloween displays through
the nostrils of Frankenstein's nose.

"So did you have an okay Halloween after all?" my dad said, carrying me upstairs to my bedroom. I nodded and got into my pjs, then
pulled the covers over my face and let him bite my nose through the
blanket like he did every night. Later, when I could hear him snor-
ing through the wall, I took the bag of candy from my dresser and
tiptoed downstairs to what used to be our living room. There was a
stove hooked up to each of our three chimneys, one which was cold,

one with some embers inside, the third filled with flames. I opened the door to the flaming stove and thought about throwing my whole bag in there, but then remembered the rule: wood and paper only. Besides, I had an entire Snickers bar in there; I wasn't insane. I sat for a long time, eating chocolates one by one in front of the fire, then plunged my hand into the stove to see how far it could go before it really started to hurt.

Inside "The Littlest Hitler": From Preparation to Evaluation

One time I asked a really stupid question. I was 20 years old, attending Lollapalooza in the eastern half of Washington state. Rage Against the Machine played. So did Dinosaur Jr. In one part of the dusty parade grounds was a tent where lecturers discussed matters of interest to people who'd driven several hundred miles to see Tool. You know, heavy academic stuff. One of the speakers was Dr. Timothy Leary, the man most responsible for the popularity and eventual criminalization of LSD in the 1960s. I was aware that Dr. Leary had recently become a sort of evangelist for "cyberspace" and "virtual reality." Also "smart drugs," which is an early nineties term for "Jamba Juice boost."

Dr. Leary spoke for a while to a rapt audience of people who would have otherwise been watching Babes in Toyland on the main stage. I can't remember a single thing he said. Then came the Q&A. I raised my hand and in all seriousness asked: "Dr. Leary, is it possible for there to be more space *inside* a computer than *outside* a computer?"

You would think that the guy who'd turned on the world would have a snappy comeback to this line of inquiry. But the psychedelic shaman regarded me with his deep-sunken eyes, shrugged, and said, "I don't know. I guess so?"

★★★

I think of Timothy Leary's response to my stupid question as I'm confronted with the task of writing about this short story I wrote in 1998, "The Littlest Hitler." The sentiment "I don't know. I guess so?" could sum up my attitude about questions concerning its origin, the choices that went into its craft, themes, all that writerly jazz. The anecdotal truth is that I was finishing my last semester in Bennington College's Master of Fine Arts program when I wrote it. I started the story while sitting in my car waiting for my wife (then girlfriend) to finish her workout at the gym. I started writing it in a notebook and later transferred my handwritten draft to my computer, an Apple LC 520, a model that looked to be suffering from elephantitis of the monitor. I printed this later draft and included it in my final packet of work to Amy Hempel, my faculty adviser that semester.

What an exciting anecdote this is turning out to be!

So a couple years went by and the story got published in *Mississippi Review*, then in *The Best American Nonrequired Reading*, then in translation in an Italian magazine called *Il Diario*, an English composition textbook called *The Longwood Reader*, then in my debut collection of short stories of the same name. And now here. I've seen dramatic stagings of the story by high-school drama clubs. I've had to explain to a number of people that I never dressed up as Hitler for Halloween (I'm looking at you, *Seattle Times*). Can I explain how it works or its "craft"? I suppose I could, but I fear I would sound about as intelligent as I did when I asked whether there could be more space *inside* a computer than *outside* a computer. Or rather, explaining it is not really my job. My job was just to write the damn thing. And I punched that card back in 1998.

★★★

Recently I've been reading a book by artificial intelligence pioneer Marvin Minsky, *The Emotion Machine*, in which he speculates about the parts of the brain that operate subconsciously. Minsky says it's not necessary for our conscious minds to be aware of how these parts of the brain work any more than it's necessary to know how an internal combustion engine works to drive a car. He describes a mathematician, Henri Poincare, who in the early twentieth century noticed patterns to how he solved complicated problems. First he'd endure torturous sessions of getting nowhere. When he finally grew tired of this, he'd take a break and forget about the problem. After a while, a solution would appear in his consciousness when he least expected it to. Solution in hand, he'd spend a considerable amount of time analyzing and testing it until he was satisfied that it was sound.

Minsky spells out the four stages of this process: preparation, incubation, revelation, and evaluation. This process struck me as precisely what artists go through when creating work. Perhaps for "The Littlest Hitler," the preparation and incubation periods were graduate school and arguably my whole life up to that point. My revelation happened while listening to Smashing Pumpkins in my car in the parking lot of Pro Fitness. The evaluation period included several rounds of revision and incorporating feedback from Amy Hempel and others.

There's an element of this enterprise, writing stories, in which I don't know what the hell I'm doing. And I'll defend that element as vitally necessary. I love the part of the writing process that is mysterious, and I start to tense up when I encounter too much determination to solve the mystery. It's like the fable of the goose that laid the golden eggs. Any attempt to get inside it to figure out how it works results in a dead goose and no more of those wicked cool eggs. Another way to put it is that any violation of the incubation stage of the process results in the whole system breaking down. However, that's not to say I haven't learned how to better manage this process. Here are some guiding principles that help me write stuff:

1. **Let the first draft be a disaster.** The key with a first draft is to let the good ideas I'm not aware of land on the page with as little interference from me as possible. If I'm fussing over commas and semicolons in draft number one, it's a sign that the ideas haven't incubated long enough.

2. **Don't beat up on yourself when you get stuck.** If I come to an impasse in a story, I simply set it aside and tell myself that the solution will present itself when it's ready. This can be startlingly effective.

3. **Be grateful.** When I write something I'm proud of, I often say "thank you" out loud. I'm convinced that this is a practical method of reinforcing the subconscious processes responsible for coming up with ideas, even though it sounds like some sort of hippie-ish, mystical hoo-hah.

Of course, while these tips (or whatever they are) seem to work for me, they could be completely wrong for you. A blissful writing experience beats high-minded advice about writing just like paper beats rock. When you're in thrall of a story's creation, there's not really any thinking involved in the commonly accepted sense. You're just interfacing with an experience. Craft, sentence structure, plot arcs, and denouements were absent from my thoughts when I entered Davy's world and followed him around for a day.

Finally, yes indeed it's possible for there to be more space inside a computer than outside a computer. Totally.

 WRITING EXERCISE

Write the definitive history of your Halloween costumes throughout the years. What kind of evolution developed? Did you go from robot to witch to Hitler? If so, why? What about you changed? How did your inner changes manifest themselves in Halloween costumes?

JUDY BUDNITZ

Immersion

We live in a small town a train ride away from the big city. Our father works there. We've never been there. Our mother says the city is full of infections and diseases waiting to pounce, waiting particularly for children, particularly in the summers. People out here get sick too, my sister Lily says. But not like in the city, where everybody's packed in on top of each other, our mother says. Out here, maybe things are a bit old-fashioned, but at least there's room to breathe.

Breathing in the germs is what makes you sick. Or if you lick a doorknob a sick person has touched. Germs like liquids; they can swim around in them. Lily can fit an entire doorknob in her mouth, which is unusual. I have to keep her from trying to impress people with her trick in public places. You can also get diseases from kissing, which is something we don't have to worry about yet. The diseases you get in the city can leave you dead or in a wheelchair or inside a big metal machine that pumps you in and out like an accordion. Cripple fevers, people call them. Brain swellers. Infantile paralysis. The other problem with Lily's trick is that it is not ladylike.

It is not ladylike to pull at the collar of your Sunday dress but sometimes it is unavoidable, especially when the collar is lacy and itchy and too

tight, especially when it's a hot day and not even a Sunday. Especially on the first day of summer.

On the first day of summer the pool opens and if the lifeguard's any good he'll go through the proper rituals of opening the gates and letting everyone line up on the concrete ledges with their toes hanging over, letting them get good and hot, maybe tossing a silver dollar in the water for a prize, waiting till the proper minute to blow his whistle and break the spell and officially open the pool. At that moment we all jump in screaming, every single one of us wanting to be the first to hit the pure, untouched turquoise water.

We're not in the water, we're pulling at our collars (in Lily's case, purely out of solidarity) in the heat of the train station. We've got our bathing suits on under our dresses. Vain hope; train late. We're here to pick up our cousin Mattie. We have to make her feel welcome, our mother says.

Cousin Mattie—not really a cousin at all. She's the orphaned daughter of an old friend of our father's. She lives in the city but is coming to spend the summer with us to escape the heat and contagion and the boredom that is like a disease for a girl that age. So they say. We suspect there are other reasons. She's older than us. Older girls have needs. One of these needs is privacy. For this reason, she gets our room and we are banished to the sleeping porch for the rest of the summer.

The beds on the sleeping porch are always dewy-damp. We hate sleeping there. All the nighttime clicks and twitters sound like they are right there in the bed with you. Moths come and cling to the screen and sleep there all night. Every now and then an extra big one will crash into the screen with a soft heavy sound like a big paw tapping. It's enough to make you scream.

Lily screams when the train comes. She can't help it; any time there's noise she has to add to it. She's a copycat to the bottom of her soul. The train crashes and hisses to a stop. They unload Cousin Mattie off it. It's our first time seeing her. She's a thick column of a girl, a stout log, a dense cylinder from head to toe. Her thick legs too short to negotiate the train steps. They have to lift her and set her down on the platform. Beside her they set a fat bulging suitcase that looks like another section of the same log she's been cut from. She stands there, waiting for us to come to her.

Welcome, Mattie. We're so glad to have you. This is Catherine. And this is Lily.
    Hello, Cousin Mattie.
    Hello, Cousin Mattie.
    Hi.

She has highfalutin city ways, you can tell. We hate her right away. She keeps scrunching up her nose to keep her glasses from slipping. New-fangled glasses with sparkles in the frames. She ends each sentence with a little grunt like she's out of breath. What's there to do around here? she says, looking around (our!) bedroom and putting her folded clothes in (our!) bureau. The swimming pool, Lily says. Cousin Mattie looks at me, knowing Lily cannot be trusted. It's not so great, I say. Cousin Mattie says, I like to swim. I like pools.

Why don't you like the pool any more, Lily asks when we're lying in our soggy beds on the sleeping porch. She's all ready to change her opinions the second I do. I don't want to have to take *her*, I say. Lily does lying-down jumping jacks in her bed. Sometimes a bat will come slamming into the screen, grabbing at the moths and devouring them. The bats have squashed snouts and pointed ears exactly like Satan. There's a lot of clicking and squeaking, flapping and snapping.

Cousin Mattie's red plastic sandals flap and slap against the pavement. Lily and I are barefoot. Lily's body in her bathing suit is a solid block, it doesn't go in or out at all.

Kids are already jumping in and out of the water when we get there. Everything's in place, it's all exactly the way it is every summer—turquoise water, grown-ups on deck chairs sitting in the sun, the lifeguard on his high stand with his sunglasses and whistle and white beak of zinc oxide. The stammer of the diving board and kids yelling, nonstop, shrill, like the puppies at the pound who don't know you but want you to take them home.

We try to pretend we don't know Cousin Mattie. The first jump is always the best, cold bracing plunge and bubbles up your nose. Simon and Knobby and the Creavey twins are playing Alligator in the deep end and we go to join them. There's a clumsy splash and Cousin Mattie's right there with us. She's wearing a nose clip that pinches her nostrils together. It's fastened by a strap around her head. Her bathing suit fastens around the neck and is yellow with ruffles that make her big behind look even bigger.

The bigger kids sit at the far end of the pool near the snack bar. She should be with them. She's too big to be with us. We dive down deep, swim like spies underwater, taking lots of turns and doublebacks. We come up for air and she's right behind us. It's nice, right? she says with a little grunt. Then she points to the fence and says, who are those kids?

Those kids are Cheryl and Melinda and Marcus and Brick and some others. They stand behind the fence watching us the way they do every summer. This is a public pool but only white kids swim here. The black kids watch from behind the fence. They do it every summer. They watch for a little bit and then go away. They look hot, Cousin Mattie says. I don't say anything. I recognize a lot of them from school. I make my face seem like I don't. They do the same. That's manners.

Their faces are shiny with sweat. They probably don't know how to swim, I say. They are watching Lily jump up and down, bright spangles of water flying off her. I don't know what they're thinking. Soon enough they'll let go of the fence and go away.

Come in, Cousin Mattie calls. She paddles over to them and says again, why don't you come in? She invites them by raising her arm. A sudden silence descends, so complete that the lifeguard looks around to see who drowned.

I'm holding my breath even though I'm not underwater. The black kids let go of the fence. They're going away. No they're not. They're walking around to the gate. Everyone watches them but they don't move slow or fast. They walk across the concrete and right up to the edge of the pool. The smallest kid crouches down and very gently puts his fingertips on the surface of the water. Brick takes off his shirt. We all stare at his chest, his nipples, his belly button. Hey Phil, one of the grown-ups yells to the lifeguard. The lifeguard says to Brick, You kids have to have proper bathing suits to swim here.

Brick acts like he doesn't hear. He takes off his pants. Underneath he's wearing blue bathing trunks covered with red stars. The others get undressed too and they pile their clothes neatly together. Marcus has a green bathing suit. As he jumps in he lets out a yell so loud it makes my teeth rattle in my head. The others slip in quietly, cautiously, as if the water might bite them. They slip in one by one.

As one, we all move to the ladders, to the sides of the pool. As one, we all get out. What are you doing? Cousin Mattie says. We're getting out, I say. Come on, Lily says, hurry.

The black kids are unhurriedly spreading out through the pool, dispersing themselves, stretching their arms and legs, bobbing up and down the way Lily does so the water flies sparkling in all directions.

Mattie doesn't seem to know how to follow directions. Come on, we say, but she lingers by the ladder. She watches the other kids climbing out of the water, heaving dramatic sighs of relief as they flop down on the grass. She looks longingly at the black kids, at Melinda doing a hand-

stand in the water with her toes perfectly pointed. Why ...? Cousin Mattie says. You can never be too careful, says Lily in our mother's voice.

There's not a sound but the voices and splashings of the black kids. The
rest of us sit and watch them. They play the same games we always play,
Alligator and Marco Polo and Go Fish. If you close your eyes you'd
think the pool was the same as always. I look over at Simon, whose
hair is sticking up in orange spikes. He has an old tennis ball in his
hand. When the lifeguard looks away, Simon sends the ball whipping
low across the pool, missing Cheryl's head by inches.

The adults are inching over to the lifeguard's stand, whispering at him.
He's shrugging and shaking his head. He's a new lifeguard, hard to tell
what he's thinking behind the sunglasses.

Clouds slide in front of the sun, but the black kids stay all day, until
six when the pool closes. We all stay to watch. When the lifeguard
blows the closing whistle, the black kids climb out, dress hurriedly,
and disperse. The grown-ups cluster around the lifeguard. There's
nothing I can do, he keeps saying. They're allowed to come here.
Well, I hope you *scrub* this pool tonight is all I can say, one of the
mothers announces, and the bunch of them murmur in agreement.
It's like they can't stop talking, even for a second, they make a con-
stant bubbling babble.

We walk home not talking. I don't have the swollen content feeling
I usually have after a day at the pool. I feel hot, crumpled, scratchy
like I've been starched. Cousin Mattie limps, her red sandals cutting
into her heels. Why did we have to get out? she says. Because, Lily
replies firmly. Then doesn't know what to say next. Mattie looks perplexed. Lily looks perplexed that a big girl like Mattie doesn't understand something so obvious it defies explanation. I know that in my
thinking I am somewhere between the two of them but don't feel like
trying to bridge the gap.

Next day, I'm showing Lily how I can spit water through the gap where I lost one of my dog-teeth. We've been in the water about ten minutes when the black kids show up. They've brought friends. There's at least a dozen of them. They come in briskly, take off their clothes and jump in. We jump out. Cousin Mattie is the last to come. But why? she keeps saying. Lily and I pretend we don't know her.

I don't know what the lifeguard's thinking. He sits impassive on his chair, occasionally twirling his whistle on its string around his finger. I wonder if he's blind behind those sunglasses. We sit, sweating in the sun, and watch them play in our pool all day.

Not one of us leaves, for the whole entire day. No one goes home for lunch, even. We don't talk. We just watch. The lifeguard looks at his watch and blows the closing whistle. Only then do we grab our towels and head home, our bathing suits absolutely dry.

The next day they stay dry too. The same thing happens. The black kids come first thing in the morning. We all watch in silent protest.

I don't care, Cousin Mattie protests. I'm hot, I'm getting in. Don't you dare, I say. What are you gonna do? she says. You can't, Lily says, you're one of us. I'm not one of *you*, Cousin Mattie says disdainfully. We'll tell our dad, I say. He won't like it one bit.

Bit by bit, strange things can start to feel normal. We now have a new summer routine: put on our bathing suits and go to the pool and watch the black kids play and bring in friends and more friends so they can occupy the pool in shifts so that it is never empty. Even on cloudy days, rainy days they come. One morning they're late and we all pour into the pool. Maybe it's dirty and tainted from the day before, we don't care. Then the black kids show up, just a few minutes behind schedule, and we retreat to dry land. They ignore us.

We watch their games so intently we feel like we're the ones playing. Each of us has a counterpart that we secretly root for. Mine is Cheryl. She's missing a dog-tooth too. *Yes*, I catch myself whispering, when Cheryl races and beats all the boys by an arm's length.

This is too boring, Cousin Mattie says, stretching her fat legs out in front of her on the grass. Let's do something else, she says. No! Lily says. We can't! Why not, says Cousin Mattie. *Why not*, mimics one of the Creavey twins, who are sitting behind us. Fatty wants to know why not, says the other twin in a nasty voice. Both twins pinch their noses with two fingers, like Mattie's nose clip, and give nasal laughs. We can't just give in, Lily says incredulously. We watch Cousin Mattie's face go red and hot.

It's a lot cooler out here, Mattie says that night, stepping out onto the sleeping porch in her nightgown. Her nightgown looks like a lamp-shade on her. It's a lot cooler than the house, she says, maybe I'll join you. There's no room, Lily says. We are all quiet. The insects shrill and scream and grind stuff in their tiny jaws. Have you ever been night swimming, Cousin Mattie says suddenly. It's wonderful. Like flying. I say, No. She says, We could sneak into that place, easy. Just climb over the chain-link fence. Lily is quiet, waiting to hear what I will say.

We wait, hot, dry, staring at the cool water, day after day. It's a stand-off. Neither side will budge. The summer grows hotter. Our skins burn and peel and burn and blister and turn a deep burnished brown. All of us except Cousin Mattie, who just gets pink and pinker. I'm al-most as dark as *them*, Lily says, admiring her brown arms. You'll never be as dark as them, I say. I'm watching Cheryl. She can swim, all right. She can go the whole length of the pool underwater without a breath. It's not fair.

It's not fair, we tell our father. We've never been to the city. *She's* been there her whole life, why does *she* get to go? Cousin Mattie's homesick, she misses her friends, our father says. I'm taking her back for a quick visit so she can see them. We don't believe it. Cousin Mattie couldn't possibly have any friends. Our mother packs the special overnight case and tries to curl Cousin Mattie's limp hair. We watch everything and say nothing and make hate blare out of our eyes in flashes like signal lights. We've been doing it all summer, we're pretty good at it by now. Our father goes on the train with her to the city. We hope he leaves her there.

Here's Cousin Mattie. Back already. Can we swim yet? she asks with her little grunt. Not yet, we say. Eventually they'll get tired of the pool and go away, Lily says hopefully. There's no hope of that. The black kids show no signs of getting tired. Now it's a matter of principle, a battle of wills. When will the lifeguard do something? Either kick out the black kids, or shove us in the water with them. Either would be preferable to what he's doing. Which is: sitting there, uninvolved, impassive, sunglassed, blind.

Cousin Mattie stumbles out to the sleeping porch without her glasses. Her body glows in the dark, round, luminous, like a giant moon, a mutant firefly. I imagine an enormous bat swooping down and biting off the top half of her. Wormy bits of intestines would pop out. There's something tired and battered and saggy about her face. You can tell what she'll look like as an old lady. Let's go, she says. Take a swim. I really need a swim tonight. No, I say though I'm dying to go. I don't want to give her the satisfaction.

This is the summer of denial. The days trickle away. The vision of the pool floats before our eyes like a mirage, distant, untouchable. We dream of the soothing balm of chlorinated water with Band-Aids floating in it. Cousin Mattie grunts and mutters her discontent. I don't say a word; Lily whines enough for the two of us. The past few weeks have been an eternity. The weeks ahead stretch out interminably.

I've had it, Cousin Mattie says—I'm getting in, I'm *so* hot. She's awfully red in the face. There's a whistle in her breath, in addition to the usual grunt. I hold one wrist and Lily holds the other. We keep her sitting on the grass without too much trouble. No one notices a thing. On the way home she keeps rubbing her wrists and sniffling. Aw, don't be a baby, I say, we didn't hurt you. Cousin Mattie tries to catch her breath. Her face is very red, splotches popping out on her temples and the sides of her neck. I feel a little afraid of her. After all, she has seen Death and we haven't. That gives her power over us. Our mother told us all about it before Mattie arrived. How Mattie left the dinner table to answer the phone, and came back to find her father slumped over facedown in the mashed potatoes, stark dead. So remember that and be kind to her, our mother said. Remember that she's looked into the Face of Death. You have no idea what that's like. Lily was listening, rapt and horrified. I wanted to say that *technically* that wasn't true, if her father had been facedown in his dinner. She probably only saw the back of his head. I'd forgotten about Death, but now, looking at Mattie's red face, I remember and get a chill. I look at her glasses and small pinkish eyes and wonder how Death felt, looking back at her.

The next day Mattie won't go back to the pool with us. I don't feel good, she says, and lies back down in (our!) bed. She's making too much of the wrist-twisting. We barely touched her. We go to the pool without her and stare at the black kids hard enough to count as three people. Maybe even four.

When we go home at six Mattie is still in bed. She stays in bed the next day too. On the third day our mother calls the doctor. You know what *this* means, I tell Lily. Yeah, she says wisely. A second later she says, What does it mean? She's got *it*, I say, one of those diseases, those summer fevers that eat up your nerve endings, she probably got the germs when she went to the city to visit, probably from one of her friends. I say this just to scare Lily, but then our mother says, I want you two to stay away from her. What she has is very serious and I don't want you to catch it. She could die or end up in a wheelchair. You hear? And don't tell anyone, our mother says. I don't want people thinking I don't keep a clean house.

That night as soon as the house is quiet and asleep, I wake Lily and say, It's time. She says, For what? Get your bathing suit, I say. I go to (our!) bedroom, where Cousin Mattie is muffled up under the covers though it is stifling. Our room smells funny, Lily whispers. It does. It smells like it isn't ours. Come on, I tell Cousin Mattie. Time for a swim. She looks up at us, eyes swimming around, all unmoored without her glasses. All right, she says.

Cousin Mattie says night swimming is like flying. I don't know if she's lying or not. I'm watching her and it doesn't *look* like flying. But maybe it *feels* different. Maybe the way the dark falls into the water makes you feel like you don't know where one ends and the other begins. Maybe the way the stars are reflected in the water's surface makes you feel like you're surrounded by stars rather than beneath them. I'm just guessing. One day I'll find out for sure.

I'm not sure about this, I have to guess, because right now I am *not* night swimming. I'm standing on the concrete ledge next to Lily, watching Cousin Mattie night-swim in the darkened, deserted pool. We watch her dive and swoop and float on her back. She stretches her arms wide, she seems to grow and stretch, stroking from one end to the other, spreading herself everywhere. Why can't we get in? Lily whines. We got our bathing suits on and everything. It's part of the plan, I whisper. What plan? Lily says. Secret plan, can't tell you, I say. Come on in, Mattie calls, fly with me. I'm too cold, I answer, it's colder than I thought, I changed my mind. Scaredy-cat, Cousin Mattie yells. It's all I can do to keep my mouth shut.

The waters open, swallow, recede, buoy her up like a mattress. Dark shadows swim beneath her, around her, over her. She laughs in an enticing, frightening way. A grown-up laugh. Beside me, Lily quivers with longing. She'll never get in without me. I hate her, Lily moans, and I hate you too. Cousin Mattie climbs out of the water, and we take her home, shivering and shaking, and put her to bed.

She stays in bed, still sick. We go to the pool every day, grim and defiant. We will not move, we will not leave, we will not say a word.

Nothing happens. For a while.

One day I notice that the red-and-blue starry shorts are missing. Brick's not there. I've been watching the black kids all summer, I know them like I know my own family, and I notice immediately that Brick and two of the younger boys, regulars, aren't there. Three missing.

The next day the three have become five.

And then the five become eight.

And then the kids trickle away steadily, none of the missing ones reappearing, they dwindle and dwindle until there is only Cheryl and two boys darting nervously about in the water, looking anxiously behind them as if they're being chased. And then only one holdout is left, one forlorn little boy, the same boy who first touched the water with one tentative hand. He stands shivering in the water for a full day, not knowing what to do with himself but not wanting to give up. Then the next day he too is gone.

They're all gone. They're out. It's time for us, finally, to get back in. We come to the pool early, expectant. We find the lifeguard chaining the gates shut. There's an outbreak of fever spreading through the community, the lifeguard says. He can't allow kids to congregate and pass germs around. He pins up a notice that declares the pool closed for the rest of the summer.

Maybe it's closed, but we still won. We held out to the end, didn't we? Now we don't get to use the pool, but neither do they. So now we're even. Fair and square.

We hear lots of stories. We hear about lots of kids getting sick. White and black both. We're not allowed to leave the yard, or play with anybody, or even go in to see Mattie. As if we'd want to! Our mother puts smelly stuff in little cloth bags that Lily and I have to wear next to our skin, on strings hanging around our necks and dangling down inside our shirts. I don't see how it can help—the stuff doesn't even keep away mosquitoes. They're calling it an epidemic, health department workers pinning warning signs on everybody's doors. I don't know if it's as bad as all that.

We've heard that lots of kids are dying, or ending up in wheelchairs, just as our mother always said. We know some of them. I wonder if this counts as looking Death in the face. We hear that a lot of black kids have died. More than half of the ones that came to the pool— Brick and Melinda and a bunch of others.

Nobody's saying it, but I know they're thinking it—those kids got what they deserved, justice has been dealt. Just like in the Bible. They shouldn't have come in, they should have stayed behind the fence, same as always. When you break rules, even unspoken ones, there are always consequences. Nobody will admit they're glad some kids are dead, but I know they're thinking it, deep down secretly they *are*.

Not that I'm claiming credit, or anything. Not me. I didn't have anything to do with it. It was all Mattie. Mattie did it. Maybe I had a plan, but *I* didn't go to the city and then spread myself all over the pool. It's Mattie's fault. Mattie's guilty. Mattie's the one to bring an end to everything.

Which is fitting, since Mattie is the one who started the whole thing in the first place, Mattie with her invitation to come in, her little wave. Which is why I am glad she is sick too.

When people talk about the sickness, they talk about dying, about the wheelchairs and the iron breathing machines. They never seem to talk about the fourth possibility, which is getting better. Which is what Mattie seems to be doing. Has Cousin Mattie said something to my mother about me? About the plan? But what could she possibly say without incriminating herself? Nothing. And yet ... and yet .... Just a little while ago my mother looked at me, studying, and for a split second her face did a strange thing, scrunching up and smoothing out again but the imprint of the crumple is still there, like when you squeeze a paper bag in your fist. Then she looked away.

We're lying in the backyard, Lily and I, trying to catch a little of the breeze that blows through the pine trees. We're wondering when Cousin Mattie's going to leave. We want our room back. Lily is very quiet. I'm thinking about the classroom at school, guessing how many seats will be empty. We won't have to share readers any more. Lily's lying flat on her back, staring up at the cloudy sky. Her face is flushed. Doing jumping jacks again? I say. No, dummy, she says scornfully. I can't remember her ever disagreeing with me before. What are you doing, then? I say. I'm just ... *remembering*, Lily says and closes her eyes. Remembering what? Night swimming, she says. It really *is* like flying. How do you know? I say, looking at the red flush blooming along her neck and around her ears. From *personal experience*, Lily says loftily. Lily, you didn't, I say, sitting up. You wouldn't, you couldn't, not without *me*. Her pupils are huge and her breath smells strange and even before I touch her I know her face will feel scorching hot. When? How? Lily, you didn't, I say. And Lily says, I *did*, and it *is*.

Inside "Immersion": Word Games

This started out as an attempt to do that Alice Munro thing of conveying a novel's worth of depth and scope in a short story. She's a dangerous author to try to emulate because she makes it look so easy; she makes you think that if you just cram together enough characters and incidents and relationships and twists, your story too will magically coalesce into a Munro-esque compressed epic. And of course it never does.

In the first draft, the story had the frame of an elderly woman looking back over her life, reviewing her past misdeeds and reassessing how aware she was of her guilt at the time. There were more characters playing larger roles, and I envisioned a whole complicated web of relationships and motivations among them. Mattie, for example, was not simply a friend of the family's; she was the product of a years-long affair the narrator's father had had with a woman in the city. The woman had recently died, the affair had come to light, and the narrator's mother had invited Mattie to live with them—ostensibly out of the goodness of her heart, but really so that she could wave her own selflessness and martyrdom in her husband's face at every opportunity. There was a lot of competition among the girls for the father's affection, but at the same time the father was sinister and possibly abusive, so the sisters both wanted and dreaded his attention and were secretly relieved when Mattie took the brunt of it off them. There was an older brother, too, climbing out of his window at night and getting into trouble, and a dozen other plot threads involving the neighborhood kids, their parents, the lifeguard, other neighbors.

It was kind of a mess, and I knew the voice wasn't right—I couldn't settle on how much distance to put between the adult-narrator looking back and the child-narrator experiencing the events. Hitting that perfect *To Kill a Mockingbird* balance is no easy feat. I didn't feel good about the story—I had that bad cringing feeling of not even wanting to read it over. But I sent the story to my agent Leigh anyway, and she read it and responded with her characteristic frankness that she had no idea what was going on. But she said she could tell that there was something in there, something that was tugging at me and compelling me to write the story. She suggested I figure out what that was, write only about that, and jettison the rest.

So I gave the story a hard look, and it was immediately clear to me where the tugging was coming from—not from the familiar clichés (infidelity, abusive father, etc.), but from a minor thread: the swimming-pool protest, the reverse sit-in. Combining unspoken racism with fears of disease and contagion, the obvious water imagery—it all made sense. And it became clear to me that I needed to get rid of the frame and stick closely to a child's point of view. I wanted the narrator to try to justify what she does by claiming it's for the greater good, insisting she's merely preserving the status quo, but I also wanted her to have hints of conscience, a growing awareness of the enormity of her crime. I needed a child in order to retain some degree of reader sympathy. An adult who knowingly does what she does would be a monster, but a child who is only partially aware, and grows to full awareness, could be sympathetic, even tragic.

I didn't want to confine myself to historical accuracy—I have no idea if polio scares really coincided with desegregation tensions. I simply wanted to get the *feel* of the story right. So I relied on a setting and atmosphere that was familiar to me—a hot summer in the South, a swimming pool, a little sister. That's my childhood in a nutshell, so it was easy to gather the sensory details to ground the story in a tangible world.

I wrote another draft, but I still couldn't get the narrator's voice right. I was using a child's point of view, but I was using past tense and that implied some kind of gap between the action and the telling, and that gap allowed time for reflection. I didn't want the narrator to have a chance to reflect, and perhaps revise her version of events, shift her degree of complicity, for her audience. I wanted her to be reporting events just as they were happening. I knew I needed to use present tense, but was reluctant to. It's so hard to get present tense just right. I like the immediacy of present tense, but I hate the language that I tend to fall into whenever I use it—that dreamy, stream-of-consciousness floridity.

So I did something I often do when I'm stuck. I gave myself a distraction, a sort of word game to think about instead of obsessing over the problem at hand. I gave myself a challenge and some strict parameters to work within. I told myself: Instead of writing straight prose, I'll arrange the text in small sections, surrounded by white space, like islands surrounded by water. I'll need something to help the reader bridge the gap from one section to the next, so what I'll do is use a repeated word. It doesn't have to be the very last word of one section and the first of the next one, but it should be a word somewhere in the last sentence of one section that will be repeated somewhere in the first sentence of the next.

It sounds needlessly complicated, but it helped—planning the "islands" and the "bridge" words kept the scurrying, superficial part of my mind occupied so that the more intuitive, unconscious part could relax and let inspiration sneak in. The story finally started to come alive.

After a while I decided to change the parameters a little, to keep my brain busy. I told myself that whenever the story took an unexpected turn, when events veered out of the narrator's control, I would use antonyms, rather than repeated words, as a "bridge." I don't remember if I stuck to my own rules all the way through. I doubt the device adds anything to the story. I'd like to think the repetition helps create a rhythm, a kind of incantatory effect. But I don't know. Every time I meet someone who has read the story, I ask if they noticed the "bridge" words, and I'm met with *no*s or looks of incomprehension. Maybe that's a good thing. If the device were noticeable, it would probably be intrusive and annoying; it would break the spell. At any rate, the game served its purpose—it got me unstuck, got the story out of me.

Before I hit on the game, I didn't know how to resolve the story satisfactorily. I knew I wanted the narrator's actions to rebound back on her, I wanted her to shoot herself in the foot, but I wasn't sure how. I knew the pool's closing would be a bit of a punishment, but it wasn't enough; I needed retribution to hit *her*, particularly, right where it hurt. But where was that? As I was writing along, it became obvious—she had to endanger her sister, the person she cares about most, her alter ego, her echo, practically her self. And I saw that there had to be a double realization at the end—not only does she realize that she's infected her sister, but she realizes she's not omnipotent. The narrator had always thought she knew her sister's every action, every thought; Lily's secret night swimming comes as a shocking betrayal. The narrator discovers she doesn't have all the answers, she's not always right. It's the moment of dawning realization that I was seeking in that first faulty draft, with an elderly narrator reaching it through a review of her memories; but I think it makes more sense happening this way, to a child on the cusp of adulthood, about to be thrust from the security of childhood omnipotence into the precarious adult world of uncertainty and consequences and moral fallibility. Now that I think about it, it fits neatly into the classic coming-of-age paradigm.

Now I can reread this story without cringing, which means I did something right. It's not a perfect story by any means, but I feel that I served the idea as well as I possibly could. Every time I reread it, I notice new details I don't remember putting in there—things I didn't consciously choose, but some unconscious part of my brain decided would work and stuck in there anyway. Like Mattie's little grunt, and the buggy, batty sleeping porch, and the ill-fitting sandals that cut into one's heels. I named the sister Lily simply because it felt right; it was only later that I noticed the obvious associations and implications of the name. And the scene where Mattie is night swimming, laughing her frightening grown-up laugh, while the sisters hesitate on the edge of the pool, Lily quivering like a little puppy—well, now I see that it's an obvious brink-of-adulthood metaphor. But when I wrote it, I wasn't thinking about any of that. I was just writing the scene the way it needed to be written, the only way that felt right.

 WRITING EXERCISE

This is an exercise several of my writing instructors assigned to me when I was a student, and I, in turn, always assign it to my own students. It's a useful exercise to do when you're staring at a blank page (or screen) and can't seem to get started.

What you do is write ten (or twenty) "first" sentences. Don't write (or think) beyond that; simply write ten openers as quickly as you can. Be as playful or nonsensical or abstract as you wish. It can be surprisingly liberating to write a "first" sentence when you know you don't have to commit to the idea for another twenty pages.

Put the sentences aside and look at them again later. You'll see how even the simplest sentences, seen in isolation, become freighted with implication and portent. A single sentence can set off a cascade of questions that you can spend an entire story answering. (Here's an example: "He thought about cutting off the other leg." What leg? Whose leg? Why? How's he going to do it? What happened to the *first* leg he cut off? Why's he still thinking about it and not *doing* it—what's stopping him? Who *is* this guy?) Hopefully you'll discover a couple of ideas worth pursuing.

Usually when I assign this exercise to students, I give them a list of examples to get them going. So you might find it helpful to look at the opening sentences of some of your favorite stories. One of my favorite examples is from "Big Bad Love" by Larry Brown. The first sentence is "My *dog* died."

DAN CHAON

Prodigal

Mine is the typical story: I used to despise my father, and now that he is dead I feel bad about despising him. There's not much more to say about that.

When I was young, I used to identify with those precociously perceptive child narrators one finds in books. You know the type. They always have big dark eyes. They observe poetic details, clear-sighted, very sensitive: the father's cologne-sweet smell, his lingering breath of beer and cigarettes, his hands like ____. Often farm animals are metaphorically invoked, and we see the dad involved in some work—hunched over the gaping mouth of a car, straightening the knot in his salesman's tie, pulling himself into the cab of his semi-truck, on his hands and knees among the rosebushes. We'll see a whole map of his wasted, pathetic life in the squeal of his worn-out brakes, in the wisping smokestacks of the factory where he works, in the aching image of him rising before dawn to turn up the thermostat. The mom will peer from behind a curtain as he drives away. Her hands tremble as she folds clothes, washes dishes, makes you a sandwich. Something you don't quite understand is always going on and you press close to the bathroom door she is locked behind. You'll probably hear her weeping.

★★★

Now that I have children of my own, this bothers me. This type of kid. Sometimes, when I feel depressed and stare out the window while my kids pester me for attention, or when I lose my temper and throw a plate or whatever, or when I'm in a good mood and I'm singing some song from the radio too loudly and too off-key, I think of that gentle, dewy-eyed first-person narrator and it makes my skin crawl. It doesn't matter what you do. In the end, you are going to be judged, and all the times that you're not at your most dignified are the ones that will be re-called in all their vivid, heartbreaking detail. And then of course these things will be distorted and exaggerated and replayed over and over, un-til eventually they turn into the essence of you: your cartoon.

★★★

My father is a good example. My father used to whistle merry little tunes when he was happy and soft, minor key ones when he was sad. I can't remember when exactly this began to annoy me but by the time I was eleven or twelve, I could do a pretty amazing parody of it. I'd see him coming, loping along with his hands behind his back and his eyes downcast, whistling some dirge, and I could barely contain my private laughter.

Once, when he was visiting, he began to whistle in an elevator, com-pletely oblivious to the obvious codes of silence and anonymity that gov-ern certain public places. The second the doors slid shut, he abruptly puckered his lips, like a chaste kiss, and began to trill, filling the air with melody, accenting the tune with grace notes and a strange, melodra-matic vibrato at the climatic parts, until everyone nearby was turned to stone with horror and embarrassment, staring straight ahead and pretend-ing they couldn't hear it.

He was on his last legs by that point—"last legs," he said, as if he had more than one pair. I didn't believe him at the time, in part because those words seemed so trite and goofy. I felt that any person really facing death would conceive of it in much grander terms. Even my father.

★★★

One time my father hit my mother. I wish you could've seen his face: the bared teeth and bulged eyes, the mottled redness of the cheeks and forehead, the skin seeming to shine like a lacquered surface. If someone had been there to take a photograph, to freeze the expression in the moment before his hand lurched up to grab my mom by the neck, in a purely objective picture, you would not be able to identify the emotion in that look as rage. You might assume that it was pain or terror. There's a great photo from the Vietnam War—you know the one, of the guy screaming as he's shot through the head. That's what my dad looked like at that moment.

I never saw him look like that, before or after. But if I close my eyes I can see that face as clearly as I can picture the school portraits of my children on the coffee table, or the blue LeSabre that is waiting for me in the garage, or my first and only dog Lucky, who, on the night of my parents' fight lay under the table in the kitchen, his long snout resting warily on his paws.

I'm sure that my father never realized how easily I could graft that face over his gentle one, how much more easily I could conjure up that image instead of some thought of his good qualities. It probably would have made him cry. He wept easily in his last years. I recall seeing him sitting in his easy chair, touching his fingers to his moist eyes as he watched a news special about poor orphans in Romania. When he and my mother had their fiftieth wedding anniversary, and he stood up to make a speech, his voice broke. "This woman," he said, and he choked back a sob. "This woman is the first and only love of my life."

I don't know. It's hard to decide if the waver in his voice was authentic or not. Who knows what he was really thinking as he spoke, as he stood there with my mother beaming, glistening-eyed, up at him— whether that strangled "love of my life" was tinged with regret, self-pity, whether it was because he was standing in front of all these people who knew that he and my mom hadn't had the most pleasant of lives together. But it also might be that he said it with true, honest feeling. In the end, there probably isn't much difference between being in love and acting like you're in love.

I don't mean this as a put-down either. I really don't believe that it's possible to be in love all of the time, any more than it's possible to always be good. So you must go with the next best thing. You try to pretend.

There are times when I would do anything to be a good person. But I'm not. Deep down, most of the time, I'm not. What can you do? You have a flash of goodness and you try to hold on to it, ride it for all it's worth.

There was this one time that my kids and I were playing with clay, the three of us together. I don't know why this moment was special, but it was. We were all quiet, concentrated on our work, our fingers kneading and shaping. We were making an elephant and I remember how excited they were when I rolled out its trunk, a careful snake between my palm and the surface of the table. My youngest was about three at the time, and I remember how he rested his cheek against my arm, watching me. I remember how soft and warm that cheek felt. The older one was pounding out a flap for the ear, and I can recall my voice being gentle and perfect when I told him how great it was. He gave it to me; I pressed it to the elephant's head.

But it didn't last for long, that moment. I am sure that neither of them remember it as I do, for pretty soon they started arguing, whining about who had more clay and so on. It was a jolt; I could actually feel the goodness moving out of me, the way you can feel blood moving when you blush or grow pale. "Come on guys," I said, "let's not fight. This is fun, isn't it? Let's have fun." But my gentle voice was just an imitation, I was mimicking the tone of those enlightened parents you see sometimes, the kind who never seem to raise their voice beyond the steady monotone of kind patience, like the computer in that movie *2001: A Space Odyssey*.

But even parents like that won't be forgiven, you know. My wife's friend is a psychologist and she spent her life explaining things in the most calm, reasonable voice you can imagine. She never raised her voice. Even when her kid was two years old, she was out there saying things like, "Please don't run in the street, because, even though you're excited and it's hard to pay attention, some people drive their cars too fast and they might not see you," etc. Now, naturally, her adult son won't talk to her. At all. He finds her unbearably manipulative. Repressive. Repulsive. Good words like that.

I recall when my wife's friend first told us about this. How old was I? Twenty-three or twenty-four maybe, and the son might have been twenty. I was sitting at the kitchen table across from this old, heavy, smooth-talking gal, the leader of some women's group thing my wife went to, and I was holding my sweet, sleeping baby in my arms. I can recall giving her that stern, bored stare I used to reserve for people I thought of as adults. She was almost my father's age, and her angry son was only a few years younger than I. She was a failure, I thought then. I stared down at my sleeping baby's face, the long-lashed eyes, the softly parted lips that moved slightly, as if he dreamed of nursing, and I thought: that will never happen to me. I will never let them hate me.

★★★

Now, as they are growing older, I am aware that hatred is a definite possibility at the end of the long tunnel of parenthood and I suspect that there is little one can do about it.

Not long ago, when I insisted that he come down to dinner, my youngest son called me a "Stupid Idiot." I did not spank him, or wash his mouth out with soap, as my own father might have done; I simply set him up on the "time-out" stool—our preferred method of punishment—and scolded him while he kicked his legs and sang defiantly. His eyes sparked at me, and I could clearly see the opening of a vortex I would eventually be sucked into, against my will.

Once, I recall, when my oldest son was about five years old, he asked me if he could have my skeleton when I was dead. He told me that when he was grown up, he wanted to own a haunted house. He would cover my remains with spider webs and charge people five dollars to look at them.

"Sure," I said. "Whatever." I even smiled, as if it were cute. I did not act as if I were offended. But the truth is, my throat tightened. You'll be sorry, I wanted to say. You'll be sorry when I'm gone!

★★★

Do you know how sorry I was? You should have seen me at my father's funeral. I look back on this with some embarrassment, because I truly lost control. I wailed and tore at my hair. My children may have been too young to remember seeing this.

When my grandfather died, my father wept silently. Tears ran out of his nose, and I remember that it took me a long time to figure out that he didn't simply have a cold. At the funeral, he stared straight ahead, rigid, almost glaring, his jaw set.

One time, I remember, we were at the county fair. We were walking back to our car through the parking lot, when a group of older teenagers began to make fun of us. This was in the early seventies, and the teens were what we then called "hippies"—shaggy, raggedly dressed, full of secrets. As a child, I was warned to stay away from them, as they might kidnap me in one of their Volkswagen vans and force me to smoke marijuana.

In any case, they were amused by us. We must have looked ridiculously corny to them, and I remember one of them calling out, "Look! Here comes Mother, Father, and The Children!" And the others joined in: "Hello, Mother! Hello, Father! Hello, Little Wally!"

My father acted as if they weren't there, though his face became fixed stiff and his eyes fixed harshly on some point in the distance. He just kept plodding forward, as if he couldn't hear them. That was the look, I thought, that he had at the funeral.

The times in my childhood that I remember seeing him cry, they were always because of music. He was frequently brought to tears by some old, unbearably sentimental song. I remember this one called "Scarlet Ribbons," and another which went:

O my Papa!
To me he was so wonderful!
O my Papa!
To me he was so good!

This song, in particular, used to drive me crazy, and when he would play it I would leave the room, if possible. It wasn't only because of the maudlin tremor in the singer's voice, or because of my father's solemn canonizing of my grandfather, a man who had once burned my father's arm with a red-hot fork, leaving a scar which still remained. ("It taught me a lesson," my father said. He was being punished for having cruelly burned his younger sister with a match.)

It wasn't the hypocrisy that repelled me. It was simply that I understood the implications of the line: "To me he was so wonderful." By which the singer meant, "No matter what, my father seemed wonderful to me." And I knew that my father wasn't weeping because he was extending this grace to his own father. No, he was weeping because he was wishing it for himself. He hoped that I would someday sing "O my Papa!" He cried for himself, and each tear said, "Someday you will love me unconditionally. Someday you will forgive me. Someday you will be sorry."

Which was something I didn't want to hear at the time.

★★★

I've suffered a little. Along with his sentimental side came a nasty temper. I got my share of what my father called "lickings," a term which, even in the extremity of my punishment, would cause me to smirk into my hand. I was beaten with a wire brush, a belt, a length of hose. And I was the victim of verbal and emotional abuse. I don't know whether I mentioned this or not, but once my father hit my mother. I stood by watching.

Nowadays, I meet a lot of people who were never beaten when they were children. They never witnessed any sort of violence in the home, and the idea of striking a child is so aberrant to them that I enjoy shocking them with tales of my abuse—most of which are quite true.

My father would have been just as outraged to hear of a parent who didn't use corporal punishment. You couldn't really reason with a child, he would have reasoned, but you had to make sure they obeyed. They had to learn to respect before they learned to think. The idea of a world filled with unspanked children would have made him frown grimly. For what would become of society, once these children grew up? The children would be spoiled, and the world would be filled with rude, disrespectful, dishonest, shiftless adults.

He worried about me being spoiled. By *spoiled*, he didn't mean what my mother means when she says that she can hardly wait to see her grandchildren at Christmastime. "I'll spoil them rotten," she says devilishly, and I say, "Oh, they're already so spoiled it's not funny." And we laugh.

To my father, the word still retained a large part of its older, more serious connotations: *spoiled* meant "ruined," and the act of *spoiling* had flickers of its archaic meaning—to pillage, to plunder. In my father's estimation, a man who spoiled his children was robbing them, for a spoiled child would never be capable of the higher emotions: love, patriotism, self-sacrifice, honor, duty. Though he wept when the father made the son shoot the pet deer in *The Yearling*, he felt that the father did the right thing. We got into a heated argument about this one night about a year before he died. "It had to be done!" my father had insisted, and his voice rose, almost cracking with emotion. "That's how it was back then, damn it!"

"Well, do you know how it is now?" I said—I immediately saw the opening I'd been waiting years for, my chance to educate him. "Do you know what would happen to a man who burned his child with a red-hot fork? He would be jailed and his children would be taken by the state!"

My father could not help but look at his scar—the tattoo of his father that he would still be wearing as he lay in his casket.

(I saw it there—I pushed up the sleeve of his jacket, smoothing my fingers over that paper-dry corpse skin, and there it was. I touched the scar, and that was the last time I touched my father.)

My father stared at the five smooth lines the fork had left just above the wristband of his watch. "Do you think my dad loved me any less than you love your kids?" he said. "Is that what you think?"

And we were both silent.

★★★

I don't know the answer, even now. Maybe love, like suffering, is relative. My wife's psychologist friend once told me, judgmentally, that sarcasm is more damaging to a child's spirit than a slap across the face. Emerson once said that the civilized person actually suffers more than those primitive people who are inured to hardship because the genteel person is more acutely aware of pain. I used to call this Emerson's Princess and the Pea Theory but maybe it's true. We all require a certain amount of pain to justify ourselves later, and if we aren't lucky enough to have parents who beat us and force us to shoot our beloved pets, the stab of an unkind word or a neglectful shrug of the shoulders will do just as well.

Still, sometimes when I hear the stories of other people, I feel a little ashamed for complaining. I once knew a girl whose father raped her, regularly, when she was between the ages of two and six. Another of my friends, a guy from Cambodia, lost his mother and four brothers to the Khmer Rouge; his own father informed on them. Listening to such stuff, I feel like an anorexic in a country of starving people. Why was I so angry at my father? What's the point of my complaint? I've suffered very little, relatively speaking, so why do I feel so bad, so maudlin?

I'm not even sure I'm going to die right away. I might easily—75 percent chance—recover. According to the books, "the five-year survival rate for patients with localized disease is 75%." But I could live twenty more years. Or fifty! What's the point in even wondering?

★★★

That's what my father used to say when I asked him about death: There's no point in wondering, in worrying about it. It will come to all of us, sooner or later, he said, very solemn and sage-like, though I was thinking, *Duh—I* know *that.* You could get hit by a truck tomorrow, he continued, and I sort of shut him off after that, his thoughtful droning. Why had I even bothered to ask?

Actually, I do remember one other thing he said—though whether he said it that time or another I can't recall.

"Our children relive our lives for us," he said. "That's the only kind of afterlife I believe in, just that we live on through our children. I don't know whether that makes any sense. It probably doesn't now, but it will. You try different things, you make different choices, but it's still all the same person. You. Me. Your grandpa. We get mostly the same raw material, just recycled. We're more alike than different, you know."

At the time, the thought seemed ridiculous. *I'm not you,* I thought. I knew for a fact that I was much smarter and more capable than he'd ever be.

★★★

I wonder how my own children would react if I told them my father's theory. I doubt if it would make any more sense to them than it did to me, though they are not old enough yet to be repulsed by the idea, I don't think.

Still, it's hard to guess what they imagine I am. I doubt if they think of it much; I am "Dad," that's all. It's strange how easily we fall into those roles—the form-fitting personalities that my children think of as "Mom" and "Dad." As they've grown, we have increasingly given over pieces of our lives to these caricatures, until the "Dad" part of me casts a shadow over what I think of as my "real" self. I feel like an old soap opera actor who, after years of playing the same part, begins to feel the character taking on a presence in his soul. My wife and I have not yet taken to calling one another "Mom" and "Dad," as my parents used to, but much of the time this is how we think of one another. We are already lost, even to ourselves. We slip helplessly into parody.

There is no way for my sons to know this, no possible way. They don't even really believe that the world existed before they were born. They know it intellectually, of course, but at the same time it's as unfathomable as infinity, or zero.

I start my chemotherapy tomorrow, and they don't know that either. They know that I am going to the hospital, but very little else. We have decided, my wife and I, that it would be too much for them to handle. And so they go on with their everyday lives: playing outside, squabbling at the dinner table, watching some cartoon on television and laughing uproariously, interrupting me as I talk on the phone to the doctor. I turn to my youngest fiercely, cupping my hand over the receiver. "Will you shut up! Can't you see I'm on the phone?" And in that moment, I see him blanch, hurt and resentment flickering across his face. One more piece of me disappears.

Later, standing at the edge of their bedroom, watching as they play checkers, I want to tell them. I want to say: "I might die soon." I want to shake them. "Can't you see me? Can't you see that I'm real?" But what I say is, "Hey, Bud, I'm sorry I was sharp with you when I was talking on the phone. I didn't mean to snap like that."

He shrugs his shoulders, absorbed in his game. "S'Okay," he says. He doesn't look up.

★★★

Once, my father hit my mother and I stood by watching, smirking into my hand. For a long time in my life, every bad thing that happened seemed bitterly hilarious. I felt that I had a heightened sense of the absurd. When my father was dying—dying of the same cancer I now have, if you want the truth—I was almost giddy with the terrible irony of it, the sarcasm of God. It was about two months after the retirement he'd been talking about, hoping for; for years he had been planning to buy a Winnebago, to go traveling across the country with my mother. He was diagnosed shortly after he'd purchased the thing.

That time he hit my mother, they had been arguing for a long while. I don't remember what it was about. It must have been very important to them at the time, but I saw how minuscule it was, how little it mattered in the grand scheme of things. What could I do but try to contain my private laughter? Back then, I believed that I had no connection to these strangers, these two foolish people who didn't realize that they were already summed up. Their lives were already over, I thought then. Nothing they ever did could change things.

And so, in giddy and adrenaline-fueled shock, I clamped my hand over my mouth. I saw my father's face twist as he turned to me, and I wonder what he thought I was thinking. His eyes widened and his

83

mouth moved. We looked at one another; I think now that he hoped that I could save him.

★★★

Why do we think that, we parents? Why do I think it even now, standing in the dark, watching my sons sleeping? *Save me, save me,* I think. And yet they can't, of course. Already I am halfway gone. Even from the beginning, when their infant eyes begin to focus on your floating face, the way a cat will watch the moon, already you are a ghost of yourself.

He must have known that, too, my father. He must have seen it in my face as I stared back at him. I sit down on my youngest son's bed, as my father might have sat on my bed late one night when I was a child. We look down, we touch the child's ear, watching him stir a little.

But no matter how hard we try, we are disappearing. Oh my child, you will never save me. You will never be what I wanted to be, you will never love me in the way I need you to, you will never give me myself back.

And yet, I forgive you. You won't know this until a long time later, my little narrator, my wide-eyed camera. You won't know it, but I forgave you a long time ago.

Inside "Prodigal": The Fictional Essay

Back when this story was written, I was going through a period of feeling hostile toward the nonfiction memoir. The form was enjoying a lot of popularity, and I decided that I bore a grudge against it.

In this case, I was particularly irritated by the dysfunctional childhood narrative, and I decided that I was going to write an essay, basically making fun of the genre. There was a certain kind of prose that I wanted to denounce, that melancholy but sweetly funny, innocent-but-wiser-

84

now poetic style, which, I decided, was essentially a kind of elegant way to express adolescent self-pity. I was going to call my essay "Mommy Drinks Because You Cry," and I even had a good opening line: "When I was young, I used to identify with those precociously perceptive child narrators one finds in memoirs." I had an idea of a certain kind of acrid, wry, incisive voice that would quote from and then dismantle a variety of books that I didn't like. I imagined, excitedly, that my essay would cause a lot of controversy!

But sitting down to write the essay was another story. Actually, it wasn't as much fun as I thought it would be. Creating an intelligent analytic review is a lot of work, and, to me, it's not enjoyable work. The more I tried to explain why I was irritated by a certain kind of memoir, the more I realized that my grudge was idiosyncratic and kind of illogical in a way that didn't make a very good critical review. I found that, again and again, the essay seemed to ramble off away from the books I was supposed to be critiquing and into long asides. I found myself telling anecdotes, rather than drawing upon examples from the various texts that I was supposed to be reviewing.

As my rant against memoir dwindled away, I began to discover that what I was *really* interested in was the "voice" itself—the snarky, aggrieved monologue, which had slowly stopped being the person I thought of as "me," and had become, without my knowing at first, a persona.

We all do this, of course, when we are telling stories. We exaggerate aspects of ourselves for effect, or to make a point, or to get a laugh, and I think this is particularly true in the personal essay. I often wonder what newspaper columnists and famous essayists are *really* like, in the flesh rather than on the page. How much of their authorial voice is like their real personality, and how much of it is a put-on?

As for me, it wasn't long before the whole thing had become an act. The "personal examples" I was giving weren't entirely true, even from the beginning, and the further I went along, the more confabulated they became. Soon, I began to see the first-person narrator of my essay as a fictional character I was inhabiting, and it was at this point that I realized that I probably wasn't really writing an "essay" any longer. I was flat-out telling lies. I was writing a story.

It's funny, because once the burden of truth was lifted, I felt as if the narrator was more alive than when I was writing as "myself." One of the reasons I've avoided nonfiction is because it always seems as if there's a kind of weird stiffness to my "personal" writing, a self-conscious awkwardness. But once the character wasn't "me" any longer, the voice seemed both more natural and more complicated.

And more interesting. One of the problems with writing nonfiction, for me, is that it always seems to draw out a little genie of self-loathing. I'll try to tell a humorous anecdote, and the genie will whisper: *Oh brother! Do you really think you're funny?* I'll write a poetic metaphor and the genie will sigh. *How precious that sounds!*

But once my narrator was a fictional character, I found that I could actually make good use of this kind of dual-consciousness. I felt more sympathy for him, as a character, than I probably would have felt for myself; and looking at him from outside, I could see both his humor and his crankiness as a kind of defense mechanism. Looking at him from outside, you could see that he was revealing himself in ways that he didn't intend.

This unreliability, of course, was another thing that pushed the piece further into fictional territory. It seems to me that the essayist is attempting to encapsulate and explain a moment, and thus takes on a kind of authority that a fictional character can never have. To me, the fictional first person is almost always about subjectivity and unreliability in one form or another.

At the same time, because it had started out as an essay, this story was also structurally quite different from the kind of fiction that I usually wrote. I found myself playing around with the digressive, conversational style that is common in the personal essay, the sense that the author is speaking directly to the reader, an illusion of intimacy, and that led me toward more essay-like structuring devices as well. In general, most of my stories are structured around a chronological sequence of events, starting with some kind of incident, and proceeding to follow the characters as they react and respond. This piece was different because it tended to revolve around a thesis, and so I found myself using more rhetorical and argumentative transitions, rather than plot and sequential transitions. I found myself especially attracted to the "rhetorical question" as a way of moving the story forward—which turned out to be useful because I didn't always know what the answer to the question was, and that, in turn, led me deeper into the story and into the character.

It turned out that this method was a lucky accident for me, since it forced me to take this character, initially conceived as comical, into increasingly dark and emotional territory. It's strange, because I started out going for laughs, and by the end, it became one of the most sentimental pieces that I've ever done.

It's something I never would have gone for if the story were more straightforwardly plot-oriented. Like most writers of my generation, I'm kind of horrified by sappiness, and I can't imagine permitting myself to write a line like "Oh my child, you will never save me." in a traditional story. In a more narrative version of this piece, I probably would have gone for a colder, more ironic ending. I would have had to place the father and son together in real time, for one thing, and I would have had to create scenes that developed some kind of mounting tension between the two of them, and I imagine that I would have ended with the father and son at an awkwardly sad and depressingly hilarious impasse.

And if I'd written it as an essay, I'm sure I wouldn't have had much room for sentiment. It would have been a tart, unforgiving little hack job, perhaps with some kind of melancholy downturn at the end to soften it a bit.

Still, one of the problems with trying to create a hybrid of fiction and essay forms is that fiction really seems to demand some kind of climax or turn. That was the hardest aspect of this story for me. I realized that somehow the piece had to have an "occasion"—some sort of present-time reason for the monologue to exist, a place that the voice was speaking from, and that was when I decided that the character was sick, and was about to begin chemotherapy.

Yes, I know. I was definitely worried about making use of cancer as a device, which I realize has the potential to be both corny and clichéd. I resisted it for quite a while, trying to think of something better—but ultimately, I decided that it was necessary, that the story needed another complicating development, something urgent and dire that would cast a new light on the rest of the monologue. Ultimately, despite my uneasiness, I decided that cancer had the right kind of gravity, without requiring a great deal of background explanation to make it believable. I planted this revelation right about in the place where, in a traditional story, the climax would have been, and I liked the way it tangled up and muddied some of the narrator's earlier declarations. He was scared—that's what I understood when I went back to revise.

Looking back on the story now, there are, of course, a lot of things that I still have doubts about and maybe I would make some different choices, but I still feel pretty happy with the piece, all in all, not least because I think I learned some things from it. And I'm glad I never wrote that essay. I like the memoir form better now, thanks to people like David Sedaris and Lauren Slater and John Edgar Wideman, and though I personally still don't like to write about my own life, I've grown to respect those who can do it well.

WRITING EXERCISE

I find that many beginning fiction writers can be broken into two categories: those who are writing thinly veiled autobiography, and those who are completely avoiding it (which, usually, includes people who are interested in genres like fantasy or horror). I think that it's often useful for both types of writers to move outside of their comfort zone, so here's something to try.

1. **Start with an incident that happened in real life.** Write it in first person, in the form of a kind of summary or précis, in one sentence. For example: "My dad and I were driving to Mammoth Cave, in Kentucky, for a little father-and-son bonding time." Or "My girl-

friend and I were talking about breaking up." Or something like that. Just think of something personal that's been on your mind.

2. **The next sentence should be a lie, and probably kind of a big one.** "My father was a former movie star, and though he hadn't been in a film in more than a decade, he still worried about being 'recognized' by the public." Or "I have actually been dead for the last few years, but I hadn't told my girlfriend about it because I didn't want to scare her." You get the picture. Have some fun with your lie—you can even make it fantastical—but make sure it's got enough weight that you can make it convincing.

By the end, the world of the story should be almost entirely fictional, but with just enough patina of reality from that first sentence that you can make use of it. The idea is to think about how characters can develop depth, but also how they can become more fictional and dramatic.

BROCK CLARKE

The Apology

Wyatt and Dave were in Wyatt's attached garage, searching for a croquet set Wyatt insisted he bought, once, long ago, and had to be in the garage *somewhere*, and while they were looking they got to talking, idly, about the weather, baseball, the status of their job searches, and the conversation took a surprising turn or two and soon Wyatt and Dave discovered that they had both been abused by Catholic priests when they were boys.

Once that was out in the open, Wyatt and Dave forgot all about croquet. From the mouth of the garage they could see their wives—Susan and Rachel—smoking Merits under the last remaining mature oak in Shady Oaks, which was the name of their subdivision. Wyatt's two sons were playing a complicated game involving a frisbee, a dog, a detached piece of rusty gutter extension, and someone's hat. They all of a sudden seemed very far away, as if they were someone else's wives and children, as if Wyatt and Dave were very far from the selves they once were. Wyatt could smell the chemicals from the slow-burning charcoal fire he'd set earlier. As was the case with every barbecue he hosted, Wyatt had already made a big speech about cooking with charcoal and not propane. But now that he and Dave had ripped open their chests and revealed their tortured hearts, he felt very far from the man who had been so adamant about the superior taste of ground beef cooked over charcoal, too.

As for Dave, he felt something different. He and Rachel's baby son had died just two months earlier. He had died of crib death. The doctor had told them that it happened more often than people think, but news of its surprising frequency did not make Dave or Rachel feel any better. The doctor had also asked them if they had put their son to sleep on his stomach or his back. "He liked to sleep on his side," Dave said. The doctor had nodded sadly, as if sleeping on one's side were the problem, which pretty much ruined what was left of Dave to ruin. Every night Dave had sneaked into his son's room to watch his son sleep on his side and in the doing so had begun to feel the blossoming of his own loving, fatherly self. Now that he and Wyatt had told the truth about their abuse, he could start thinking about that and stop thinking about his dead baby.

But he didn't say any of this. Instead, he said, "I don't want to be like one of those guys on TV." He was talking about the many other men who'd been sexually abused by Catholic priests in their youths, those legions of sad, wide-eyed men you see on TV who told their stories in public for reasons—money? attention? forgiveness? peace of mind? the well-being of other would-be victims?—that seemed mysterious, even to them. No, Dave didn't want to be those men, didn't want what they wanted.

"But what do we want?" Wyatt asked.

"We want an apology," Dave said.

He was right. They simply wanted an apology. So Dave and Wyatt abandoned the garage and set off for St. Anthony's.

Rachel and Susan were finishing their cigarettes when they noticed their husbands walking down the street, away from the garage and the smoldering charcoal briquettes and their chirping children and their smoking wives.

"Dave, where are you going?" Rachel asked.

"We're going to St. Anthony's."

"What for?"

"To demand an apology," he said, and then they kept on walking.

★★★

This was not the first time Dave and Wyatt had demanded an apology. Dave had demanded an apology from his bank for sandbagging him with hidden withdrawal fees. Wyatt had demanded an apology from his children's teachers for making assumptions about how much time Wyatt did or did not spend with his sons going over their homework after school. Dave and Wyatt had both demanded apologies from Lance Paper Co. for transferring them from jobs in Utica, New York, and Worcester, Massachusetts, respectively, to Clemson, South Carolina, without giving them a real say in the matter, and then they demanded an apology from their new bosses in South Carolina for laying them off not six months after they'd uprooted themselves and their families. When Dave and Wyatt were done demanding their apologies, they had apologized to their wives for not getting the apologies they felt they deserved, or for getting the apologies and then being disappointed that those apologies didn't make the sun any brighter and the grass any greener and their lives any happier.

So Dave and Wyatt had demanded other apologies. But this was the first time they had walked to demand one. It was a longer walk than they'd reckoned. For one, Dave and Wyatt never walked anywhere anymore, a fact their physicians couldn't say enough about vis a vis Dave's and Wyatt's hanging bellies and high blood pressure and diminishing life expectancies, and every quarter mile or so Dave and Wyatt had to pretend to look at a bird or something so that they could stop and catch their breath. For another, Shady Oaks didn't have sidewalks. Plus, theirs was one of those pickup truck subdivisions and when the S-10s roared by, going well above the posted thirty miles per hour limit and sending Dave and Wyatt diving into the open sewers their taxes had been raised for, Wyatt—whose belly was bigger than Dave's and whose blood pressure was higher—even raised the possibility of turning back and just driving to the church in their own S-10s, or maybe just making the trek some other time, when the sun wasn't so high and the heat so oppressive and the traffic so heavy, and when he and Dave were in better physical condition. But Wyatt's suggestion didn't have much conviction behind it and Dave knew it was just nervousness talking. Because they knew they were doing what they had to do, and as Dave pointed out, that they were walking instead of driving was a testimony to their seriousness of purpose. Besides, Dave said, there was something Biblical and symbolic about their walking, and Wyatt agreed that he couldn't really imagine Moses driving around the desert for forty years in a detailed truck with running boards and cupholders.

They kept walking. It took Dave and Wyatt over an hour before they got to St. Anthony's. In fact, they almost walked right past it, because neither of them were actual members of the church or had even attended mass there and had only had a vague idea of where it was located. Besides, it looked nothing like the churches they'd been abused in—nothing like Sacred Heart in Utica with its spire reaching five stories high and the cross at its peak reaching another story; nothing like Our Lady of Assumption in Worcester, which was made of native granite and which took up a whole city block and was so grand and massive that it seemed like even God wouldn't be able to destroy it when the day finally came. No, St. Anthony's was more or less a brick ranch house, and they would have missed it entirely had Wyatt not said, "Hey, there's a crucifix over the front door of that brick rancher," and he and Dave turned around, gathered themselves, and then knocked on the church's front door.

Who knows why they didn't just go right in instead of knocking? Why is a vampire in the movies unable to enter a house unless he's been invited? Even a vampire wants to feel wanted. They knocked and knocked, and finally, a priest opened the door. He wasn't wearing a collar or even those black casual clothes priests wear: he was wearing jeans and flip flops and the kind of collarless button down shirt that makes you think of a rich person on vacation. But Dave and Wyatt knew he was a priest—because of course he had answered the church door, but mostly because he looked remarkably like the priests who had abused them: he had a full head of curly reddish brown hair and a cautious fatigued smile and raised eyebrows and Dave and Wyatt both took a step back, because the priest looked much like both of their abusers, as though they had summoned those priests to appear before them in a single body.

"Can I help you?" the priest asked. His voice was tired, resigned, as if he knew the answer to the question before he even asked it.

"Yes," Dave said and explained how he and Wyatt had been abused by Catholic priests in their youth and now they wanted an apology.

★★★

Dave and Wyatt really had been abused. Their abuse had run the gamut. Dave had been fellated on retreats, and the same priest had also more-or-less innocently and chummily draped his arm over Dave's shoulders during church school's discussion of the Virgin Birth and didn't remove the arm until the lesson was through. Wyatt had been fondled in empty church gyms after CYO basketball games, and the same priest, in front of Wyatt's parents, had simply remarked that Wyatt was a "good looking boy." Dave and Wyatt had been forced to do some things that they couldn't talk about, even now, even with each other. They sometimes still woke up in the middle of the night yelling, "It hurts, it hurts," and had to be comforted by Rachel and Susan, who thought their husbands were merely having garden-variety nightmares.

Wyatt hadn't told Susan about his abuse, but he'd told his three previous wives. His first wife had wondered immediately if the abuse had turned Wyatt homosexual, or if it had happened because he had already been homosexual. Wyatt's second wife had used the abuse as a trump card, and if their checking account was empty when it came time to pay the mortgage, or when Wyatt accidentally spilled wine on the white lace tablecloth his second wife had had in her family centuries before they'd immigrated from Donegal, the second wife said, "Don't worry about it, Wyatt. It's nothing compared to what that son of a bitch priest did to you." Then there was Wyatt's third wife, who had been purely supportive when he first told her. She'd said, "It's better that you told me. It can't hurt you anymore. Life will be different now." But their marriage turned out to be something less than the happy, healthy thing she thought it would be, and whenever Wyatt drank too much at dinner parties and took long, loud stands that were somehow both offensive and boring, or whenever he failed to get the raise or promotion that he felt sure he would get, Wyatt would say, "I'm sorry, I don't know what happened, it's not really my fault," until finally, his third wife accused him of subconsciously using the priest's abuse as an excuse for all his subsequent failures and shortcomings. Wyatt hadn't told Susan, his fourth wife, which seemed to Wyatt the only smart thing he had ever done.

Dave hadn't told Rachel, either, and didn't think he ever would, for exactly the reasons that Wyatt had had four wives to his one, and for exactly the same reason that he never, ever talked about his baby son's death, either. In the case of both his abuse and his son's death, Dave was afraid that once the truth was out there in the open it would be promptly lumped in with other unpleasant truths and its importance would be diminished; and he was also afraid that it wouldn't be lumped in with all these other truths, that it would dominate the others and that once it was visible no one, not even Dave, could ignore it if he wanted. Dave was afraid too that he'd be accused of using his abuse and his son's death as an excuse, and that, at some level, there would be some truth to the accusation.

So Dave told no one about the abuse and he never talked about his dead son, either, not even with Rachel. They instead talked idly. They had so many conversations about the weather that Dave had begun to feel the same way about Rachel that he did about the television weatherwoman—sometimes she wore clothes that were understated and flattering, sometimes garish and unbecoming; sometimes he found her encyclopedic knowledge of tornadoes fascinating, sometimes dull. But he did not feel love for Rachel anymore, which before their son had died had been pretty much the only thing he'd felt for her. But at least he didn't talk to her about their dead son, at least she didn't make him admit to his terrible, true feelings—that the only thing that mattered anymore about their son was that he was dead; and not once did Dave tell her or anyone else about being abused, until he told Wyatt, and then the priest at St. Anthony's.

★★★

The priest listened, head down like a man in deep thought or deep regret, and when Dave and Wyatt were done he said, "I see," and then said, "It doesn't sound like either of you were abused in this church, though."

"Even so," Wyatt said. "We'd like an apology."

"Can you come back tomorrow?" the priest asked. "Or maybe the day after?"

"No," Dave said. "We've waited twenty-five years already. We want it now."

"Okay," the priest said. "But I'll have to talk to the bishop first. He'll have to talk to the cardinal. Lawyers will have to be consulted. It might take a little while."

"That's fine," Dave told him. "We have plenty of time."

★★★

And it was true that Dave and Wyatt had plenty of time. They could have waited there all night and into the morning for their apology. Because even though the next day was Monday, Dave and Wyatt had no jobs to go to. They hadn't looked for work since they'd been laid off six months earlier, even though they both had new houses and crushing mortgages and Wyatt had children who would eventually have to get their teeth straightened and go to college. Dave and Wyatt weren't old, either; they were still in their late thirties; they had the relevant college degrees; they could have gone out and found something: there were paper companies everywhere, and someone needed to work for them. But Dave and Wyatt didn't even bother looking. It was as though they had lost their will to do something about anything. It wasn't that they were lazy, exactly; it was that they felt that being ambitious wouldn't amount to much. Besides, Wyatt had the kind of oversized garage designed to accommodate the speedboat Wyatt talked about buying but knew he never would. Wyatt and Dave liked to set up folding chairs in the garage and leave the country music channel playing softly on the transistor radio and not talk and watch Wyatt's grass seed wash away in the warm, monsoonal spring rains. The rain made a nice, fat, bonging sound on the garage's tin roof; it was comfortable in the garage, safe. Why would they want to go out and look for work when they could stay in the garage?

Wyatt's and Dave's abuse at the hands of their priests might have had nothing to do with this lethargy. This was yet another thing they were afraid of: that they wouldn't know what was the product of abuse or what was simply part and parcel of being a normal thirty-eight-year-old American man disgruntled and living far away from his true home with no job, not even one he disliked. They would never know what was connected to the abuse and what was not. They would never be sure. This was another thing they would demand an apology for.

★★★

The priest made them wait in the church basement. Wyatt griped about this at first. The basement was carpeted and the carpet smelled of something wet and long dead and the glaring overhead fluorescent light kept flickering and if it were to go out Dave and Wyatt would be in complete darkness, because there were no windows and no other lights that they could see. Wyatt said, "After all we'd been through, we deserve better than to be stuck in a church basement." Wyatt hadn't been in a church in ages, and spoke longingly of the seed-oiled wood pews, the stained glass, the votive candles, the towering pipe organ, the holy water, the veined marble pulpit and stations of the cross. "I wouldn't mind waiting so much," Wyatt said, "if we could only wait in the church itself."

But Dave said, "No, it's better that we wait in the basement. It's better this way," and the subject was dropped.

They waited. They waited a very long time. They did not speak to each other. Wyatt breathed heavily through his nose, then whistled in the distracted manner of a person unaccustomed to introspection. Dave was crying softly, so softly that Wyatt couldn't hear it over the white noise of his nose breathing and whistling.

Dave was crying because he had started thinking about the apology— how satisfying it would be to finally get it after all these years and how maybe he could then forget about the priest, the retreats, everything,

97

how maybe once the apology was tendered he could then start living his life—and then realized that he had never asked anyone to apologize for his son's death. It had simply never occurred to him. He had demanded apologies from everyone and for everything imaginable, and yet he had not demanded one for his son. It was yet another way he had failed his son: he had failed to keep his son alive, and he had failed to demand an apology for his death. This was why he was crying; he cried for what seemed like hours, until the crying exhausted itself. You couldn't cry forever, Dave knew this from experience; and once you stopped crying, you had to do the only thing you were capable of doing. The only thing Dave was capable of doing was to wait for the priest's apology, and that apology would have to double for the apology he should have gotten for his son.

Just then Wyatt and Dave heard voices. The basement door opened; there was the sound of someone walking down the stairs. They both rose to their feet without realizing that they had risen to their feet. They expected it to be the priest, of course, apology in hand. But it was just Rachel and Susan, their wives.

Wyatt was glad to see Susan, because he had begun to think his and Dave's mission was a big mistake: they had begun the quest for their apology together, on the same page, but they were not on that same page anymore. There was something about Dave's gloominess Wyatt could not penetrate. Wyatt knew about Dave's son, of course, and was so grateful that nothing bad had happened to any of his three boys, but he had not realized until now how much greater Dave's pain was than his. It had not occurred to Wyatt that all pain is not equal, and that one's pain didn't give one a greater insight into someone else's. Dave's and Wyatt's abuse had brought them together, but it could not do so completely, or forever, and so while Wyatt felt sorry for his friend, his best friend, he also felt alienated.

As for Dave, he was not thinking about Wyatt; he was thinking about Rachel, how beautiful she was with her hair swept back in the messy ponytail that would always make her look like a twenty-year-old girl just back from the beach, how she was much too lovely to be in this musty basement, how her beauty didn't make him feel any better and in fact made him even more sad because the beauty didn't matter to him anymore, and how he wanted her to leave immediately.

"What are you doing here?" Dave asked them.

"We're here to get both of you to come home," Susan said. "The kids are waiting in the van. We saved some hamburgers for you back home."

"Is the priest up there?" Dave asked.

"Yes," Rachel said.

"What's he doing?"

"He's just sitting in a pew, staring into space. When we asked him where you were, he put his face his hands and said, 'Basement.'"

"He seemed a little freaked out," Susan said.

"Good," Dave said.

"Dave," Rachel said, "what are *you* doing here?"

Dave shot a look at Wyatt, who sighed his big man's sigh and nodded, and so Dave told the story. He spoke for himself and for Wyatt, looking at his feet the whole time. When he was done telling the story, he didn't look up.

"I'm sorry," Wyatt said to Susan. He knew his history, and could see the end of their marriage looming in the distance like a dark cloud.

Susan shrugged and said, "That's okay," because she was more than a decade younger than Wyatt, and her generation was relatively comfortable talking publicly about the bad things that had been done to them. "No big deal," she said. "I still love you."

"Do you know what I hate?" Rachel said to Dave.

"What?" Dave said. But she didn't answer him back until he lifted his head to look at her.

"I hate when I tell people that Nick died of crib death, and they ask, 'Where did it happen?'"

Dave smiled then, he really did. But when Rachel said, "I want you to come home," he shook his head, and the smile disappeared and he said, "No, I'm going to wait for this apology."

"I miss him, too," she said. "And I'm truly sorry about what that priest did to you. But I want you to come home."

"I can't," he said.

"I wish you'd come home with me right now," she said, very slowly, as if speaking to someone addled or retarded. "Because I don't think I'm coming back to get you." They looked at each other for a while, their gazes steady, unblinking. It was the way people stare at each other not when they're in love, but afterward, when they finally realize all the many horrible and beautiful things locked up within that love. But Dave didn't move, and Rachel finally broke the eyelock and ran up the stairs, two at a time.

Wyatt was on his feet; he was already thinking of how lucky he was to have this younger fourth wife and his spacious garage and his kids and suddenly the apology didn't seem so urgent anymore: he had waited so long, he could certainly wait a little longer. And even if Wyatt never got his apology, then maybe that was all right, too: it seemed to him that he had gotten what he wanted, somehow, without getting what he wanted, and he marveled to himself about how resilient the human animal is and thought that he might even work on his resume when he got home, maybe check the employment ads in the morning.

"I'm going home, buddy," he said to Dave. "You should, too."

Dave shook his head. "It's all right," he said. "I'll catch up with you later."

They shook hands, then Wyatt took Susan's and they walked up the stairs, closing the door behind them.

When they were gone, Dave turned off the light and lay down on the rug. He was thinking of the future. His wife and friends were gone; it was undoubtedly too dark to walk home, and besides he didn't want to go there anyway. But maybe he could stay in the basement. It wasn't as nice as Wyatt's garage, but overall it didn't seem such a bad place to stay. There was an old Frigidaire humming in the corner. There was a bathroom with an exhaust fan. He could conceivably stay in there forever. Maybe he would ask the priest if that were possible. Maybe he could attach it as a rider to the apology. Dave fell asleep, rolling over on his side in the fashion of his dead son, and his last thought before falling asleep was that he would waive his apology if God would just let him die in his sleep, just as God had let his son die in his sleep, just as God had let so many other things happen.

But Dave didn't die in his sleep; he woke up when he heard a door open at the top of the stairway. He got up and walked to the foot of the stairs. The priest was standing there, illuminated from above by the chandelier in the vestibule. The priest saw Dave, but he didn't move, and neither did Dave. It seemed possible that they would stand staring at each other forever; but that was fine with Dave. Because there was nothing left for him to do but wait for his apology, which was the only thing standing between the life he had lived up until now, and the life yet to come.

Inside "The Apology": Starting With an Image

I love free newspapers—in part because they're free, and in part because they're often sloppily edited or misleading or melodramatic and, as such, are good for a cheap laugh or, as is the case here, an idea for a short story.

One of the free newspapers I read is my campus newspaper, and I was on my way to a poetry reading (I don't recall the poet or his reading, although I have perfect recall of that issue of the newspaper, which probably says something about the poet and his reading) when I picked up a copy of my campus paper. This was during the height of the priest abuse scandal, and you couldn't pick up a newspaper, or watch the TV, or listen to the radio, without hearing the story of one of the victims, or of one of the priests, or one of the apologists for the priests, or one of the lawyers of the victims. To be honest, I had no especial interest in the subject: I'd grown up a Roman Catholic, and while I had long ago given it up, that had nothing to do with what I'd read in the paper. I had never been abused, nor had I ever known anyone who'd been abused. Nor did I have a difficult time believing all the stories in the newspaper were true. When I read about the victims, I thought, *Poor people*. When

I read about the victimizers, I also thought, *Poor people.* I pitied them, in other words. And in my experience, nothing is less conducive to engagement, and to fiction writing, than pity. Which is probably why I hadn't written a story on the subject. In fact, it had never occurred to me to write one.

Until I picked up the campus paper that day. Amidst all the outraged editorials about the sorry performance of the university's sports teams and the paucity of good bars within lurching distance of campus, I saw this headline: CATHOLICS LEFT WAITING FOR AN APOLOGY. And I immediately had an image of a group of Catholics sitting in a dark room, hands folded in their laps, waiting patiently for someone, anyone, to come and apologize to them. I loved everything about the image: the pathos, the sadness, the absurdity. I also loved, in terms of story potential (and fiction writers are among the most mercenary people on the planet—they're always looking at everything in life with an eye for what kind of story they can get out of it. Only memoirists are more mercenary, although they tend to be not as good at it, or at getting away with it. But that's another story, another essay), the inherent drama of the situation: Something terrible had happened to these people. That fact, I (and the reader) would know. But what the reader wouldn't know was: Would they get the apology? And if they did, would they feel better once they'd gotten it? And if they didn't get it, then what would they do?

Well, I didn't read the article that came with the headline. I went to the poetry reading, but the whole time I was thinking of the story I would write. I was in the middle of writing a series of stories set in South Carolina and Georgia, stories about people from the Northeast who had their troubles and hoped by moving to the South, they'd leave those troubles behind. Obviously, the story I had in mind fit this theme, or could fit it as long as I could stay away from melodrama, from self-righteousness. As long as the story could be irreverent without being flippant. As long as I could have the story be about specific characters, with specific problems, and not about an issue. Which is why in "The Apology" I never did get a scene with a group of Catholics sitting in one room, waiting for an apology. But I did come up with Wyatt and

Dave: guys who'd been abused by priests, but also guys who were apology junkies. Guys who'd been wronged, guys who'd had terrible things happen to them, but also guys who'd done some suspect things themselves. Guys you could care about, who you could root for, even if the rooting might not do any good. At least that was my hope, and still is.

WRITING EXERCISE

Watch a five-minute segment of a soap opera and rewrite the scene so it feels like serious literary fiction. Which is to say, avoid cliché; avoid the expected. If there is a person in the story, or in the situation, who seems like he or she is set up to be a victim, then make it difficult for that person to be considered a victim, or only a victim. Likewise, if there is a hero or heroine in the scene, make it difficult for your readers to believe so simply in his or her heroism. The purpose of this exercise is not to debunk, but to complicate. There are no tired situations, only tired treatments of these situations.

MICHAEL CZYZNIEJEWSKI

Janice the Mantis

Three years after skipping out, my father pulled up to our house in a pink monster truck, strolling up our walk and holding hands with a very tan, blond, and muscular man. Just before ringing our doorbell, they leaned into each other for a kiss, the very moment I knew I had to get the F out of Dodge. There was my chance to tell the bastard what I thought, to exorcise some demons with a pointed remark and a door-slam in his face. Instead, I snuck out the back, slipped through the neighbor's yard, and waited at the corner for my friends, leaving my mom to deal with Dad, his new gay lover, and their twenty-foot-tall monster truck.

Goog and Glasscock, like the converging crowd, wanted to know why there was a monster truck on my lawn, the mailbox smashed underneath, everyone's dogs barking their asses off. I told them I didn't know, and when they asked if I wanted to check, I told them to shut the fuck up.

"It's really pink," Goog said. "Even the wipers."

"What about your mom?" Glasscock said.

"Drive."

We headed to our high school to work out for open Saturdays. Goog, Glasscock, and I were on the baseball team, but in three previous seasons, had not cracked varsity. Hoping to avoid ultimate humiliation—seniors on JV—we were hitting the cages four times a week, taking extra fielding, and playing long toss till it burned. We were behind the eight ball on making the team, none of us pitchers or catchers, and unless you were 6'14" and had arms like thighs, you had to be in the battery to make the big-boy team. Glasscock was a first baseman who couldn't catch, I was a left-handed shortstop, and Goog, well, Goog kept score. More than likely we'd be anchoring the JV squad yet again. Still, dicking around in the weight room gave us something to do, all of us already accepted to good schools, just biding the months, waiting for that bright future.

"Cheerleaders date varsity guys," Goog said more than once.

"Sluts, too," Glasscock said. "Varsity gets you BJs and HJs."

Goog and Glasscock had their focus and I had mine. Some major breakdown notwithstanding, I was going to graduate salutatorian (behind Goog), planned to kick it at Cal Tech, and in four years, be a mechanical engineer. I'd make good if not great money. I'd buy a condo and drive a decent car, probably a Mazda, and before long, I'd figure the rest out. The fact that I played sports, even JV, would separate me from the *Star Trek/Wars* fanboys I'd partner with in labs. That was more important to me than girls, to not walk into a physics lecture with Vulcan ears. Really, anything but that.

★★★

After the gym, we found the monster truck parked on the street instead of the lawn. I imagined a scene, Mom at some point threatening to get her gun, in the same drawer as her Bible and vibrator. I imagined my dad rationalizing his actions with a support program, his visit fulfilling a step, his sponsor—maybe the guy he kissed—insisting he rectify. Mom would have laughed at such sincerity, or bullshit, whichever she determined it to be.

"Martin, who's that Hulk Hogan-looking guy in your window?" Glasscock said.

My dad's boyfriend stood in the picture window. He was flexing, just ripping it up for all the neighborhood to see.

"Maybe it's actually Hulk Hogan," Goog said. "The Hulkster could very well drive a pink monster truck."

I told them to shut the fuck up and got out of the car. Goog pulled next to the pink monstrosity and they stared at it, not leaving until I whipped the newspaper from the porch at Goog's Hyundai.

I didn't know what to say when I saw my dad. I'd really hoped, the entire time working out, that he'd be gone when I got back, that Mom would make it all go away. No such luck. I wanted to run off again, maybe hang with Goog or Glasscock for a while, until my father re-disappeared. I probably could have done that, too, until Mr. Universe spotted me and waved. Then I pretty much had to go in.

I treated my dad like the cable repairman. "Hey," I said as I got juice from the fridge, never making eye contact, not really listening if he answered. I asked Mom if dinner was ready, told her the boys and I were going to the movies. I also said that her hair looked nice, that her shirt—this old purple thing she wore to do errands—brought out her eyes; to note, I had no idea what color my mom's eyes were.

"Your father and I would like to talk to you," Mom said.

"Goog and Glasscock in forty," I said. As if struggling against a great wind, I turned my head toward my newly gay father's general direction.

"You're taller, Martin," Dad said.

The best he could come up with was this. No *Good to see you!* or *I missed you!* or *I'm so fucking sorry for abandoning you!* Instead, something factual anyone could have assumed. From anywhere.

"You look more *here*," I said.

Sarcasm—from a teenager! I'd earned a little bit of that, but after three years, you'd think I'd brandish better game.

Mom explained the situation: Dad was there to make peace, to re-connect, to be my father again. But most of all, to get a divorce. He was engaged—to the man in the other room.

"California, Hawaii, or Massachusetts?" I said.

"I don't follow," Dad said, then fetched his boy from the living room, once again holding the tan, muscular, blond guy's hand.

"I'd like you to meet my fiancé," Dad said. I'd never encountered an actual gay person, just a few guys at school from the drama club who dressed sharply but weren't officially out. Now I was meeting two, in my kitchen.

I reached my hand out to shake, then realized that I'd been wrong all day. I'd made a huge mistake.

"This is Janice," Dad said. "She's been very eager to meet you."

★★★

More than ever, I hoped Glasscock could filch something from his parents' stash. The fall before, they'd caught him leaving with a fifth of peppermint schnapps in his jock. According to him, he actually told his mom he had a boner when she saw the bulge in his jeans. It would have worked, too, had the bottle not slipped down his leg and shattered on the driveway. Even though his dad had to ground him, he thought it was hilarious and started calling Glasscock "Glasscock" ever since. For seventeen years, he managed to stay nicknameless, just Kevin Torres, "Kev" at worst. Then he was Glasscock and always would be. Whenever I'd drop by, his dad would yell upstairs, "Hey, Glasscock, Martin's in the foyer." Glasscock didn't like being called Glasscock, which is exactly why we called him Glasscock every time we called him anything.

"Sloe gin," Glasscock said when I got in the Hyundai. "For fizzes."

Amazing. Glasscock risking another grounding for such shit.

"What about that Maker's Mark?" I said. "The Crown Royal?"

"They'd miss that. They've had this shit since before I was born."

We parked in the back of the multiplex lot and hit the sloe gin, which tasted like melted lozenges. We mixed it with Diet Sunkist, which Goog for some reason brought, agreeing to fuck the movie. Goog and Glasscock asked me a thousand times who the monster truck belonged to, and a thousand times I answered, "Not Hulk Hogan."

I did a number on the sloe gin myself, and when it was gone—Goog and Glasscock still sober as stone—I insisted we attempt to buy.

"We're eighteen but look fifteen," Goog said.

"Gus Diaz buys at the GoGo Mart," Glasscock said. "He wears his freakin' letterman jacket, too."

"Gus has a full man-beard," Goog said. "And he's on varsity."

After I bitched and moaned a while, Goog and Glasscock convinced me to go to a movie. I didn't know what we walked into, but halfway through, a guy in a red vest and bowtie shined his flashlight in our eyes and told us we had to get out. I remember throwing some popcorn from the floor at the guy, which proved as effective as it sounds. The next thing I knew, Goog and Glasscock were dragging me up my front steps, digging through my pockets for my keys.

"Left ball, corner pocket," I said.

When they opened the front door, my mom was standing in front of us in her housecoat. I said, "That housecoat brings out the color of your hair," then vomited onto the welcome mat, an orange and purple swirl that was really quite beautiful, for a pile of steaming puke.

★★★

The next morning, I found out the deal: Mom was flying to Reno to procure a quickie divorce. That's how you divorced right away, in Reno. Vegas had wedding chapels and Reno had the opposite. I wondered how many people got married while drunk, sobered up, then drove to Reno to hit backspace.

"We'll get a nice settlement," she said. "We can buy you a car."

"Monster trucking must be lucrative," I said.

"Gets you girls, too," she said. My mom sucked in her stomach a bit and pushed her chest forward, staring into her coffee. "What do you think of her?"

"I thought she was a guy the first time I saw her," I said. My mom came up behind me and started to rub my temples. At first, I just wanted to sit still, my feet flat, but the rubbing made the room stop. "Goog thought she was Hulk Hogan."

Mom made her way from my temples to my neck. Right at the tip of my collar, she squeezed a deep pimple till it burst.

"Nasty," she said.

Mom would be gone three days and two nights, making a trip out of it since Dad was paying.

"You're vacationing with them? Honeymooning?"

"Janice isn't going," Mom told me. "I guess if she doesn't lift eight to ten hours a day, she begins to lose mass."

It occurred to me Janice not only looked like a man, but fit the exact opposite description as Mom. Janice was 5'9", platinum blond, skin the color of wet sand, while Mom was barely five feet, grayed years ago, and couldn't have been paler if she were a worm. Since Dad left, she'd purchased a treadmill, a cross-country skier, and three ab rollers, all collecting bug eggs in the garage. What made Dad take such a distinct departure? How do you just like tiny brunettes one day and then fall for Janice?

With her Cherokee in my possession while she was gone, Mom had one rule: not to drink and drive. After the sloe gin, the thought of alcohol made bile rise in my throat. I assured her I'd be safe, accepting a fifty-dollar bill for food and gas.

"Or four bottles of delicious sloe gin," she said, goosing me as I stumbled toward the shower. "My plane leaves in four hours."

★★★

The next day in homeroom, announcements included the place and time for baseball tryouts, just a week away. Next to me, Glasscock wrote "BB tryouts" in his date planner. I grabbed the planner and wrote "JV" before the BB, then gave it back.

"Only for you," Glasscock said, and wrote "Avoid gay ass raping by Martin!" underneath the tryouts note.

In first period, AP Cal II, Goog told me who the man in my living room was.

"Janice the Mantis," he said. "He's a girl."

"I know."

"She's big on the monster truck circuit. We couldn't see it ground level, but there's a bitching logo on the hood."

Goog handed me a printout, from Google, of the Mantis's trademark. A giant green mantis with a pink bikini and blond hair was biting the head off another mantis, assumedly a man mantis.

"Why was Janice the Mantis in your house, Martin?" Goog said.

"That was Hulk Hogan," I said. "He's helping me get ripped for try-outs."

★★★

During last period, AP Physics, Goog and Glasscock and I talked about upping the routine for the week: running more, lifting some, doubling swats in the cage.

"We should have done that all winter," Goog said. "It's probably too late now."

In the weight room after school, there was a big circle of guys crowded around the bench press. We figured it was one of the linemen going for a school record, maybe some kid who put too much on the bar and dropped it on his throat. Instead of a record or fatal injury, we saw Janice. Janice the Mantis. She was pumping around three hundred pounds—quick thrusts, too, not slowing down or breaking a sweat.

"She's been here all day," someone said.

"That pink truck in the lot is hers," another kid added.

I turned to get out of there, mumbled something about doing sprints, but Goog and Glasscock weren't letting me go.

"Tell us now. Or we'll make you watch *Akira* again."

I explained how my mom was in Reno, about my dad's return, and Janice, my soon-to-be stepmom.

They stared at me for a second until Goog said, "Your mom's in Reno?"

"We're having a party there in like twenty minutes," Glasscock said. "Why didn't you tell us?"

My friends seemed to forget about our workout, about running till we puked and lifting till we couldn't raise our arms over our heads. Not to mention, the dad part of my story, how he'd come back after three years of dead-beating, the thing that traumatized me for years. They'd even forgotten about the monster truck and woman growing larger before our eyes. They just wanted my house: Parties had girls and drinking, and in their minds, chicks + booze = sex.

"We have to tell people," Goog said, then corrected himself: "We have to tell *girls*."

I didn't want to talk to Janice, not in front of every jock in my school. I guessed she, or more likely my dad, had made some deal to use the school's facilities. I pictured a monster truck assembly coming soon. I felt like I should almost say hello, at least some kind of "Reno, huh?"-type acknowledgment. But I didn't.

Goog spread the word about the bash while I drove Glasscock to his place, scoring as much booze as we could carry. His parents would notice for sure, their bar suddenly empty, but Glasscock said, "I can take the heat," then dropped some vodka on the kitchen floor, another bottle biting the dust.

Goog met us at my house and said he told over twenty girls about the party, instructing them to bring all their girlfriends. A half an hour later, ten of those girls were in my house—and at least sixty guys: Ekrich Fest 3000. Some guys I knew, from the team, from our classes, but most were total strangers. Even freshmen and sophomores. One other guy looked twenty-five, like he'd just been in prison and a room full of drunk high-school boys was his dream come true. More guests knocked on my door every minute, fewer and fewer of them female.

"We couldn't get laid in a gangbang," Goog said.

"Think positive thoughts," Glasscock said. "Girls sense surrender."

By 9 o'clock, we were out of booze and people started to leave. At 10, everyone we knew was gone, including all the girls, leaving just a few geek underclassmen behind, guys like me, Goog, and Glasscock, two or three years removed. The nerds sat on my couches and chairs with empty cups, in awe of what was going down, a terrible failure of a party they would still count amongst the greatest experiences of their lives.

Just when I was going to kick them out, start cleaning up and opening my wrists in the tub, Janice the Mantis arrived in her monster truck and approached the house, wearing a matching pink tube top and bike shorts. Everything was so tight it looked like she'd put it on when she was skinny and just worked out around it.

"I saw your light on," she said.

For a second, I thought about trying to hide the party, then realized Janice had no bearing on my life. Mom wasn't going to ground me because Janice squealed. Mom just didn't care, off in Reno getting smashed on free Cape Cods and dropping my car money in the slots.

"Come in," I said. "Wicked party winding down."

Immediately, the glasses-clad, vodka punch-drunk dorks squared their shoulders and hid their cups under the cushions.

"This is Janice," I told them. "She is the Mantis."

Janice wanted a glass of water, but asked if I had a straw or two to put together. She couldn't bend her arms far enough to drink normally anymore, she explained, and needed an extra-long straw.

"I lift weights," she explained.

Nobody had the guts to talk, let alone leave, as if Janice sensed only motion and was waiting for movement to strike. She sat on a folding chair and asked a lot of questions, pointing to the shivering boys who wanted to be anywhere but there: "What year are you?" "What's your favorite subject?" "Do you ever lift weights?" The boys used one word at a time, staring at the door as they answered: "Freshman." "Math." "Never."

When Goog and Glasscock said they had to split, everyone else jumped up, too, using the opportunity to escape. I was surprised that my two buds wanted out, assuming they were in for the long haul, the Janice scenario taking another severe plot twist.

"We have diffy q," Goog said.

"My dad's probably sold all my stuff by now," Glasscock said.

Janice stood and shook everyone's hands. I thought she was going to crush some nerd phalanges, but she didn't. She was gentle, taking their hands like a lady, giving a gentle nod. Seeing these skinny freaks lock hands with Janice was like witnessing Adam reaching his finger up to God for a touch of life. I'm not sure if they were leaving to do their homework or jack off all night, but if word got around that Janice had stopped by, my post-party rep would go from pathetic to odd and uncanny.

Janice accepted her eighth glass of water when it was just us, and when I offered food, she said she ate only parsley, wheat germ, and raw steak. We didn't have those things, so I offered her some wheat bread. She declined.

"A moment on the lips, forever on the hips."

Janice asked me the same questions she did the boys, and then I decided to ask her some things, too.

"How'd you meet my dad?"

"He's my manager," she said. Janice blushed, smiling for the first time since we'd met.

"We traveled together, sharing lots of Best Westerns, and eventually, asked for the queen instead of two twins. Your dad curls his toes when he sleeps—did you know that?"

Janice, mutant party crasher, was telling me secrets about my dad. Girl stuff. I couldn't remember him as anything but a walkout. I guess he also drank a bit too much, coached Little League one year, yelled a bit too much, and once in a while, like on my birthday, confirmed I was *at least* good in school. With the same man, this enormous woman, giggling like an eighth grader, had fallen in love.

"He bought me the Mantis," Janice said, pointing outside. "He came up with the name and designed the logo, too."

I peeked out the window at the Mantis, also the name for the truck, again parked on our lawn. I wondered if Janice could help herself from climbing things. I decided she could not.

"Would you like to go for a ride?" Janice said. She stood and pulled a set of keys, complete with Mantis keychain, from her sports bra. "You can even drive—if you don't tell your dad."

★★★

At first, Janice drove, providing a quick tutorial on how to handle something that size. The Mantis had eight gears instead of five, but it was unlikely I'd need that many. I didn't want to destroy, just test it out.

"Your turn," Janice said. We were on the outskirts of Tucson, a lot of nothing to kill but cacti and rocks.

The Mantis didn't handle like a normal car, made for smooth rides to and fro. Whoever designed the monstrosity built it to lunge forward with great bursts of speed. Tapping on the gas pedal meant shifting up. It was easy to picture it smashing normal cars. Or buildings. The world.

"When I was just a bodybuilder, I didn't have anywhere to funnel my power," Janice said. "There was nothing to put in your hands. You just stood on stage, pointing."

I hadn't thought of it that way. When athletes get big, it's usually to hit something harder. Unless she was going to become a gladiator or tear out trees with her bare hands, having so many muscles was kind of senseless.

"Is that why you stopped competing?" I asked.

"I got busted for steroids. Twice. Bye-bye, Ms. Olympia circuit."

If Janice was one thing, it was candid. Modesty didn't get you to the point in life she was at.

"I still take them every day," Janice said. "I could set you up, if you think it would help you make varsity."

I didn't know how Janice knew about varsity, or that I played baseball. Maybe she'd asked around at the gym. Maybe my mom had told my dad and my dad told her.

"Not right now," I said.

"It's probably for the best," Janice said. "I don't think your dad would approve."

"That would be a reason to do it."

Janice let me drive laps into nothingness. Around midnight, my phone rang—Mom—and I pulled over and cut the engine. Mufflers, on monster trucks, were hardly the point.

"Just checking in," Mom said. "Remember, 11:15 tomorrow night. Southwest Terminal."

I asked my mom if she was divorced yet and she answered, but I couldn't hear. In the background radiated loud disco music, "I Will Survive." I told her that I'd see her at the airport, to not worry, and just as I hung up, Janice's phone rang.

It was my father, I knew, because Janice had her phone mounted on the steering wheel and on speaker. I stayed quiet. I thought about what my father would think if he knew Janice and I were hanging out, so late at night. Just the two of us.

"I'll be back tomorrow night," he said. "Then we're outta there."

Janice asked if he was divorced yet, and my father said that he wasn't, that he hadn't even seen my mother since he'd gotten there. Without a doubt, in the background, I heard "I Will Survive." Dad was out discoing in Vegas. With my mother.

For less than a second, I considered not telling Janice what I'd heard, weighing the consequences. For me, there were no consequences. So I told her as soon as she hung up.

"That son of a bitch," she said.

"Yeah," I said.

Janice and I switched places and we drove some more. She revealed more things about my father, some I knew, some I didn't. Dad liked to build model airplanes. He liked squash. He also spent some time in jail, though that wasn't why he left me and my mom.

"Bad checks," Janice said. "Eight months in Springer."

"He just gave my mom a big check," I said.

Janice and I kept driving, talking more about my father, basically how big of an ass he was.

"We've never even had real sex," she said. "We only kiss, and that's rare."

Janice pulled into a Circle K for gas. It cost over a hundred bucks to fill the tank, she said. While I waited, I thought about Janice and my father not having sex, which of course led to me thinking about them *having* sex. I started to picture it, being with Janice that way, when I couldn't before.

"How old are you?" she asked, back inside, back on the road.

"Eighteen," I said. "Missed the cut-off for school by two days."

"I have an idea," Janice said.

Considering what she'd said before, I was sure Janice wanted to have sex. For her, it would be sweet revenge, against my father *and* my mother. For me, there would be no better revenge against my father. It wouldn't hurt his feelings all that much—he didn't have any—but the message would be clear. I could think about it for a week and not come up with anything better. I could major in it at Cal Tech and not come up with a better answer.

"We're driving to Vegas to get married," Janice said.

Janice didn't seem to be giving me say: She was using a declarative sentence. I asked her if she was serious and she said she was always serious. She explained that this was the one and only response to the situation, what any sane, rational person would do.

"I hope you have ID," she said.

Janice directed the Mantis toward the highway, and before I knew it, I was headed north to get married. I would miss school in the morning, and if we stayed longer than a day, I'd miss a couple of tests. With anything but straight As in my classes, I would slip out of the number two spot, even out of the top ten. But that was beside the point. My dad's fiancée was taking me to Vegas to marry me. Diffy q, varsity, and class rank became very childish very quickly.

"Maybe it was just a coincidence," I said. "They could have been at their hotel bar. They could have been on opposite ends of the room."

Janice reached over and squeezed my knee. Hard. "This is the best idea," she said. I looked out the window and wondered if I could roll out, make it home across the desert. Janice squeezed harder, pressed deeper into the gas.

In five hours, I'd be married to Janice. I didn't know for how long, or what would happen after. Maybe we'd get a room, for the honeymoon, or maybe just sleep in the Mantis, a long night behind us. The next morning, we'd drive to Reno and get divorced. Or maybe not. I wasn't getting a say. Either way, anything that got in our way, we'd crush.

Inside "Janice the Mantis": Creating Conflict From Character

"Janice the Mantis" started out like a lot of my stories, with an image or an idea that I wanted to write about—in this case, a monster truck. In college I had seen a monster truck rally inside the university's basketball arena, a surreal experience I could never relay literally, and it was some-

116

thing that had been in the back of my head for a while. Eventually, those memories turn into story elements, and when I was looking to start a new piece, it was just the monster truck's turn.

Once I have an impetus, I try to figure out what sort of conflict/relationship the story's characters will have, and for this story, I ran through some different scenarios and eventually settled on son-absent father. I knew I was going to have a teenage boy as a protagonist, probably a high-school kid, and this is one I'd never used before.

Just about all of my stories' first lines combine the motif of choice with the conflict of choice, so as soon as I had the monster truck and the father-son conflict, I had a first line, something like "Three years after deserting us, my father drove up to our house in a huge monster truck." I wanted the story to start with the father's sudden return, and the twist would be the monster truck would be too cool for the kid to ignore, no matter how mad he was at his dad. This combination of idea and conflict almost seems like 90 percent of any story, and from there, I can usually write and write until I have a finished draft. The remaining elements fall into place as I go—or the story isn't working and gets put into a limbo file. Fortunately, this one kept rolling.

Early on, I thought the story would be more about Martin and his father. I envisioned a plot sequence where the dad tries to win Martin back by giving him steroids so he can make his varsity baseball team. (I played freshman and sophomore baseball in high school but didn't bother trying out for varsity my junior year and have regretted it ever since, another element from my past I've always wanted to sneak into a story.) After a page or two, the banter between son and father seemed thin, so I invited a second conflict in, the father returning with a new love and needing a divorce from the mom, giving me an ulterior motive for his sudden appearance.

Before long, I had Janice, female bodybuilder and consort. At first, I thought she would be lost in the background, that I'd have her in every scene just standing off to the side, flexing, doing push-ups, posing in front of the monster truck, but never speaking. Basically, she would be a running visual joke and not a real character. Her sexual ambiguity also served a function, and since Martin was a high-school boy not interested in girls, Janice seemed like a nice foil.

Before long, it was easy to see Janice as way more interesting than the dad, especially from Martin's point of view. She drove an awesome vehicle and was a successful athlete, two things Martin pursued. She was also blond and tan over all those muscles, Barbie run amok. In short, she was what Martin wanted, or was expected to want, but extrapolated in every way. As if on steroids.

Once I refocused on Janice, I wrote the rest of the story in one sitting, at least until the ending. I was literally lost, the two of them driving circles around Tucson, stuck in the same holding pattern as my creativity. I had to start thinking of the possibilities, what *could* happen. I knew they couldn't just have sex, because this story wasn't going to be about sex, some quest to lose Martin his virginity. I considered them running over something with the truck, maybe Goog's car, even the varsity baseball coach's car (for some reason I'd explain), but thought that was too easy, too, maybe even easier than having them have sex.

As soon as I thought of them getting married, the story made perfect sense to me, in terms of believability and theme, and I wrote the rest as soon as I could. The last line is probably my favorite, and when I typed it out, I knew I was finished.

WRITING EXERCISE

When I begin a story, I start with a concept. It has to be an attention-getting concept, something I want to write about, but it also has to lend itself to elaborate description, be workable as a plot element, and even have an air of mystery. The concept can be a thing, such as a pink monster truck, or an image, such as, say, a thousand cantaloupes smashed against a brick wall.

I then establish a conflict-ready relationship. Most end up being husband and wife or boyfriend and girlfriend—if I feel like writing about romantic relationships—but the connection can also fall under "other," like teacher-student or employee-boss, or any combination of family members.

Lastly, I weave these two into a first sentence, such as "Three years after my father deserted us, he pulled up to the house in a pink monster truck." Or "Seconds after telling my boss I'd slept with his wife, we drove past a health club that had at least a thousand cantaloupes smashed against its wall."

This gives me an image to build on, a relationship to explore, and best of all, a conflict, all in the first sentence.

Keep a log of as many interesting concepts as you can think of, a log you're always adding to whenever something inspires you. At the same time, keep a list of relationships that are prime for conflict, for emotional overload, for intrigue. Whenever you're ready to begin a new story, refer to these two sources and generate as many combinations as you can, writing out as many first sentences as it takes for you to be enamored, for you to want to move forward and write the second sentence, and the next, and the next.

Field Trips

We took two field trips in grade school. The first was a tour of the Bridewell House of Corrections and the Cook County Jail. The prison complex was on Twenty-sixth and California, only blocks away from St. Roman's School, so, herded by nuns into an orderly column with the girls in front and boys bringing up the rear, our fifth-grade class walked there. The nuns must have thought it a perfect choice for a field trip as not only was there a suitable cautionary lesson, but it saved on bus fare, too.

Filing from school at midmorning felt like a jailbreak. Paired up with pals, we traipsed down California, gaping like tourists at the familiar street coming to life—delivery trucks double-parking before greasy spoons, open doors revealing the dark interiors of bars still exhaling boozy breath from the night before. Some of the kids like Bad Brad Norky—already twice convicted of stealing the class milk money—were hoping to see various relatives who were doing time at County. Others, like my best friend, Rafael Mendoza, were hoping to catch a glimpse of a mob boss, or a mass murderer, or the infamous psychopath Edward Gein, a farmer from the wilds of Illinois who supposedly cannibalized his victims and tanned their skins to make lampshades and clothes. Gein fascinated us. Some years later when I was in high school, I bought a pair of hand-stitched moccasin-top gray suede shoes that when soaked with rain turned a cadaverous shade, and my buddies took to calling them my

Gein shoes. That, in turn, developed into a neighborhood expression of appreciation for any article of clothing that looked sharp in an unconventional way: *muy Gein, man* or *Gein cool!* At the same time, the term could also be used as an insult: "Your mama's a Gein."

Even more than the murderers and celebrity psychos, the main draw at County, at least for the boys, was getting a look at the electric chair. We'd heard it was kept in the basement. Local legend had it that a sudden burst of static on the radio or a blink in TV reception, say, during the *Howdy Doody* show, meant that the power had surged because they'd just fried someone at County. We thought maybe we'd get to shake the hand of the warden or whoever flipped the switch at executions. But, if there was an electric chair there at all, we never got to see it.

Surprisingly, the most memorable part of the trip occurred not at County where the men, penned in what the tour guide informed us were sixty-square-foot cells, mostly ignored us, but rather at Bridewell when they took us through the women's wing. The inmates there, prostitutes mainly, saw the nuns and had some comments about being Brides of Christ that were truly educational:

"Yo, Sisters, what kinda meat do the pope eat on Friday? Nun."

"Hey, Sister Mary Hymen, when I dress up like that I get an extra fifty!"

The nuns didn't respond, but their faces assumed the same impassive, inwardly suffering expressions that the statues of martyrs wore, and they began to hurry us through the rest of the tour.

A hefty female guard rapped the bar with her stick and shouted, "Pipe down, Taffy, there's kids for godssake."

And Taffy laughed, "Shee-it, Bull Moose! When I was their age I was doing my daddy."

And from another cell someone called, "Amen, girl!"

★★★

The next year the nuns avoided the jail and instead took us to the stockyards, a trip that required a bus. A rented yellow school bus was already waiting when we got to school that morning, and we filed on, boys

121

sitting on the left side of the aisle, girls on the right. I sat next to a new kid, Joseph Bonnamo. Usually, new kids were quiet and withdrawn, but Bonnamo, who'd only been at St. Roman's for a couple weeks, was already the most popular boy in the class. Everyone called him Joey B. His father had been a marine lifer and Joey B was used to moving around, he said. He'd moved around so much that he was a grade behind, a year older than everyone else, but he didn't seem ashamed by it. He was a good athlete and the girls all had crushes on him. That included Sylvie Perez, who over the summer had suddenly, to use my mother's word, "developed." Exploded into bloom was closer to the truth. Along with the rest of the boys, I pretended as best I could not to notice—it was too intimidating to those of us who'd been her classmates for years. But not to Joey B.

"Like my old man says, 'Tits that size have a mind of their own,'" he confided to me on the way to the Yards, "and hers are thinking, 'Feel me up, Joey B.'"

"How do you know?"

His hand dropped down and he clutched his crotch. "Telepathy."

"Class," Sister Bull Moose asked, "do you know our tradition when riding a bus on a field trip?"

"A round pound?" Joey B whispered to me.

No one raised a hand. We didn't know we had a tradition—as far as we knew we were the first class from St. Roman's ever to take a bus on a field trip.

Sister Bull Moose's real name was Sister Amabilia, but she had a heft to her that meant business, and she wielded the baton she used to conduct choir practice not unlike the guard we'd seen wielding a nightstick at Bridewell a year before, so my friend Rafael had come up with the nickname.

From within her habit, a garment that looked as if it had infinite storage capacity, she produced the pitch pipe also used in choir practice and sustained a note. "Girls start and boys come in on 'Merrily merrily merrily' …"

Joey B sang in my ear, "Row row row your boner …"

★★★

At the Yards there was a regular tour. First stop was the Armour packing plant where the meat was processed into bacon and sausage. I think the entire class was relieved that the smell wasn't as bad as we worried it might be. We knew we had traveled to the source of what in the neighborhood was called "the brown wind" or "the glue pee-ew factory," a stench that settled over the south side of Chicago at least once a week. My father said it was the smell of boiling hooves, hair, and bone rendered down to make soap. I'd once dissected a bar of Ivory on which I'd noticed what appeared to be animal hair to see if there were also fragments of bone and if beneath the soap smell I could detect the reek of the Yards.

We left the processing plant for the slaughterhouse and from a metal catwalk looked upon the scene below where workmen wearing yellow hard hats and white coats smeared with gore heaved sledgehammers down on the skulls of the steers that, urged by electric prods, had filed obediently through wooden chutes.

Every time the hammer connected, my friend Rafael would go, "Ka-boom!"

The steer would drop, folding at the knees as if his front legs had suddenly been broken.

"That has to smart," Joey B said.

For the finale they took us to where the hogs were slaughtered. A man with hairy, thick, spattered forearms, wearing rubber boots and a black rubber apron shiny with blood, stood holding a butcher knife before a vat of water. An assembly line of huge squealing hogs, suspended by their hind legs, swung past him, and as each hog went by the line would pause long enough for the man to slit the hog's throat. He did it with a practiced, effortless motion and I wondered how long he'd had the job, what it had been like on his first day, and if it was a job I could ever be desperate enough to do. Up to then, my idea of the worst job one could have was bus driver. I didn't think I could drive through rush-hour traffic down the same street over and over while making change as bus drivers had to in those days. But watching the man kill hogs, I began thinking that driving a bus might not be so bad.

With each hog there was the same terrified squeal, but louder than a squeal, more like a shriek that became a grunting gurgle of blood. A Niagara of blood splashed to the tile and into a flowing gutter of water where it rushed frothing away. The man would plunge the knife into the vat of water before him and the water clouded pink, then he'd withdraw the shining blade just as the next squealing hog arrived. Meanwhile, the hogs who'd just cranked by, still alive, their mouths, nostrils, and slit throats pumping dark red gouts were swung into a bundle of hanging bodies to bleed. Each new carcass slammed into the others causing a few weak squeals and a fresh gush of blood.

The tour guide apologized that we couldn't see the sheep slaughtered. He said that some people thought the sheep sounded human, like children, and that bothered some people, so they didn't include it on the tour.

It made me wonder who killed the sheep. We'd seen the men with sledgehammers and the man with a knife. How were the sheep slaughtered? Was it a promotion to work with the sheep—some place they sent only the most expert slaughterers—or was it the job that nobody at the Yards wanted?

"Just like the goddamn electric chair," Rafael complained.

"How's that?" Joey B asked.

"They wouldn't let us see the chair when we went to the jail last year."

★★★

At the end of the tour on our way out of the processing plant they gave each of us a souvenir hot dog. Not a hot dog Chicago style: poppy seed bun, mustard—never catsup, onion, relish, tomato, pickle, peppers, celery salt. This was a cold hot dog wrapped in a napkin. We hadn't had lunch and everyone was starving. We rode back on the bus eating our hot dogs, while singing, "Frère Jacques."

I was sitting by the window, Joey B beside me, and right across the aisle from him—no accident probably—was Sylvie Perez. I realized it was a great opportunity, but I could never think of anything to say to girls in a situation like that.

"Sylvie," Joey B said, "you liking that hot dog?"

"It's okay," Sylvie said.

"You look good eating it," he told her.

It sounded like the stupidest thing I'd ever heard, but all she did was blush, smile at him, and take another demure nibble.

I knew it was against the rules, but I cracked open the window of the bus and tried to flick my balled-up hot dog napkin into a passing convertible. Sister Bull Moose saw me do it.

"Why does there always have to be one who's not mature enough to take on trips," she asked rhetorically. For punishment I had to give up my seat and stand in the aisle, which I did to an indifference on the part of Sylvie Perez that was the worst kind of scorn.

"Since you obviously need special attention, Stuart, you can sing us a round," Sister said. Once, during our weekly music hour, looking in my direction, she'd inquired, "Who is singing like an off-key foghorn?" When I'd shut up, still moving my mouth, but only pretending to sing, she'd said, "That's better."

"I don't know the words," I said.

"Oh, I think you do. '*Dor-mez-vous, dor-mez-vous, Bim Bam Boon.*' They're easy."

Joey B patted the now empty seat beside him as if to say to Sylvie, "Now you can sit here."

Sylvie rolled her pretty eyes toward Sister Bull Moose and smiled, and Joey B nodded he understood and smiled back, and they rode like that in silence, communicating telepathically while I sang.

Inside "Field Trips":
'Like This Really Happened'

In college, I had a friend named Ron who was an entertaining raconteur despite his habit of prefacing stories with the phrase: "No shit, you guys, like this really happened."

I'm not sure why his declaration of authenticity began with a "no shit." Maybe by admitting the possibility of disbelief on the part of his audience, he hoped to nip it in the bud. Obviously, he ascribed a primacy to what "really happened" over something made-up. Still, there's that qualifying use of "*like* this really happened." Is "like" a hedge or merely a verbal tic? Ron was the kind of guy who said "you know" and "man" a lot, too. He employed the "no shit" gambit so often that friends would interrupt whatever crazed tale he was spinning with questions such as, "Ron, like no shit, man, this *really* really happened?"

Despite—or maybe because of—his insistence that he was telling the truth, Ron had triggered in his listeners what Hemingway called the "crap detector," a device he claimed a writer needed. He should have included editors, talk show hosts, and news anchors, not to mention the population of the United States under the reign of Bush/Cheney. Saying a story is true is not the same as making it credible. All that said, what I want to tell you about "Field Trips" is no shit, like it really happened.

At least, that's how I remember it happening, but then, more than the qualifying use of the word *like*, saying something happened in memory is the ultimate hedge. We know that despite the best intentions to be accurate, memory is notoriously unreliable, selective, subjective. Thanks to Google, it is easier than ever before to verify facts, but how can a writer claim to accurately remember something so elemental as dialogue to the "show, don't tell" axiom of storytelling? To claim a remembered story really happened is a relative, not an absolute, truth; forms of nonfiction such as memoir and the personal essay are not about objective or absolute truth.

Fiction avoids these potentially distracting concerns by *not* making a deal with the reader that "this really happened," even when often it did. Before the story begins, fiction offers a disclaimer as to the reality of the events and people portrayed. It's a way of not getting sued. It is also a way of saying that fiction's first allegiance is not to memory, but to imagination.

The events in "Field Trips" happened, but that doesn't in and of itself make it nonfiction. I could have published it as fiction as I have published any number of other stories that are autobiographical. Many of the stories in my novel-in-stories, *I Sailed With Magellan*, for instance, are family stories that my brothers and I would often retell before I ruined such sessions by writing them down. "Field Trips" is nonfiction because I made the decision to work with the material in that genre, availing for the story the particular relationship that memoir strikes up with a reader. It was an aesthetic choice, a craft decision.

Even when a writer defines his work as fiction, it seems that the reader remains curious as to just how autobiographical it is. That urge to look for "real life" in stories is, I think, heightened when stories are told in the first person. It is part of the special power of the first-person point of view to forge an intimate, confiding connection with the reader, and that happens whether reading nonfiction or fiction, but in nonfiction, because the reader expects what's told to be true, that expectation becomes part of the reading experience.

I think one of the elements that makes "Field Trips" engaging is the somewhat incredible idea that adults would, in the name of education, bring children to a slaughterhouse. I could have heightened credibility there by including the fact that, at one time, those trips to the Chicago Stockyards were the most popular tourist attraction in the city known as "Hogbutcher for the World." The slaughterhouse was Chicago's version of the Grand Canyon. Nonfiction naturally allows for the inclusion of such facts, but because I wanted to tell the story in a way that conveyed the spontaneity of firsthand experience, and to keep the story firmly at the level of a childhood point of view, I left out such "adult" facts.

While the reader can get caught up in the differences between fiction and nonfiction, once the writer is past the initial decision, the concern is telling a story, and the techniques of telling the story in fiction and nonfiction are basically the same—the creation of scenes, settings, and characters; the treatment of point of view; etc. Every story, fiction or nonfiction, takes risks that create problems for the writer to solve. If a story doesn't take a risk, then there's something off about the conception.

The risk I was most aware of with "Field Trips" was how to connect the two anecdotes about visiting the jail and visiting the slaughterhouse into a single, coherent story. I began this essay talking about a friend who was a raconteur. A raconteur usually deals in anecdotal stories. If the anecdotes have a laugh or a punch line at the end, that is all that is required to satisfy a listener. But more is required from anecdotes when you write them down. Besides being entertaining, anecdotes need to resonate, to have a larger meaning. The intention to raise the impact of comic anecdotes from childhood experience to a level of universal significance has little to do with whether a piece is fiction or nonfiction, and everything to do with the art of telling a story.

WRITING EXERCISE

Without question, a wide gap exists between an oral story and one confined to paper. Next time you're at a family gathering, take special note of *how* a story is told. Where does the voice inflection lie? What types of gestures are included? Has the person told the story before, and if so, what clues you in to this fact?

Next, attempt to transcribe the story to paper. Taking a simple familial anecdote and giving it more substance, more story, is a daunting task that requires a keen observer's eye and unbiased discretion. Which memories make the best scenes, and which can be edited out? How many omissions are you allowed before truth blurs with fiction? Experiment with this blurring. Find which details are necessary to achieve authenticity and which ones are excessive.

MICHAEL MARTONE

The Spirit of St. Louis

L eaving the funeral home with his small son, he saw the sun closing on the horizon. The parking lot contained a few baffles of cars at angles to each other. Beyond the cars, the sun fell to the point where he could now see it more clearly. The sun sank and grew small. He was allowing it to cool to match the cold day. To his small son, he wanted to say that you could almost touch it, but, what he said was, "Do you want to stay up late tonight?"

"Would Mommy mind?" he answered.

"No, I don't think she would."

"What can we do?" He was watching the sun fall from his father's shoulders and roll down his arm. He wanted to touch the sun.

"We could play games," his father said.

"What kind of games?" he answered. The sun was a gem on his father's hand.

"Hide and seek, blind man's bluff?"

"I'm too old, Daddy, and besides, there are only two of us. Can we watch TV?"

"No, let's not watch TV."

"What then?"

"Let's do something special." The sun was disappearing. He had been standing watching it go. He studied the sunset.

"Let's go," his father said walking the rest of the way to the car.

"What are we going to do?" he said to his father. He looked in the window of a car close to theirs and discovered a very nervous dog, rigid and tense, looking back at him.

"Let's build a model," his father answered.

★★★

He stopped the car at a hobby store on the way home. Clouds gathered behind the parking lot lights, making two kinds of blackness in the sky.

The store was a labyrinth of shelves stacked with plastic-wrapped boxes of plastic models. Model planes hung from the ceiling. On the wall were prints of airplanes falling off the wall, burning and cartwheeling to crash on the floor. The faces of those pilots in those punctured and bleeding cockpits looked nervous, with burning planes corkscrewing through clouds with blacker oily clouds. The victorious planes must be somewhere else, thanking-god-for-this-time-victory-rolling over their own fields, tuned engines sighing with those on the ground.

He looked at all the models with his son, who liked the sleek fast jets climbing off the box art into the thin, empty air. Their silver bodies were slivers in the sun. Most of the boxes illustrated the vintage, prop-driven planes plunging at disintegrating enemy craft, strafing helpless boxcars, bombing wincing cities.

"The Spirit of St. Louis" was among the carnage. The peaceful nature of its flight was distorted by the box art. The game little plane struggled to get out of the picture. Avoiding huge clouds and tracers of lightning, it limped over a boiling Atlantic. The kit was made by "Hawk." It would be small and cheap.

"What about this one?" he asked his son.

"What is it?" his son asked looking up from a picture of a B-29 called "BochsCar" dropping the bomb on Nagasaki.

"It is a small plane called 'The Spirit of St. Louis.'"

"What is that?"

"It was a plane that a man named Charles Lindbergh flew to Paris. He was the first man to do that. He was alone for a long time, and when he landed he never was alone anymore. And they made up a dance and

130

named it after him. He lost his son—his son was kidnapped. The plane is in a museum hanging from the ceiling."

He had been staring at the box while he talked, moving it at odd angles. The light reflected off the plastic wrapping. It looked violent.

"Yeah, but what is it?" he asked his father. His father's glasses were turning slowly into goggles. A dry confetti snow descended heroically outside.

"Is what?" his father asked.

"Is the Spirit of St. Louis?" he answered.

★★★

The snow fell very fast, and they could hardly see it. In the car it was easy to pretend that they were pilot and copilot, and they went though a very professional exchange: "Ignition switch on. You say, *contact*." "Contact." His son sat very close to him holding the model of "The Spirit of St. Louis." No one was out. They skimmed silently over the first layer of powdered snow. The bank tower blinked coldly behind them. To him it seemed, of course, that they were all alone. And when they got home, there was no one there either. Before they went in the house, he picked up his son and rubbed his nose, all the time calling, "The Lone Eagle, come in Lone Eagle." He twirled around and fumbled for his keys. His son giggled so hard that he almost dropped the model. He laughed so hard he almost dropped his son. And the snow dropped softly.

Old Mrs. Witham came out from next door. She was wearing pink slippers and stood on the little porch. She wrapped her arms around herself, her hands inside her sweater sleeves. She looked very cold. She had been waiting for them to get back.

"I'm sorry, Mike," she said.

"Thank you," his father said.

"Mike, when you get time, later not now, could you look at the water heater? Later, when you've had time, not now."

"Sure, Mrs. Witham," his father said.

"Have you been a good boy?" she said to him. "Would you like a piece of candy?"

He looked at his father and understood.

"No, thank you, Mrs. Witham," he said.

"I'll have rhubarb this spring, and I will make a pie," she said.

"That would be nice, Mrs. Witham," his father said looking at the pink slippers.

"It is cold," his father said.

"Yes." She went inside her house.

The pink slippers were the exact color of the crabapple blossoms that bloomed every year. In the dark, he wondered how he knew this.

★★★

They worked on "The Spirit of St. Louis" that night on a small TV table in the living room. His father put on records.

"It was good you didn't take the candy. Your hands would be dirty and then what would we do about our model?"

"Mrs. Witham's a nice lady," his son said.

"Yes, but she still has cold water," he said.

He followed the directions the best they could. He had spilled glue on them and the lettering ran. Without letting on, he improvised a great deal. He pointed out to his son that the plane had no forward-facing window because Lindbergh had put in another fuel tank. He laughed to himself when the theme from the movie "The High and the Mighty" came on, whistling around the room. And he laughed out loud when his son clapped about the room with outstretched arms buzzing and whistling. "The Lone Eagle," he called. "Come in Lone Eagle." And his son flapped up to the table and, in an efficient but clumsy landing, bumped the table sending the plastic parts skittering across it.

"You left something out," he said, his engine still running.

"What is that?" his father asked.

"The man," he said, dipping his wing and rolling away.

★★★

It was very late. He had even put the decals on the wings. But by that time the Lone Eagle had nested, curled up in the rocking chair, the rocking chair with wings. He got up from behind the table and put the records back on. He woke his son and gave him "The Spirit of St. Louis."

"Don't fly too high," he said.

It was time to go to bed. But his son was awake now, and he took off around the room holding the model over his head. He shouted, "The Lone Eagle" like the Lone Ranger.

His father came at him like the sun. And then he was in air with his plane, and a man was whistling somewhere sad, soft, and lonely.

His father put him down on his bed. His father took "The Spirit of St. Louis" and tied it to a light fixture on the ceiling with some string. The heat coming from the register kicked up a small turbulence.

His father said, "Get undressed and into bed." And then he turned to the window.

He didn't get undressed but watched his father's back melt into the night outside his window.

It was still snowing. His son was very quiet behind him. It was all very quiet. It was dark. What was it he heard? The Spirit of St. Louis. How did it ever get back across the Atlantic? Outside, a car plunged through the darkness with a scream and the snow fell like feathers.

Inside "The Spirit of St. Louis": Beginning With an End

First Things First, Last Things Last
My grandmother, dying, had waited for me to die. Start again. Had waited to die, herself, I mean. Had timed her death upon my arrival bedside. Or so we all told ourselves after she had died. This dramatic scene. Me *rushing* into the assisted-living turned assisted-dying facility in Fort Wayne. My surviving family—mother, father, brother, uncle, aunt, grandfather—in tableaux around my grandmother in bed, laboring. And that is the first thing I noticed. She looked to be in labor. My wife—in Syracuse, New York, where I had *rushed*—had recently labored, giving birth to our second son. I had attended that labor, too. Breathing, labored. Eyes, closed. Both faces masked in sweat. Here, I whispered to

my grandmother through that numbed penumbra of death and dying. I told her I was here, there, beside her. She had raised me. Her daughter, my mother, a teacher absent during the days of my childhood. Grandmother labored. That pant. And I did, I did tell her to let go. Give up. Stop. And she did as if on cue. And, suddenly, as she died, I realized that this was a first, the first time I had witnessed this. Of course, I had seen death represented hundreds, thousands of times in movies, television, books. This was the first and still the only time I had seen someone die. I myself, a writer in middle age, had killed numerous characters, arranged a variety of deaths, thinking, I thought, I knew what I was doing. I didn't. It didn't, real death didn't, still, seem real.

Having Killed My Grandmother in the Opening Scene, We Continue With a Discussion of Introductions and the Granting of the License to Kill

First days of beginning fiction-writing workshops often begin with introductions and an open-ended question. Why do you write? What do you want your writing to do? Shy, new to each other, the writers in class most often answer with cheery optimism. I would like to entertain, to tell stories that matter, that connect with the reader, that create sympathy or understanding, that solve problems, that bring solace, and that express an emotion. The answers verge on the scientific, are couched in a positive manner, are reasonable if distant. Everyone is very polite. I got into the business, I tell them dramatically, to kill people. And, I tell them, I suspect you did, too.

Art with its power to simulate the world grants the possibility to alter the world. I started writing when my high-school girlfriend, a cheerleader, broke up with me to date a power-forward. During free writing in an English class, I found I could reorder that order, send the power-forward powering over a cliff in a senseless accident, say, or to then have a character somewhat like me effortlessly console someone somewhat like my former girlfriend in her stunningly rendered and extensive grief. There is often, in those introductions, some talk of emotion—but in the abstract, a nebula that pulses perhaps, that floats and shimmers, not the black hole so heavy no light escapes. Soon after the introductions, the young writers try on this power to create, yes, but to murder also. The carnage in a workshop can become, by the end of a term, prodigious. The catharsis from such violence, cathartic. Death all day.

The Nonsense of an Ending Ending or Ending in the Middle of Things

My ten-year-old son is scared to death of death.

He is at that stage. As the sun goes down each night, the color drains from his face, and he races to the bathroom to kneel by the toilet, waiting to throw up. I go in after him, sit on the floor next to him while he, hunched over, concentrates on the cramps of his own body waiting. "It's not fair," he says.

"No," I say, "it's not." I imagine this death sickness is, perhaps, chemical, sparked by his own dawning hormonal changes. He is losing his body fat. His teeth are falling out.

Poor kid. What can I say to him? On the floor waiting as time passes I think of Thomas Aquinas. I consider how the saint came up with his own accommodation with this drama. Death is an ending to the story, he reasoned. Death exists to give meaning to life. Without death, there would be no distance to regard the course of events in order to make judgments, to make meaning.

I think better of sharing this insight with him while he is engaged in a struggle with his own reality, of life becoming real to him. It also seems rather lame now in the cold light of the bathroom.

My students struggle with their narratives. Their lives do not lack for drama. There is plenty of drama to go around. What they do lack is the ending. They are in the middle of things. The solution, of course, is to construct an artificial coda, to draw arbitrary parentheses around a particular period of life being lived. Childhood, say, one bounded moment that can, now, be made to mean.

Death as the Beginning of the End

Listen: Start with death. The short story form does not do well with death, even less well with acts of violence. Death isn't an ending in stories so much as it is a lens that focuses attention on that one pristine and perfect telling gesture. It is in the still moment after a death that we who survive, our characters and ourselves, are most alive. Death foils life in both senses: defeating life, yes, but death also serves as it foils, in that other sense, making life in contrast stand out all the more. Too often I see my students use death solely as the foiling foil. Curses, foiled again. They have struggled mightily to bring their characters to life, to animate the characters and their conflicts, their motives, their drives, and their desires. Their characters attain character. Those characters have what the reader senses as "depth." The characters are "complex." At this point, the point of coming alive, the young writer kills the character. He is run over by a bus. Often it is a bus. Out of nowhere, a bus. The Frankenstein Stratagem. The monster has come to life. Kill it! And they do. Foiled. At the point where a character is beyond the control of the writer, a consciousness has been activated, an intelligence. It lives! Kill it! Listen: If you have that feeling, that urge to kill the character you've created just as the character comes to life, just as the character surprises you with a life you never expected, kill the urge to kill and start the real labor. Start the real labor right there.

 ## WRITING EXERCISE

Once I asked a student to give me a rough outline of a plot of a story he was going to write. First, he told me how the story was about a television remote cameraman who was always getting in the way of the police at accidents, filming recklessly the gore of the wreck, hindering the brave emergency workers. He asked me then if I could guess what would happen. Yes, I said, the cameraman will be called to a deadly crash and rudely butt his way in to film the victims and only then discover the mangled remains of his dead wife and infant child. My student was stunned I had predicted the outcome of the story. How did you know?

I told him I gathered from the way he described the cameraman that he didn't like the cameraman much. It turned out, of course, that the writer's father was a traffic officer and complained endlessly about newspaper reporters and cameramen getting in the way of his job when they were doing their job. I told the student I could tell he wanted to use the story to punish his character. He might have started, I suggested, from that moment that was his ending, imagining a cameraman who is just trying to do his job and finds he has to film while remaining objective and professional and he must do so in the midst of filming something that is incredibly subjective and personal. There is an interesting beginning of a story—a man who has had to document the death of his loved ones. What happens then? How does the character go on? How does he live with that?

Begin a story with a horrific death, an agonizing scene of violence, then use the story to track the trauma, its aftermath. One track unavailable to you is vengeance or retribution. There is to be no further violence; no one else dies for the duration of the story. The story is to be about the living, with the death happily or not, ever after.

Here on Earth

"This is where we bought the pregnancy test," Darcy's mother told her. "It was positive the next morning. Your father didn't believe it. I brought it to him in bed, little test tube of pink urine. By then, we had our furniture."

"Huh." Darcy watched the grungy drugstore pass, unwillingly imagining her parents walking out the door together, sack between them, the two of them the next morning in bed with no clothes on. She was thirteen years old. She didn't want to hear about pregnancy tests at all, but especially ones involving herself or her mother and father. The word *urine* hung in the air like a bad smell.

Reclining in the front seat of the rental car, Darcy fantasized they owned it and she lived here in Chicago. Busy and fast, trains rattling through and people rushing on the streets, the sky a ponderous, profound gray. Apartments stacked on one another, lined up on endless blocks, all the red bricks it had taken to build them: the overwhelming sense of numbers and density. Of never being able to know it all. She felt herself opening up as the kitchen and bedroom and living room windows rushed by, this life, another life, yet another on top. How many beds must there be in one high-rise alone? And just behind them, Lake Michigan, another stretch of the mind's capacity for volume, a lake that might as well have been the ocean, full of fish and junk and sunken ships and drowned people.

Darcy had never been to a city like Chicago, old; it thrilled her as much as it made her resentful. When she demanded to know why they'd ever left such a worthy, wondrous place, her mother gave her an endless account of the worst public schools in the nation and ungodly bad weather. They'd moved to Arizona when Darcy was two. She felt badly treated, taken against her will, bereft of her birthright. Chicago seemed like home. She'd thought so since they landed at O'Hare. The three teenagers who'd sat in front of her and her mother in the flight had talked nonstop about the radio stations in Chicago, how much they'd missed the music during their visit to Phoenix.

"We just did it all wrong," her mother explained. "We bought when we should have rented, we took the first job your father got instead of really thinking about day-to-day things like could we stand to live in a place where people have to clean up after their dogs. We were young. We had a dog." Her mother laughed as if she'd said something funny.

Her mother had been sent by the Phoenix City Council to Chicago to attend a seminar on recycling plastic containers. She had to present her findings next week. Darcy joined her because the airline's promotional pitch this summer was to offer free trips to children. They were staying at the Ramada Inn next to the airport, a disappointing location. From their window, Darcy's mother was quick to point out to Darcy (as if she were three instead of thirteen), they could watch the planes land. Driving on Michigan Avenue, in the heart of the city, Darcy had seen many more intriguing hotels in which to hold a conference.

"I can play hooky today," her mother had told her that morning. "They're talking about recycling tires." So they'd decided to tour the old neighborhood, Rogers Park, on the far north side. Darcy navigated, astonished each time the street on the map would materialize in front of them. They visited the Loop, then sped up Lake Shore Drive, onto Hollywood, past Touchy, circling back to Sheridan. Her mother pointed out landmarks: the place they'd bought a television, an air conditioner, the buildings they'd looked at apartments and condos in, the office her obstetrician had occupied. Apparently, the whole three years in Chicago had been, for her, a time of becoming a mother. Her memories had little else in them.

"And you went to day care right there," her mother said, pointing at what Darcy had learned was called a brownstone. "You loved Debbi. Remember Debbi?"

"No, why should I?"

"First you said Mommy, then Daddy, then Debbi. Your grandmothers were hurt. Debbi cried when we moved away."

"Maybe we should go back downtown and eat lunch on top of the Hancock building. Maybe it revolves."

"There!" her mother exclaimed. "Right there on the corner!" She pointed to a brick apartment building with a fake turret on top. "That's where you were conceived!"

Not "That's where we lived" or "That's our old condo," but "That's where you were conceived." Darcy felt like jumping out the car door. She looked at the building, giving her mother the silent treatment. The turret was a mossy green and had leached its color down the drainpipes surrounding it.

"We only had a futon for the first week, and we were painting everything white. Your father wanted it all white, so it would look bigger than it was. But I insisted on one pink window. After you were talking, you could say, 'Pink window.'"

Someone honked at them. A black man gave them the finger as he passed, yelling things in the vacuum of his air-conditioned car interior. Darcy felt her face heat like fire. There weren't many blacks in Phoenix; she felt this man had superior claim to the road and was embarrassed when her mother, white, ignored him. Her mother leaned over Darcy to ogle the building some more, her head nearly in Darcy's lap. Darcy started down at her mother's coarse, cantankerous hair and made a face.

"The first thing we said when we looked at the place was, 'It will be fine as long as we don't have kids.' Nine months later, boom, there you were."

"Ironic," Darcy said. "Could you move? Your dandruff is getting on me."

140

Her mother sat up and looked hurt. Now ashamed, Darcy tried to make amends. "Where was I born?" she forced herself to ask.

Though she didn't say anything, her mother began driving again.

"Didn't you say there was an earthquake the day I was born, Mom?"

"Yes."

"Isn't that kind of weird in Illinois?"

"Yes." Her mother had set out on today's adventure with Darcy enthusiastically, but her eagerness had waned. One thing that kept Darcy on her toes was her mother's sudden mood changes. Now she began cursing other drivers. Darcy, conversely, had cheered up as she made conversation. She was just on the edge of discovering the push-me, pull-you relationship she and her mother would share the rest of their lives together.

After thirty minutes of circling and reading signs, they gave up on the hospital search and went to an Italian restaurant her mother remembered ("They love kids, always gave you crayons and cookies") but which had turned into a foreign auto repair shop in the intervening eleven years. They sat in the parking lot while her mother squinted in deep thought, muttering the names of streets she could remember and swearing over the ones she couldn't. It was almost perverse how her mother's anger made Darcy feel better.

"Let's have a picnic instead," Darcy suggested. "We can go to that store." On the corner at any angle from them was a small grocery that advertised lottery tickets and bourbon. A bum (a drug addict, Darcy thought) sat on the curb. Her mother looked skeptical. The trash in the streets only made Darcy feel sophisticated; Phoenix was so *sanitary* compared with this. She felt real here. "Come on. We'll get Vienna sausages and American cheese slices and circus peanuts."

Her mother finally smiled. These were things she was not, as a grown-up, supposed to enjoy.

"When I was pregnant with you," she said, "I made your father buy me circus peanuts in the middle of the night."

"Yeah, I know."

"Don't forget to lock your door."

"Duh."

With their groceries, they drove south along the lake, looking for a suitable spot for a picnic. The wind blew and the water was a deadly, churning gray. Darcy could not get over the fact that you could not see to the other side.

"When I was pregnant, I cried about everything. One time, taking the train down to the city, I saw these three boys standing over a grave in the cemetery. They were skinheads, you know, shaved skulls and black jackets and what not. I burst into tears. The woman sitting next to me got up, she thought I was a nut. Other times I'd cry over TV commercials, little babies playing in toilet paper. I kept thinking the day was going to quit breathing. It was an emotional time. Raging hormones."

Darcy flinched at the mention of hormones. Her mother could tell a perfectly presentable anecdote and then ruin it with a certain uncomfortable word. Sometimes Darcy believed that was intentional, that her mother liked to embarrass her, liked to put her in situations in which she'd have to prove her frank relationship with her mother: See, they could discuss hormones. Darcy resisted, annoyed with the obviousness of the ploy. When she was young she loved to hear about birth and prenatal activity, but lately the more biological details kept cropping up, forcing her to imagine herself inside her mother. At this rate, she would not be able to stand any of it in a few years. It remained a story her mother never tired of telling. "I don't expect you to be grateful," she'd say, cheerfully. "I'm still not grateful to my mother for having me." Darcy had been a surprise baby, "a happy accident," an active kicker in the womb, a frustratingly late delivery, the one redeeming thing that had happened to her mother and father during their three-year stay in Chicago.

"But if we hadn't lived here," her mother said, "if we hadn't bought that tiny condo or that miserable futon, we wouldn't have gotten you, so I can't really regret anything we did. You see?"

"Uh huh."

"And sometimes I think if we'd never left here ..." She trailed off, though Darcy followed her logic, silently. She thought this way, too. If they'd never left Chicago, her father might still be living with them. He might not have a new wife and another family, a new baby daughter. In Chicago, there used to be just the three of them, crowded in a one-bedroom apartment with a big dog. Now, everything had flown apart. Even the dog had died.

Their car was the only one near the Loyola Park Beach. Darcy experienced the cold wind and the freezing water as something to retain for later, when she was hot in Phoenix, when even swimming couldn't cool her.

"Look, Dar! Tulips!" Her mother pointed at three straggling flowers. She found amazement in the most peculiar, ordinary things. She stared lovingly at the woeful red tulips bent sideways in the gusting wind. "Every year I think flowers are more beautiful. I must never have noticed them, growing up. I never noticed trees or gardens or nature. I look at them now and can hardly stand how spectacularly beautiful they are. How did it all happen?"

"They're bionic," Darcy said. "Little super wires in their stems. Let's eat." She sat and opened the sack, pulling out their deli sandwiches and the soda her mother had made certain was in returnable bottles.

"Doesn't it just astound you?" her mother said, joining her, biting into her pastrami. "To get something from nothing?" She chewed, not needing or expecting an answer. Darcy was, as always, a captive audience. And the only one left to listen to this upcoming particular story. "I just couldn't believe when I was pregnant that you were going to be born. Two people, your dad and me, and then a third one, you. Something from nothing."

"Not nothing," Darcy felt obligated to point out, however distasteful the thought of sperms swimming in semen toward the fat, waiting egg.

"Microscopic dots hardly constitute something real," her mother scoffed. She went on, but Darcy tuned out. Her mother could wax incredulous for a long time without needing a response.

When Darcy was younger she would request proof of her mother's love for her. If you had to choose, she would say, would you want me to die or you? Her mother always gave Darcy life; after all, she explained, she'd already led her own, and Darcy's was not yet filled in.

Darcy worried she might never grow into making such a choice, the choice that was, by virtue of its generosity, obviously the right one. It was not yet possible for her to imagine she would give her life up for anything—or one. (She would not, for instance, choose her mother's life over her own.) All the other parts were unthinkable, too, the getting married and having children parts, the putting things in her and the getting them out.

When she'd asked her father whose life he would choose, he told her the question was ridiculous. He asked her to please provide a realistic scenario in which one of their lives would be taken or spared over the other. "It's indulgent," he told Darcy, "to think that way. I'm not going to be a party to it." Her father also thought it was indulgent to tell over and over the story of their first years together, the Chicago years. Because she was half his, Darcy could be persuaded to believe he was right, that reminiscing and saying "what if" led nowhere. Still, there was that part that was her mother's.

She finished her sandwich and lay back in the damp new grass. Lake Michigan rose and dropped a few feet away. Darcy looked up, into the only hole in the wide, solid mass of clouds overhead. She blinked, her heart thudding suddenly as she thought this might be an invitation from above, an ovation she alone would be offered. She would fly away—she felt the sky pulling her—watching her mother and their lunch litter recede below her. But what was the password? She was frightened to think she might possess it. She wanted terribly to shoot away into that hole, to float above the city, to see the world in a piece. On the airplane she'd pressed her face to the glass, aching to see more, to escape the constraints around her, to pry out the glass, to climb through the porthole and stand on the wing, to see. Anyplace, no matter how wide and open, could give her claustrophobia; she sometimes felt her skin to be a kind of straightjacket.

Darcy started into the blue until it vibrated, swearing to whatever power had pushed open that hole in the sky that she would exchange her life for a glimpse. No science, no ship, no oxygen. She would not even expect the exclusive rights to the story; she'd die immediately (implicitly part of the bargain) and not tell a soul.

She thought of swimming through mute air, the Earth at last comprehensible and whole beneath her. But of course she would want to tell someone. She deflated, gravity quickly binding her once more, and watched gray clouds overcome the clear blue. Her moment passed. She knew the receipt of such a gift ought to have been more gracious than wanting to brag, but there was no denying she would want to *tell* somebody, report back to the miracle.

"When you were little," her mother was saying, here on Earth eating sticky orange circus peanuts, "you loved to say 'double-you,' the letter of the alphabet, over and over again. You'd get on the phone and say, 'Hi. Double-you. Bye.'"

"Really brilliant, wasn't I?"

"Yes," her mother said. "Yes, you surely were."

Inside "Here on Earth": Dividing the Self

This story was written when my daughter, my first child, was three years old, and when I was twenty-nine. As in the story, my husband and I had lived in Chicago only briefly, and the details of the pregnancy and birth are, more or less, factual. Our condominium was small, our dog was large, my husband's job depressed him, and the weather was awful. Jade was a late delivery, and there was a minor earthquake in Illinois—I felt it in my hospital room—on the day she was born, June 9, 1987. We also moved away from Chicago for the Southwest (New Mexico rather than Arizona).

Unfactual is the divorce (my husband and I celebrated our twenty-fourth anniversary this summer), the return trip with the thirteen-year-old (our daughter was seventeen when she first visited Chicago, and

YOU MUST BE THIS TALL TO RIDE

loved it), and any clue whatsoever I may have about what my daughter might think about her father's and my early relationship.

My daughter turned twenty-one last summer. When she was little and somebody asked her what she wanted to be when she grew up, she would say "an adventurer." She has fulfilled that, both in art and travel; she's an astonishing singer, actress, writer, and painter. Roughly a third of her birthdays have been spent on foreign soil (this most emblematic recent one in Amsterdam). It's sort of amazing to realize that she is now closer to the age I was when I wrote "Here on Earth" than she is to her childish self.

But now I am closer to the age my mother was when she became Jade's grandmother. So it goes. My way into this story was by occupying different stages of my own development. I know how I felt about my mother, and how I thought when I was a teenager, and how Chicago seemed to me, as a young adult. I postulated a fiction based on a few facts: I had experienced pregnancy and motherhood as a miracle. The two things I always knew I wanted to be, when I was young, were a mother and a writer. I also had been a resistant, unsentimental teen. The characters in this story, mother and daughter, are two versions of myself. They enact a conflict that is based on the psychology of self: of changing, evolving, disintegrating self, and of unchanging, adamant, expanding self.

John Cheever's story "Goodbye, My Brother" was one that, according to its author, in its first draft had a single character with extremely mixed feelings about his family. Cheever later revised the story by dividing the conflicted brother figure into two separate characters. Each of these men has strong feelings about his family and their summer home. The two brothers enact a dramatic conflict (rather than a cerebral internal dilemma), one that reaches crisis when the narrator bashes his brother Tifty over the head with a tree root.

Cheever's original single-sensibility narrator apparently was of two minds: He both enjoyed the old family house and the summer gathering, and he also saw it as impractical and vaguely false. Everybody experiences inner arguments; everybody occasionally is ambivalent. The see-saw between sentiment and pragmatism, between holding onto things and letting them go, between Christian and Pagan pantheons are the elements that act as binary forces in Cheever's story. It's brilliant because Cheever so wisely took a single person's ambivalence and divided it into active possibility in two different characters. This way, the reader can enjoy external drama instead of internal thought.

I'm not going to claim that my story is in any way as successful as Cheever's. It wasn't even my conscious decision to perform the similar act of dividing myself. But I see that that is precisely what I've done. A happy accident (which is often what makes a piece of fiction come together).

Flannery O'Connor's best stories situate two oppositional forces in a shared landscape. These characters, called "counterpointed," are not exactly opposites. In some way, they represent two ends of a continuum, which is a different situation than complete opposites. For instance, in her story "A Good Man Is Hard to Find," the Misfit and the grandmother are the counterpointed characters. True, they appear to be in some way complete opposites: man vs. woman, old vs. young, law-abiding vs. miscreant, and victim vs. villain. However, when push comes to shove, each displays a passion for knowledge of faith. The grandmother's has been, until her demise, a kind of superficial knowledge, and the Misfit's has been a labored, literal, concrete-minded ingestion of knowledge, but nevertheless, when the end comes, they are doing nothing less than enacting the tenets of Christian understanding. Their compatriots do not necessarily share that passion, the life-or-death significance of it, no matter the more obvious ways that each carload appears to be more similar to these two different people (the Misfit is traveling with men he was in prison with; the grandmother is with her son and grandchildren). In the end, it is the grandmother and Misfit who have the debate that proves each a closer sensibility to the other.

I would suggest that O'Connor's strategy might have mimicked Cheever's. She perhaps set up characters to be pitted against one another who have a strange (and often opaque) connection to one another. My own assessment of the best short fiction is that it operates with certain binaries in action. Of my own story, I would say that the binaries

147

present here are: nostalgia and reality; regret and anticipation; age and youth; and a desire to connect, on the mother's part, and a desire to separate, on the daughter's part.

One final thought: I couldn't really write "Here on Earth" now. I've changed, and so has my daughter, and so has my relationship with my various selves. I'm grateful to have a kind of record of who I was, back then; it's much easier to visit fiction than a diary, although I think that a lot of the confessional information is still present.

WRITING EXERCISE

Divide yourself, fictionally, by putting on the page two versions of yourself (the older one, the younger one; the angry one, the happy one; the powerful you, the weak you; the masculine side, the feminine side, etc.) and allow your selves to make some sort of drama. A journey (which features in the Cheever and O'Connor examples I provided) is perhaps a good way to ensure that your characters have a literal passage to make in addition to the more abstract emotional movement.

PETER ORNER

Pampkin's Lament

T wo-term governor Cheeky Al Thorstenson was so popular that year that his Democratic challenger could have been, my father said, Ricardo Montalban in his prime and it wouldn't have made a five-percent difference. Even so, somebody had to run, somebody always has to run, and so Mike Pampkin put his sacrificial head into the race, and my father, equally for no good reason other than somebody must always prepare the lamb for the slaughter, got himself hired campaign manager. Nobody understood it all better than Pampkin himself. He wore his defeat right there on his body, like one of his unflattering V-neck sweaters that made his breasts mound outward like a couple of sad little hills. When he forced himself to smile for photographers, Pampkin always looked constipated. And he was so endearingly down-homely honest about his chances that people loved him. Of course not enough to vote for him. Still, for such an ungraceful man he had long, elegant hands, Jackie O hands, my father said, only Pampkin's weren't gloved. Mike Pampkin's hands were unsheathed, out in the open for the world to see. He was the loneliest-seeming man ever to run for statewide office in Illinois.

It was 1980. I was a mostly ignored thirteen-year-old and I had already developed great disdain for politics. It bored me to hatred. But if I could have voted, I must say I would have voted for Cheeky Al also.

His commercials were very good and I liked his belt buckles. Everybody liked Cheeky Al's belt buckles.

Probably what is most remembered, if anything, about Mike Pampkin during that campaign was an incident that happened in Waukegan during the Fourth of July parade. Pampkin got run over by a fez-wearing Shriner on a motorized flying carpet. The Shriner swore it was an accident, but this didn't stop the *Waukegan News Sun* from running the headline: PAMPKIN SWEPT UNDER RUG.

My memory of that time is of less public humiliation.

One night, it must have been a few weeks before Election Day, there was a knock on our back door. It was after two in the morning. The knock was mousy but insistent. I first heard it in my restless dreams, like someone was tapping on my skull with a pencil. Eventually, my father answered the door. I got out of bed and went downstairs. I found them facing each other at the kitchen table. If either Pampkin or my father noticed me, they didn't let on. I crouched on the floor and leaned against the cold stove. My father was going on as only my father could go on. To him, at this late stage, the election had become, if not an actual race, not a total farce either. The flying-carpet incident had caused a small sympathy bump in the polls, and the bump had held.

Yet it was more than this. Politics drugged my father. He loved nothing more than to hear his own voice holding forth, and he'd work himself up into a hallucinatory frenzy of absolute certainty when it came to anything electoral. My mother left him during the '72 primaries. My father had ordained that Scoop Jackson was the party's savior, the only one who could save the Democrats from satanic George Wallace. My mother, treasonably, was for Edmund Muskie, that pantywaist. The marriage couldn't last, and it didn't. After the New Hampshire primary, my mother moved to Santa Barbara.

My father in the kitchen in October of 1980, rattling off to Pampkin what my father called, "issue conflagrations," by which he meant those issues that divided city voters from downstaters. To my father, anybody who didn't live in Chicago or the suburbs was a downstater, even if they lived upstate, across state, or on an island in the Kankakee River. He told Pampkin that his position on the Zion nuclear power plant was too wishy-washy, that the anti-nuke loons were getting ready to fry him in vegetable oil.

"Listen, Mike, it doesn't matter that Cheeky Al's all for plutonium in our cheeseburgers. The only meat those cannibals eat is their own kind."

Pampkin wasn't listening. He was staring out the kitchen window, at his own face in the glass. He didn't seem tired or weary or anything like that. If anything, he was too awake. In fact, his eyes were so huge they looked torn open. Of course he knew everything my father was saying. Pampkin wasn't a neophyte. He'd grown up in the bosom of the machine, in the 24th Ward. Izzy Horowitz and Jake Arvey were his mentors. He'd worked his way up, made a life in politics, nothing flashy, steady. Daley himself was a personal friend. And when the Mayor asks you to take a fall to Cheeky Al, you take a fall to Cheeky Al. That Daley was dead and buried now didn't make a difference. A promise to the Mayor is a promise to the Mayor and there is only one Mayor. Pampkin didn't need my father's issue conflagrations. He was a man who filled a suit. Didn't a man have to fill something? At the time he ran, I think Pampkin was state comptroller, whatever that means.

So the candidate sat mute as my father began to soar, his pen conducting the air.

"So we go strong against nuclear power in the city on local TV here. But when you're down in Rantoul on Thursday make like you didn't hear the question. Stick your finger in your ear. Kiss a baby, anything—"

"Raymond."

Pampkin seemed almost shocked by his own voice. He was calm, but I noticed his cheeks loosen as if he'd been holding my father's name in his mouth. Then he said, "My wife's leaving me. It's not official. She says she won't make it official until after the election. She's in love, she says."

My father dropped his pen. It rolled off the table and onto the floor, where it came to rest against my bare toes. I didn't pick it up. On the table between the two men were precinct maps, charts, phone lists, mailing labels, buttons, and those olive Pampkin bumper stickers so much more common around our house than on cars.

"Can I get you a cup of coffee, Mike?"

I watched my father. He was gazing at Pampkin with an expression I'd never seen before. Drained of his talk, he looked suddenly kinder. Here is a man across this table, a fellow sojourner. What I am trying to say is that it was a strange time—1980. A terrible time in many ways, and yet my father became at that moment infused with a little grace. Maybe the possibility of being trounced not only by Cheeky Al but also by the big feet of Reagan himself had opened my father's eyes to the existence of other people. Here was a man in pain.

They sat and drank coffee, and didn't talk about Mrs. Pampkin. At least not with their mouths. With their eyes they talked about her, with their fingers gripping their mugs they talked about her.

Mrs. Pampkin?

My inclination before that night would have been to say that she was as forgettable as her husband. More so. Though I had seen her many times, I couldn't conjure up her face. I remembered she wore earth tones. I remembered she once smelled like bland soap. She wasn't pudgy; she wasn't lanky. She wasn't stiff, nor was she jiggly. Early on in the campaign, my father had suggested to Pampkin that maybe his wife could wear a flower in her hair at garden events, or at the very least lipstick for television. Nothing came of these suggestions, and as far as I knew the issue of Pampkin's wife hadn't come up again until that night in the kitchen, when, for me, she went from drab to blazing. She'd done something unexpected. If Mrs. Pampkin was capable of it, what did this mean for the rest of us? I remembered—then—that I had watched her after Mike got hit by the carpet. She hadn't become hysterical. She'd merely walked over to him lying there on the pavement (the Shriner apologizing over and over) and the expression in her eyes was of such motionless calm that Mike and everybody else around knew it was going to be all right, that this was only another humiliation in the long line that life hands us, nothing more, nothing less. She'd knelt to him.

Pampkin's hand crept across the table toward my father's. Gently he clutched my father's wrist.

"Do you know what she said? She said, 'You have no idea how this feels.' I said, 'Maureen, I thought I did.'"

"More coffee, Mike?"

"Please."

But he didn't let go of my father's wrist, and my father didn't try to pull it away. Pampkin kept talking.

"You get to a point you think you can't be surprised. I remember a lady once, a blind lady. Lived on Archer. Every day she went to the same store up the block. Every day for thirty-five years. She knows this stretch of block as if she laid the cement for the sidewalk herself. It's her universe. One day they're doing some sewage work and some clown forgets to replace the manhole cover and vamoose. She drops. Crazy that she lived. Broke both legs. It cost the city four hundred thousand on the tort claim to settle it. I'm talking about this kind of out-of-nowhere."

My father sat there and watched him.

"Or let's say you're on Delta. Sipping a Bloody Mary. Seat-belt sign's off. There's a jolt. Unanticipated turbulence, they call it. It happened to a cousin of Vito Marzullo. All he was trying to do was go to Philadelphia. Broke his neck on the overhead bin."

★★★

When I woke up on the kitchen floor, the room looked different, darker, smaller, in the feeble light of the sun just peeping over the bottom edge of the kitchen window. Pampkin was still sitting there, gripping his mug of cold coffee and talking across the table to my father's shaggy head, which was facedown and drooling on the bumper stickers. My father was young then. He's always looked young; even to this day, his gray sideburns seem more like an affectation than a sign of age, but that morning he really was young, and Pampkin was still telling my father's head what it was like to be surprised. And he didn't look any more rumpled than usual. Now when I remember all this, I think of Fidel Castro, who still gives those eighteen-hour speeches to the party faithful. There on the table, my father's loyal head.

153

I was thirteen years old and I woke up on the floor with a hard-on over Mrs. Pampkin. One long night on the linoleum had proved that lust, if not love, had a smell and that smell was of bland soap. I thought of ditching school and following her to some apartment or a Red Roof Inn. I wanted to watch them. I wanted to see something that wasn't lonely. Tossed-around sheets, a belt lying on the floor. I wanted to know what they said, how they left each other, who watched the retreating back of the other. How do you part? Why would you ever? Even for an hour? Even when you know that the next day, at some appointed hour, you will have it again?

Got to go. My husband's running for governor.

Pampkin droned on. He had his shoes off and was sitting there in his mismatched socks, his toes quietly wrestling each other.

"Or put it this way. An old tree. Its roots are dried up. But you can't know this. You're not a botanist, a tree surgeon, or Smokey the Bear. One day, a whiff of breeze comes and topples it. Why that whiff?"

I couldn't hold back a loud yawn, and Pampkin looked down at me on the floor. He wasn't startled by the rise in my shorts. He wasn't startled by anything anymore.

He asked me directly, "You. Little fella. You're as old as Methuselah and still you don't know squat?"

I shrugged.

Pampkin took a gulp of old coffee. "Exactly," he said. "Exactly."

Either I stopped listening, or he stopped talking, because after a while his voice got faint and the morning rose for good.

★★★

Pampkin died twelve years later, in the winter of '92. The sub-headline in the *Chicago Sun-Times* ran: AMIABLE POLITICIAN LOST GOVERNOR'S RACE BY RECORD MARGIN.

I went with my father to the funeral. The Pampkins had never divorced. We met Mrs. Pampkin on the steps of the funeral home in Skokie. All it took was the way they looked at each other. I won't try to describe it, except to say that it lasted too long and had nothing to do with anybody dead. They didn't touch. They didn't need to. They watched each other's smoky breath in the chill air. Facing her in her grief and her wide-brimmed black hat, my father looked haggard and puny. It only ended when more people came up to her to offer condolences. I don't know how long it went on between them. I'm not even sure it matters. I now know it's easier to walk away from what you thought you couldn't live without than I once imagined.

She was taller than I remembered, and her face was red with sadness and January.

"Don't look so pale, Ray," she whispered to my father before she moved on to the other mourners, her hand hovering for a moment near his ear. "Mike always thought you were a good egg."

Inside "Pampkin's Lament": The Loser Hero

In my family, politics—especially being on the losing end of politics—runs in the blood. My father, in 1972, ran for the Illinois State Senate against a popular incumbent. He got crushed in the Democratic primary. I don't remember much about the race itself, but for many years we kept a life-sized cardboard cutout of my father smiling and waving. Under my father's feet, the still inexplicable slogan: ORNER FOR THE NEW INTEGRITY. The cutout was printed a little strangely also and my father's skin had a green, martianish tint. He lived in the broom closet. He fit nicely in there. Every time we broke a glass, we'd open the door and there this green version of my father would be still smiling, still waving to the crowd. Nobody had told him that my father had lost to Seymour Simon by eighteen points. And so maybe my interest in the characters of losing politicians stems from the resiliency of a cardboard cutout of my father, a kind of beautiful resiliency. The campaign was never really over. And maybe this is the upshot of any election. Maybe when all is said and done, it has nothing to do with votes.

A brief roll call of some recent champions: Walter Mondale, Mike Dukakis, Bob Dole, Al Gore … But I also go further back and think of Adlai Stevenson, father and son, both losers. In Chicago there is a famous photograph of Wendell Wilkie just after someone threw an egg in his face. There's a dignity in Wilkie's sad, indignant face. I could go on and on. John Adams was a pioneering loser. Who needs Jefferson's flamboyance? His university and his little pigtail? I'll take plodding, hangdog Adams any day. Not only Americans. Is there a man on Earth who has lost more elections for prime minister than the Israeli Shimon Peres? Now there's greatness. Winners don't emote this kind of pathos. That sounds highbrow. I mean only that losing will always, to me anyway, make for a better story. And there are no losers like our own losers, even those (maybe especially those) we invent. Mike Pampkin, a losing candidate for governor of Illinois, is my pale contribution to a long line of heroes. I hope he speaks up a bit for failure. In politics, yes, but also for the mightiest losses of all—defeats in love.

To close the circle a little, I'll add that my father returned to politics in 1976 when he took a job running the Illinois campaign of Admiral Elmo Zumwalt for president. This is true. Zumwalt was head of naval operations during the Vietnam War. It was his decision to drop Agent Orange because he, like many others, thought that it would help protect men on the ground from the Viet Cong hiding in the dense foliage. But Zumwalt wasn't a man not to own up to his own mistakes, even one as foolish and catastrophic as this one. His own son, a swift-boat commander during the war, contracted cancer that may have been caused by contact with Agent Orange. (See the TV movie *My Father, My Son* with Karl Malden as Zumwalt.) Elmo Zumwalt was a good, decent man and he might have made a pretty good president. He had huge and very distinguished eyebrows, and in my family we loved him like an uncle. He once told me he got seasick on boats. Zumwalt never even made it to the Illinois primary. Or any primary, for that matter. His campaign for president ended before the race even started. He ended up running for the Senate in Virginia, losing.

WRITING EXERCISE

Consider your losses.

Consider your greatest defeats and humiliations and how now, in retrospect, you attempt to make sense of them.

Next, consider your victories. What are you really proud of accomplishing?

When examining losses and victories side by side, it seems as if we tend to nurse our losses closer than the times we did succeed. Why is this? What makes the losses so much more personal and lasting?

With this in mind, create a character who has lost something: a game, an election, a love. How does this character attempt to compensate for the loss? What is the character willing to risk in order to regain confidence? What does he show on the outside, and how does that differ from what he feels within?

JACK PENDARVIS

Sex Devil

Gentlemen:
I would like to give you my idea for one of your comic books. Well it is not one of your comic books yet, but it soon will be! I call my idea Sex Devil.

Sex Devil starts out as a normal high school student. Unfortunately his fellow classmates do not think he is normal. For you see, Sex Devil (real name Randy White) has a cleft palate.

Sex Devil attempts to get his fellow classmates to like him. Unfortunately he pretends that he knows karate, which is a lie. Sex Devil's lies are soon discovered. After that his fellow classmates put a thing on the blackboard. It is a picture of Sex Devil (I mean Randy White) with slanting eyes, which he does not have. Underneath the picture it says Wandy Wite, Kawate Kiwwah. Also there is a bubble coming out of Randy White's mouth. Randy White is saying WAH!

A school janitor sees Randy White's humiliation. After school the janitor who is Asian American pulls Randy White to the side. Randy White is apprehensive yet he follows the school janitor to his creepy shack. Underground beneath the shack there is a training facility for a rare form of karate called Jah-Kwo-Ton. Randy White goes there every day and learns how to fight Jah-Kwo-Ton style which nobody else in America knows except the janitor.

The janitor has vowed not to fight because he accidentally killed a man once. He has also made Randy White swear not to defend the janitor in case anything happens to him. The janitor has learned to accept his fate.

One day the same classmates who pick on Randy White accidentally kill the janitor. Well it is partially on purpose and partially on accident. Randy White attempts to aid the janitor but the janitor tells him to remember his vow. Randy White remembers his vow. Now his classmates assume that Randy White is more cowardly than ever.

Now we go forward into the future. Sex Devil can afford the right kind of medical insurance to where his cleft palate can be surgically fixed. While he is pretending to be Randy White he continues to talk like he has a cleft palate. This is just to conceal his secret identity.

All of the boys of Sex Devil's high school class have grown into manhood to become a criminal organization. They run the city under cover of darkness, plotting fake terrorist plots to keep the city in turmoil while they make their robberies. As a result some innocent Arab Americans get sent to prison.

Sex Devil is the prison psychiatrist for the innocent Arab Americans. They can tell that Sex Devil is their friend. The Arab Americans instruct Sex Devil in the ways of a secret cult to where Sex Devil now has ultimate control over his body. Now Sex Devil is an expert in two different secret cults of ancient lore. He is also a trained psychiatrist with mastery over the human mind. No one can match his prowess based on his unique balance of science, skill and sorcery.

Sex Devil finds out from the Arab Americans that the very same people who framed them are the same people who used to pick on Sex Devil all the time. Sex Devil vows revenge.

One night he goes undercover at the chemical factory of his old enemy, who now goes by the name of Black Friday. In the middle of a fight where Black Friday unfairly uses guns Sex Devil gets chemicals spilled on his genital region. Black Friday uses the opportunity to get away.

Sex Devil retreats to his underground lair, which is located beneath the janitor shack. He examines his genital region and discovers that his genital region now has amazing powers. Combined with the bodily control he has learned from the Arab Americans now Sex Devil realizes he has a unique opportunity.

Sex Devil starts out by dating Black Friday's girlfriend. This is the same girl that used to make fun of Sex Devil but she doesn't know it is the same person because he talks completely different.

First Sex Devil takes Jennifer to a nice restaurant. Jennifer is impressed by Sex Devil's worldly manners. Because of his secret mastery of bodily control he is also the best dancer anyone has ever seen. It is the greatest date ever. Jennifer asks Sex Devil if he wants to come up for some coffee. Sex Devil jokes, who knows where that will lead. Sex Devil leaves politely without taking advantage of Jennifer.

When Sex Devil gets home he has about six or seven phone calls from Jennifer on his answering machine. Please Sex Devil, I need to see you.

Sex Devil goes back over to Jennifer's apartment. On the way he stops and buys some flowers. Then he climbs up a drainpipe and enters Jennifer's bedroom.

Jennifer thanks Sex Devil for the flowers. They are so beautiful Sex Devil. Black Friday never buys me flowers. Sex Devil says enough of this talk. Then Sex Devil and Jennifer have intimacy.

Black Friday wonders what is wrong with Jennifer. She seems to be distracted all the time. He does not know she is secretly thinking of her intimacy with Sex Devil. Jennifer refuses to have intimacy with Black Friday. Intimacy with Black Friday has become hollow. Nothing can compare to the amazing powers of Sex Devil's genital region.

Black Friday becomes depressed. Black Friday loses his ability to have intimacy. He must see a psychiatrist. Get me the best psychiatrist in the city! Little does he realize it is Sex Devil.

Black Friday unburdens the problems of his soul to Sex Devil. On the outside Sex Devil is concerned. On the inside Sex Devil is ha ha ha!

Black Friday can no longer do his criminal activities because he has lost all worth of himself as a human being. Black Friday can no longer perform intimacy because of his crippling depression. Every time Black Friday leaves the house Sex Devil comes over and has intimacy with

Jennifer. Please Sex Devil I love you, can't we get married? No Jennifer, I am married to my work.

At the end of the first issue Black Friday falls off a cliff. Now Sex Devil must go to work on the rest of the class. At the end of every issue one of Sex Devil's fellow classmates falls off a cliff or is caught in the gears of a large machine or blows themself up in an explosion or capsizes or a similar disaster. Or they are in a submarine that slowly fills up with water. It is never Sex Devil's fault but he doesn't feel bad about it because they are getting what they deserve. Every time Jennifer is like please won't you spend the whole night Sex Devil? What is with all this wham bam thank you mam. And Sex Devil is like maybe some other time baby. Because Sex Devil has more important things on his mind. And Jennifer is like I am starting to think you are just using me for intimacy like a hor. And Sex Devil is like now you are getting the picture baby.

In conclusion I hope you will start making the comic book Sex Devil because it deals with issues that young people care about today.

Inside "Sex Devil": Using the Dark

"Sex Devil" is straightforward and clear. I wrote it quickly and naturally. But it is somewhat tricky as well. The reader is required to make up the story.

The novelist Laura Lippman, writing about "Sex Devil" for NPR, put it in terms almost too flattering to cut-and-paste here, though apparently it's not going to stop me: "The subtext of 'Sex Devil' is so palpable that it's like reading a story that's been written in invisible ink, watching the letters slowly form over the heat of a light bulb ... You laugh at what's on the page; you're haunted by what's not."

That's very kindly put. But whether you laugh, cry, get haunted, shrug, roll your eyes, or throw up (it's none of my business!), you have to become a partner in the storytelling to get anything out of it. "Sex Devil" isn't the story. It isn't even *a* story. It's a scrap of evidence.

To tell you how "Sex Devil" came about, I have to go back to the story I wrote just before it.

I was watching the news, and the government had done something that seemed arbitrary. I thought, "Wow, they can do anything they want. They could throw me in jail right now if they wanted to." Somehow I made the leap to Batman. I thought, "If Batman was mad at you, or thought you were a bad guy, there would be no way to argue with him."

I started to write a story about an innocent man who is repeatedly punched out by a superhero and can't figure out why.

It was tough. Once you start writing about a superhero, you're not really writing about our world anymore. You're required to invent the environment in which your superhero exists. I wasn't up to the job.

Then something great happened to me. I read the story "Jon" by George Saunders in *The New Yorker*. The first-person narrator of Saunders's story lives in a weird, futuristic version of Earth. But he's not very bright, so he's not that good at describing it. Also, he's in the dark about a lot of what's going on. Saunders doesn't wink at the reader or intrude with explanations. Because his narrator is blinkered and painfully inarticulate, we find ourselves filling in some of the blanks for him.

Reading "Jon" changed the way I wrote. I had always admired the dramatic monologues of Robert Browning and the character-based songwriting of Randy Newman, particularly the way in which the speakers are always revealing more than they think. In "Jon," I found a new twist I could use. The narrator wasn't "revealing" anything, because he didn't *know* anything.

I changed my superhero story (eventually it was called "Attention, Johnny America! Please Read!") to the first person. Now I didn't have to make up a reason for the beatings.

Saunders obviously had an exact vision of Jon's circumstances and surroundings, and I think we see at the dark periphery precisely what he wants us to see. I am not as good a writer as Saunders, so I used his example as a fruitful excuse to be—as a writer—just as ignorant as my narrator. And my narrator and I pass our ignorance on to you. We're all in the dark. My story became a lot funnier and creepier that way, and more importantly, I was able to finish it. I didn't know it at the time, but I had just begun to write in a new way that would lead to my first publication and my first book.

With that story under my belt, my wife and I went out to see the movie *Daredevil*, based on the Marvel comic book. When Matt Murdock (who grows up to be Daredevil) is a little kid, he is bullied and tormented and blinded by chemicals. But his misfortune empowers him. Suddenly he can outsmart and physically outperform the bullies. He grows up and takes on adult bullies (criminals). I sat there watching the movie, thinking, *This is what every superhero movie and comic book is about: a child's story of murderous revenge.*

I remembered a kid who had been picked on in my high school, and how he compensated by pretending to know karate, and the mean-spirited picture that J__ H_____ had drawn of him on the blackboard. (By the way, in an early draft of my first book, every bully in every story was named J__ H_____, the real name of a guy who had made my life miserable as well. In the final draft I changed the name. *Slightly.*)

Right there, in the theater, assaulted by candy-colored screen violence and pitiful, horribly present memories of youth, I started writing "Sex Devil" in my head. It presented itself to me in such a solid fashion that I was able to type up a draft as soon as I got home. The original version probably took me fifteen minutes of straight typing. I had either the nerve or the laziness to barely change the title of the movie that had inspired me (*cf.* the bully's name, above). Without completely realizing it, I had taken the technique from my previous story to another level. In "Johnny America," we are told that the narrator is an unemployed man who has marital problems and an injured leg. In "Sex Devil," we are told *nothing* about the narrator. Did you assume he had a cleft palate? It's not in the story. You wrote that part.

I believe this explanation of the story is almost as long as "Sex Devil" itself. That's why people write fiction: so they don't have to write stuff like this!

WRITING EXERCISE

What was the last movie you saw? Write a short review of it. Now, imagine someone very different from yourself—a millionaire, a manic-depressive, a cowboy, whomever—watching the same film. How did it affect that person? Write a movie review in the voice of that character. Be true. Compare the two reviews. They should seem to be written by two different people.

BENJAMIN PERCY

Refresh, Refresh

When school let out the two of us went to my backyard to fight. We were trying to make each other tougher. So in the grass, in the shade of the pines and junipers, Gordon and I slung off our backpacks and laid down a pale green garden hose, tip to tip, making a ring. Then we stripped off our shirts and put on our gold-colored boxing gloves, and fought.

Every round went two minutes. If you stepped out of the ring, you lost. If you cried, you lost. If you got knocked out, or if you yelled, "Stop!" you lost. Afterwards we drank Coca-Colas and smoked Marlboros, our chests heaving, our faces all different shades of blacks and reds and yellows.

We began fighting after Seth Johnson—a no-neck linebacker with teeth like corn kernels and hands like T-bone steaks—beat Gordon until his face swelled and split open and purpled around the edges. Eventually he healed, the rough husks of scabs peeling away to reveal a different face than the one I remembered, older, squarer, fiercer, his left eyebrow separated by a gummy white scar. It was his idea, fighting each other. He wanted to be ready. He wanted to hurt back those who hurt him. And if he went down, he would go down swinging, as his father would have wanted. This was what we all wanted, to please our fathers, to make them proud, even though they had left us.

★★★

This was Tumalo, Oregon, a high desert town in the foothills of the Cascade Mountains. In Tumalo, we have fifteen hundred people, a Dairy Queen, a BP gas station, a Food-4-Less, a meat-packing plant, a bright green football field irrigated by canal water, and your standard assortment of taverns and churches. Nothing distinguishes us from Bend or Redmond or La Pine or any of the other nowhere towns off Route 97, except for this: we are home to the Second Battalion, 34th Marines. The fifty-acre base, built in the eighties, is a collection of one-story cinder-block buildings interrupted by cheat grass and sagebrush. Apparently conditions here in Oregon's ranch country match very closely those of the Middle East, particularly the mountainous terrain of Afghanistan and northern Iraq, and throughout my childhood I could hear, if I cupped a hand to my ear, the lowing of bulls, the bleating of sheep, the report of assault rifles shouting from the hilltops.

Our fathers—Gordon's and mine—were like the other fathers in Tumalo. All of them, just about, had enlisted as part-time soldiers, as reservists, for drill pay: several thousand a year for a private and several thousand more for a sergeant. Beer pay, they called it, and for two weeks every year plus one weekend a month, they trained. They threw on their cammies and filled their rucksacks and kissed us goodbye, then the gates of the Second Battalion drew closed behind them.

Our fathers would vanish into the pine-studded hills, returning to us Sunday night with their faces reddened from weather, with their biceps trembling from fatigue and their hands smelling of rifle grease. They would use terms like ECP and PRP and MEU and WMD and they would do push-ups in the middle of the living room and they would call six o'clock *eighteen-hundred hours* and they would high five and yell "Semper Fi!" Then a few days would pass and they would go back to the way they were, to the men we knew: Coors-drinking, baseball-throwing, crotch-scratching, Aqua Velva-smelling fathers.

No longer. In January, the battalion was activated, and in March they shipped off for Iraq. Our fathers—our coaches, our teachers, our barbers, our cooks, our gas-station attendants and UPS deliverymen and deputies and firemen and mechanics—our fathers, so many of them, climbed onto the olive-green school buses and pressed their palms to the windows and gave us the bravest, most hopeful smiles you can imagine, and vanished. Just like that.

★★★

Nights, I sometimes got on my Honda dirt bike and rode through the hills and canyons of Deschutes County. Beneath me the engine growled and shuddered while all around me the wind, like something alive, bullied me, tried to drag me from my bike. A dark world slipped past as I downshifted, leaning into a turn, and accelerated on a straightaway—my speed seventy, then eighty—concentrating only on the twenty yards of road glowing ahead of me. On this bike I could ride and ride and ride, away from here, up and over the Cascades, through the Willamette Valley, until I reached the ocean, where the broad black backs of whales regularly broke the surface of the water, and even further—further still—until I caught up with the horizon, where my father would be waiting. Inevitably, I ended up at Hole in the Ground.

Many years ago a meteor came screeching down from space and left behind a crater five thousand feet wide and three hundred feet deep. Hole in the Ground is frequented during the winter by the daredevil sledders among us, and during the summer by bearded geologists from OSU interested in the metal fragments strewn across its bottom. I dangled my feet over the edge of the crater and leaned back on my elbows and took in the sky—no moon, only stars—just a little lighter black than a crow. Every few minutes a star seemed to come unstuck, streaking through the night in a bright flash that burned into nothingness. In the near distance the grayish green glow of Tumalo dampened the sky—a reminder of how close we came, fifty years ago, to oblivion. A chunk of space ice or a solar wind at just the right moment could have jogged the meteor sideways, and rather than landing here, it could have landed there, at the intersection of Main and Farwell. No Dairy Queen, no Tumalo High, no Second Battalion. It didn't take much imagination to realize how something can drop out of the sky and change everything.

★★★

This was October, when Gordon and I circled each other in the backyard after school. We wore our golden boxing gloves, cracked with age and letting off flakes when we pounded them together. Browned grass crunched beneath our sneakers and dust rose in little puffs like distress signals.

Gordon was thin to the point of being scrawny. His collarbone poked against his skin like a swallowed coat hanger. His head was too big for his body and his eyes were too big for his head and the football players—Seth Johnson among them—regularly tossed him into garbage cans and called him ET. He had had a bad day. And I could tell from the look on his face—the watery eyes, the trembling lips that revealed, in quick flashes, his buckteeth—that he wanted, he *needed*, to hit me. So I let him. I raised my gloves to my face and pulled my elbows against my ribs and Gordon lunged forward, his arms snapping like rubber bands. I stood still, allowing his fists to work up and down my body, allowing him to throw the weight of his anger on me, until eventually he grew too tired to hit anymore and I opened up my stance and floored him with a right cross to the temple. He lay there, sprawled out in the grass with a small smile on his ET face. "Damn," he said in a dreamy voice. A drop of blood gathered along the corner of his eye and streaked down his temple into his hair.

★★★

My father wore steel-toed boots, Carhartt jeans, a T-shirt advertising some place he had traveled, maybe Yellowstone or Seattle. He looked like someone you might see shopping for motor oil at Bi-Mart. To hide his receding hairline he wore a John Deere cap that laid a shadow across his face. His brown eyes blinked above a considerable nose underlined by a gray mustache. Like me, my father was short and squat, a bulldog. His belly was a swollen bag and his shoulders were broad, good for carrying me during parades, and at fairs, when I was younger.

He laughed a lot. He liked game shows. He drank too much beer and smoked too many cigarettes and spent too much time with his buddies, fishing, hunting, bullshitting, which probably had something to do with why my mother divorced him and moved to Boise with a hair-dresser/tri-athlete named Chuck.

At first, when my father left, like all of the other fathers, he would e-mail whenever he could. He would tell me about the heat, the gal-lons of water he drank every day, the sand that got into everything, the baths he took with baby wipes. He would tell me how safe he was, how very safe. This was when he was stationed in Turkey. Then the Second Battalion shipped for Kirkuk, where insurgents and sand-storms attacked almost daily. The e-mails came less and less frequently. Weeks of silence came between them.

Sometimes, on the computer, I would hit refresh, refresh, *refresh*, hoping. In October, I received an e-mail that read, "Hi Josh. I'm OK. Don't worry. Do your homework. Love, Dad." I printed it up and hung it on my door with a piece of Scotch tape.

For twenty years my father worked at Noseler, Inc.—the bullet manufacturer based out of Bend—where the Marines trained him as an ammunition technician. Gordon liked to say his father was a Gun-nery Sergeant, and he was, but we all knew he was also the battalion mess manager, a cook, which was how he made his living in Tumalo, tending the grill at Hamburger Patty's. We knew their titles but we didn't know, not really, what their titles meant, what our fathers *did* over there. We imagined them doing heroic things. Rescuing Iraqi babies from burning huts. Sniping suicide bombers before they could detonate on a crowded city street. We drew on Hollywood and CNN to develop elaborate scenarios, where maybe, at twilight, during a trek through the mountains of northern Iraq, bearded insurgents ambushed our fathers with rocket-launchers. We imagined them silhouetted by a fiery explosion. We imagined them burrowing into the sand like liz-ards and firing their M-16s, their bullets streaking through the darkness like the meteorites I observed on sleepless nights.

When Gordon and I fought we painted our faces—black and green and brown—with the camo-grease our fathers left behind. It made our eyes and teeth appear startlingly white. And it smeared away against our gloves just as the grass smeared away beneath our sneakers—and the ring became a circle of dirt, the dirt a reddish color that looked a lot like scabbed flesh. One time Gordon hammered my shoulder so hard I couldn't lift my arm for a week. Another time I elbowed him in the kidneys and he peed blood. We struck each other with such force and frequency the golden gloves crumbled and our knuckles showed through the sweat-soaked, blood-soaked foam like teeth through a busted lip. So we bought another set of gloves, as the air grew steadily colder and we fought with steam blasting from our mouths.

★★★

Our fathers had left us, but men remained in Tumalo. There were old men, like my grandfather, who I lived with—men who had paid their dues, who had worked their jobs and fought their wars, and now spent their days at the gas station, drinking bad coffee from Styrofoam cups, complaining about the weather, arguing about the best months to reap alfalfa. And there were incapable men. Men who rarely shaved and watched daytime television in their once white underpants. Men who lived in trailers and filled their shopping carts with Busch Light, summer sausage, Oreo cookies.

And then there were vulturous men, like Dave Lightener—men who scavenged whatever our fathers had left behind. Dave Lightener worked as a recruitment officer. I'm guessing he was the only recruitment officer in world history who drove a Vespa scooter with a *Support Our Troops* ribbon magneted to its rear. We sometimes saw it parked outside the homes of young women whose husbands had gone to war. Dave had big ears and small eyes and wore his hair in your standard-issue high-and-tight buzz. He often spoke in a too loud voice about all the insurgents he gunned down when working a Fallujah patrol unit. He lived with his mother in Tumalo, but spent his days in Bend and Redmond, trolling the parking lots of Best Buy, ShopKo, K-Mart,

Wal-Mart, Mountain View Mall. He was looking for people like us, people who were angry and dissatisfied and poor.

But Dave Lightener knew better than to bother us. On duty he stayed away from Tumalo entirely. Recruiting there would be too much like poaching the burned section of forest where deer, rib-slatted and wobbly legged, nosed through the ash, seeking something green.

We didn't fully understand the reason our fathers were fighting. We only understood that they *had* to fight. The necessity of it made the reason irrelevant. "It's all part of the game," my grandfather said. "It's just the way it is." We could only cross our fingers and wish on stars and hit refresh, *refresh*, hoping they would return to us, praying we would never find Dave Lightener on our porch uttering the words, "I regret to inform you ..."

One time, my grandfather dropped Gordon and me off at Mountain View Mall and there, near the glass-doored entrance, stood Dave Lightener. He wore his creased khaki uniform and spoke with a group of Mexican teenagers. They were laughing, shaking their heads and walking away from him as we walked toward. We had our hats pulled low and he didn't recognize us.

"Question for you, gentlemen," he said in the voice of telemarketers and door-to-door Jehovah's Witnesses. "What do you plan on doing with your lives?"

Gordon pulled off his hat with a flourish, as if he were part of some *ta-da!* magic act and his face was the trick. "I plan on killing some crazy-ass Muslims," he said and forced a smile. "How about you, Josh?"

"Yeah," I said. "Kill some people then get myself killed." I grimaced even as I played along. "That sounds like a good plan."

Dave Lightener's lips tightened into a thin line, his posture straightened, and he asked us what we thought our fathers would think, hearing us right now. "They're out there risking their lives, defending our freedom, and you're cracking sick jokes," he said. "I think that's sick."

We hated him for his soft hands and clean uniform. We hated him because he sent people like us off to die. Because at twenty-three he had attained a higher rank than our fathers. Because he slept with the

171

lonely wives of soldiers. And now we hated him even more for making us feel ashamed. I wanted to say something sarcastic but Gordon
was quicker. His hand was out before him, his fingers gripping an
imaginary bottle. "Here's your maple syrup," he said. When Dave said,
"And what is that for?" Gordon said, "To eat my ass with."

Right then a skateboarder-type with green hair and a nose-ring
walked from the mall, a bagful of DVDs swinging from his fist, and
Dave Lightener forgot us. "Hey, friend," he was saying. "Let me ask
you something. Do you like war movies?"

★★★

In November we drove our dirt bikes deep into the woods to hunt.
Sunlight fell through tall pines and birch clusters, and lay in puddles
along the logging roads that wound past the hillsides packed with
huckleberries and the moraines where coyotes scurried, trying to flee
us and slipping, causing tiny avalanches of loose rock. It hadn't rained
in nearly a month, so the crab grass and the cheat grass and the pine
needles had lost their color, dry and blond as cornhusks, crackling beneath my boots when the road we followed petered out into nothing
and I stepped off my bike. In this waterless stillness, you could hear
every chipmunk within a square acre, rustling for pine nuts, and when
the breeze rose into a cold wind the forest became a giant whisper.

We dumped our tent, our sleeping bags, near a basalt grotto with a
spring bubbling from it, and Gordon said, "Let's go, troops," holding
his rifle before his chest diagonally, as a soldier would. He dressed as a
soldier would, too, wearing his father's overlarge cammies rather than
the mandatory blaze-orange gear. Fifty feet apart we worked our way
downhill, through the forest, through a huckleberry thicket, through a
clear-cut crowded with stumps, taking care not to make much noise or
slip on the pine needles carpeting the ground. A chipmunk worrying at
a pinecone screeched its astonishment when a peregrine falcon swooped
down and seized it, carrying it off between the trees to some secret place.
Its wings made no sound, and neither did the blaze-orange hunter when
he appeared in a clearing several hundred yards below us.

172

Gordon made some sort of SWAT team gesture, meant, I think, to say, Stay Low, and I made my way carefully toward him. From behind a boulder, we peered through our scopes, tracking the hunter, who looked—in his vest and ear-flapped hat—like a monstrous pumpkin. "That cocksucker," Gordon said in a harsh whisper. The hunter was Seth Johnson. His rifle was strapped to his back, and his mouth was moving, talking to someone. At the corner of the meadow he joined four members of the varsity football squad, who sat on logs around a smoldering campfire, their arms bobbing like oil pump jacks as they brought their beers to their mouths.

I took my eye from my scope and noticed Gordon fingering the trigger of his thirty-aught. I told him to quit fooling around and he pulled his hand suddenly away from the stock and smiled guiltily and said he just wanted to know what it felt like, having that power over someone. Then his trigger finger rose up and touched the gummy white scar that split his eyebrow. "I say we fuck with them a little."

I shook my head, *no.*

Gordon said, "Just a little—to scare them."

"They've got guns," I said, and he said, "So we'll come back tonight."

Later, after an early dinner of beef jerky and trail mix and Gatorade, I happened upon a four-point stag nibbling on some bear grass, and I rested my rifle on a stump and shot it, and it stumbled backwards and collapsed with a rose blooming from behind its shoulder where the heart was hidden. Gordon came running and we stood around the deer and smoked a few cigarettes, watching the thick arterial blood run from its mouth. Then we took out our knives and got to work. I cut around the anus, cutting away the penis and testes, and then ran the knife along the belly, unzipping the hide to reveal the delicate pink flesh and greenish vessels into which our hands disappeared. The blood steamed in the cold mountain air, and when we finished—when we'd skinned the deer and hacked at its joints and cut out its back strap and boned out its shoulders and hips, its neck and ribs, making chops, roasts, steaks, quartering the meat so we could bundle it into our insulated saddlebags—Gordon picked up the deer head by the antlers and held it before his own. Blood from its neck made a pattering sound on the ground, and in the half-light of early evening Gordon began to do a little dance, bending his knees and stomping his feet.

"I think I've got an idea," he said and pretended to rake at me with the antlers. I pushed him away, and he said, "Don't pussy out on me, Josh." I was exhausted and reeked of gore, but I could appreciate the need for revenge. "Just to scare them, right, Gordo?" I said.

"Right."

We lugged our meat back to camp, and Gordon brought the deer hide. He slit a hole in its middle, and poked his head through so the hide hung off him loosely, a hairy sack, and I helped him smear mud and blood across his face. Then, with his Leatherman, he sawed off the antlers and held them in each hand and slashed at the air as if they were claws.

Night had come on and the moon hung over the Cascades, grayly lighting our way as we crept through the forest, imagining ourselves in enemy territory, with trip-wires and guard towers and snarling dogs around every corner. From behind the boulder that overlooked their campsite, we observed our enemies as they swapped hunting stories and joked about Jessica Robertson's big ass titties and passed around a bottle of whiskey and drank to excess and finally pissed on the fire to extinguish it. When they retired to their tents we waited an hour before making our way down the hill with such care that it took us another hour before we were upon them. Somewhere an owl hooted, its noise barely noticeable over the chorus of snores that rose from their tents. Seth's Bronco was parked nearby—the license plate read SMAN—and all their rifles lay in its cab. I collected them, slinging them over my shoulder, then I eased my knife into each of Seth's tires, and then we were standing outside his tent.

I still had my knife out when we stood outside Seth's tent, and when a cloud scudded over the moon and made the meadow fully dark, I stabbed the nylon and in one quick jerk opened up a slit. Gordon rushed in, his antler-claws slashing. I could see nothing but shadows but I could hear Seth scream the scream of a little girl as Gordon raked at him with the antlers and hissed and howled like some cave-creature hungry for man-flesh. When the tents around us came alive with confused voices, Gordon reemerged with a horrible smile on his face and I followed him up the hillside, crashing through the undergrowth, leaving Seth to make sense of the nightmare that had descended upon him without warning.

★★★

Winter came. Snow fell, and we threw on our coveralls and wrenched on our studded tires and drove our dirt bikes to Hole in the Ground, dragging our sleds behind us with towropes. Our engines filled the white silence of the afternoon. Our back tires kicked up plumes of powder, and on sharp turns slipped out beneath us and we lay there, in the middle of the road, bleeding, laughing, unafraid.

Earlier, for lunch, we had cooked a pound of bacon with a stick of butter. The grease, which hardened into a white waxy pool, we used as polish, buffing it into the bottoms of our sleds. Speed was what we wanted at Hole in the Ground. One by one we descended the steepest section of the crater into its heart, three hundred feet below us. We followed each other in the same track, ironing down the snow to create a chute, blue-hued and frictionless. Our eyeballs glazed with frost, our ears roared with wind, our stomachs rose into our throats, as we rocketed down and felt five—and then we began the slow climb back the way we came and felt fifty.

We wore crampons and ascended in a zigzagging series of switchbacks. It took nearly an hour. The air began to go purple with evening, when we stood again at the lip of the crater, sweating in our coveralls, taking in the view through the fog of our breath. Gordon packed a snowball. I said, "You better not hit me with that." He cocked his arm threateningly and smiled, then dropped to his knees to roll the snowball into something bigger. He rolled it until it grew to the size of a large man curled into the fetal position. From the back of his bike he took the piece of garden hose he used to siphon gas from fancy foreign cars, and he worked it into his tank, sucking at its end until gas flowed.

He doused the giant snowball as if he hoped it would sprout. It did not melt—he'd packed it tight enough—but it puckered slightly and appeared leaden, and when Gordon withdrew his Zippo, sparked it, and held it toward the ball, the fumes caught flame and the whole thing erupted with a gasping noise that sent me staggering back a few steps.

Gordon rushed forward and kicked the ball of fire, sending it rolling, tumbling down the crater, down our chute like a meteor, and the snow beneath it instantly melted only to freeze again a moment later, making a slick blue ribbon. When we sledded it, we went so fast our minds emptied and we felt a sensation at once like flying and falling.

★★★

On the news Iraqi insurgents fired their assault rifles. On the news a car bomb in Baghdad detonated seven American soldiers at a traffic checkpoint. On the news the President said he did not think it was wise to provide a time frame for troop withdrawal. I checked my e-mail before breakfast and found nothing but spam, promises of great mortgage rates, cheap painkillers, increased erectile performance.

Gordon and I fought in the snow, wearing snow-boots. We fought so much our wounds never got a chance to heal and our faces took on a permanent look of decay. Our wrists felt swollen, our knees ached, all our joints felt full of tiny dry wasps. We fought until fighting hurt too much, and we took up drinking instead. Weekends, we drove our dirt bikes to Bend, twenty miles away, and bought beer and took it to Hole in the Ground and drank there until a bright line of sunlight appeared on the horizon and illuminated the snow-blanketed desert. Nobody asked for our IDs and when we held up our empty bottles and stared at our reflections in the glass, warped and ghostly, we knew why. And we weren't alone. Black bags grew beneath the eyes of the sons and daughters and wives of Tumalo, their shoulders stooped, wrinkles enclosing their mouths like parentheses.

Our fathers haunted us. They were everywhere. In the grocery store when we spotted a thirty-pack of Coors on sale for ten bucks. On the highway when we passed a jacked-up Dodge with a dozen hay bales stacked in its bed. In the sky when a jet roared by, reminding us of faraway places. And now, as our bodies thickened with muscle, as we stopped shaving and grew patchy beards, we saw our fathers even in the mirror. We began to look like them. Our fathers, who had been taken from us, were everywhere, at every turn, imprisoning us.

Seth Johnson's father was a staff sergeant. Like his son, he was a big man but not big enough. Just before Christmas he stepped on a cluster bomb. A U.S. warplane dropped it and the sand camouflaged it and he stepped on it and it tore him into many meaty pieces. When Dave Lightener climbed up the front porch with a black armband and a somber expression, Mrs. Johnson, who was cooking a honeyed ham at the time, collapsed on the kitchen floor. Seth pushed his way out the door and punched Dave in the face, breaking his nose before he could utter the words, "I regret to inform you ..."

Hearing about this, we felt bad for all of ten seconds. Then we felt good because it was his father and not ours. And then we felt bad again and on Christmas Eve we drove to Seth's house and laid down on his porch the rifles we had stolen, along with a six-pack of Coors, and then, just as we were about to leave, Gordon dug in his back pocket and removed his wallet and placed under the six-pack all the money he had, a few fives, some ones. "Fucking Christmas," he said.

★★★

We got braver and went to the bars—The Golden Nugget, The Weary Traveler, The Pine Tavern—where we square-danced with older women wearing purple eye shadow and sparkly dream-catcher earrings and push-up bras and clattery high heels. We told them we were Marines back from a six-month deployment and they said, "Really?" and we said, "Yes, ma'am," and when they asked for our names we gave them the names of our fathers. Then we bought them drinks and they drank them in a gulping way and breathed hotly in our faces and we brought our mouths against theirs and they tasted like menthol cigarettes, like burnt urinal pucks. And then we went home with them, to their trailers, to their waterbeds, where among their stuffed animals we fucked them.

★★★

Mid-afternoon and it was already full dark. On our way to The Weary Traveler, we stopped by my house to bum some money off my grandfather, only to find Dave Lightener waiting for us. He was halfway up the porch steps when our headlights cast an anemic glow over him and he turned to face us with a scrunched-up expression, as if trying to figure out who we were. He wore the black band around his arm and, over his nose, a white-bandaged splint.

We did not turn off our engines. Instead we sat in the driveway, idling, the exhaust from our bikes and the breath from our mouths clouding the air. Above us a star hissed across the moonlit sky, vaguely bright, like a light turned on in a daylit room. Then Dave began down the steps and we leapt off our bikes to meet him. Before he could speak I brought my fist to his diaphragm, knocking the breath from his body. Right then he looked like a gunshot actor in a Western, clutching his belly with both hands, doubled over, his face making a nice target for Gordon's knee. A snap sound preceded Dave falling on his back with blood sliding from his already broken nose.

He put up his hands and we hit our way through them. I sucker-punched him once, twice, in the ribs while Gordon kicked him in the spine and stomach and then we stood around gulping air and allowed him to struggle to his feet. When he righted himself, he wiped his face with his hand and blood dripped from his fingers. I moved in and roundhoused with my right and then my left, my fists knocking his head loose on its hinges. Again he collapsed, a bloody bag of a man. His eyes walled and turned up, trying to see the animal bodies looming over him. He opened his mouth to speak and I pointed a finger at him and said, with enough hatred in my voice to break a back, "Dave, I'm only going to tell you this once: *Don't* say a word. Don't you dare. Not one word."

He closed his mouth and tried to crawl away and I brought a boot down on the back of his head and left it there a moment, grinding his face into the ground so that when he lifted his head the snow held a red impression of his face. Gordon went inside and returned a moment later with a roll of duct tape and we held Dave down and bound his wrists and ankles and threw him on a sled and taped him to it many times over and then tied the sled to the back of Gordon's bike and drove at a perilous speed to Hole in the Ground.

The moon shined down and the snow glowed with pale blue light as we smoked cigarettes, looking down into the crater, with Dave at our feet. There was something childish about the way our breath puffed from our mouths in tiny clouds. It was as if we were imitating choo-choo trains. And for a moment, just a moment, we were kids again. Just a couple of stupid kids. Gordon must have felt this too, because he said, "My mom wouldn't even let me play with toy guns when I was little." And he sighed heavily as if he couldn't understand how he, how we, had ended up here.

Then, with a sudden lurch, Dave began struggling and yelling at us in a slurred voice and my face hardened with anger and I put my hands on him and pushed him slowly to the lip of the crater and he grew silent. For a moment I forgot myself, staring off into the dark oblivion. It was beautiful and horrifying. "I could shove you right now," I said. "And if I did, you'd be dead."

"Please don't," he said, his voice cracking. He began to cry. "Oh fuck. Don't. Please." Hearing his great shuddering sobs didn't bring me the satisfaction I hoped for. If anything, I felt as I did that day, so long ago, when we taunted him in the Mountain View Mall parking lot: shameful, false.

"Ready?" I said. "One!" I inched him a little closer to the edge. "Two!" I moved him a little closer still and as I did I felt unwieldy, at once wild and exhausted, my body seeming to take on another twenty, thirty, forty years. When I finally said, "*Three*," my voice was barely a whisper.

We left Dave there, sobbing at the brink of the crater. We got on our bikes and we drove to Bend and we drove so fast I imagined catching fire, like a meteor, burning up in a flash, howling as my heat consumed me, as we made our way to the Armed Forces Recruiting Station where we would at last answer the fierce alarm of war and put our pens to paper and make our fathers proud.

Inside "Refresh, Refresh": Showing Creative Restraint

Every three weeks or so, when I'm working on a novel, I need a break. "Refresh, Refresh" came out of one of those breaks. During this time, I was reading article after article, but never any short stories, about the war in Iraq. So I decided to write one. Like all of my work, it boiled out of me quickly, in a week of eight-hour days hunched over the keyboard. There are many facts underlying the fiction, over which I sprinkled a healthy serving of imagination. The setting is the setting of my youth. Hole in the Ground actually exists. My friends and I actually used to beat the shit out of each other and tear around on dirt bikes and light things on fire. As for the military base—the reservists who all at once shipped off and left behind their families—this comes from an article I read about a small town in Ohio. I cannot recall the particulars, but in one night, something like fifteen fathers and husbands and sons died in an ambush. Their loss, the bleeding cavity that appeared overnight and undoubtedly still hasn't scarred over, informs this story.

This was 2005. We're two years into the war—and I'm writing a war story. Many of my friends and family members have served, but I haven't, so I knew I couldn't write about what was happening *over there*. It's not something I completely understand. You can write about outer space if you're not an astronaut—about wizards if you've never cast a spell—about detectives if you've never worn a fedora—but when it comes to the military, no firsthand experience, no credibility. So with the Ohio tragedy at the fore of my mind, I decided to write about the battleground at home. But here's where things got tricky. I've always distrusted fiction that overtly makes a political point—about abortion, capital punishment, whatever. I didn't want to come across as an after-school special, as an editorial. So I tried to straddle a line, to show both sides, to occupy a kind of gray territory where character comes first. The boys are conflicted. They feel immense pride for their fathers even as they hate the war for pulling them away. I must have done an okay job of this because I've had such varied responses to the story. In addition to the fan mail, I've received correspondence from countless name-callers. I'm a liberal pantywaist in one—I'm a right-wing nutjob in another. One guy went so far as to say my writing was propagandist shit and he wanted to see me hang alongside Bush and he would laugh as both our faces turned blue. I've had mothers who lost their sons come up to me after readings for a hug. I've had ROTC units shake my hand. I've had hippies offer me weed and ask me to join them in a protest. So with such varied responses, I guess I was doing something right.

The original draft spanned nearly forty pages. The first published version clocks in at nineteen. I wrote the original draft as a work of magical realism. Over the course of the story the boys literally grew older—their hair graying, their bellies swelling and sagging, their joints popping and grinding with arthritis—so that in the end, they *became* their fathers. It kind of worked and kind of didn't. My agent, Katherine Fausset, is always the first line of defense—and she encouraged me to pull the fantastic quality, as it forced a metaphor and added too much octane to an already potent story. She also called me on an intensely stupid move I made. In the final scene, I had Josh shove Dave into the crater. I know, I know. It was a horrible mistake. Completely wrong. Katherine always says I'm an easy edit: I inevitably go too far, and she reigns me back in. This is the perfect example of such—and whenever I revise, that scene always rises up in my mind. If I hadn't shown restraint in revision, I would have missed one of the more important symbols in the story. That final gesture, of Josh at once pushing and pulling back, captures so perfectly his stance toward the war, the military. The art of restraint. We all need a Katherine in our lives to remind us of it now and then.

Faulkner said, "Kill your darlings." How I love this advice. But I never practiced it—never gave myself permission to kill, to truly murder scenes from a story—until "Refresh, Refresh." For this, I have Philip Gourevitch and Nathaniel Rich at *The Paris Review* to thank. They mercilessly took a scalpel to the excess flesh (twenty pages worth) and helped me make the narrative so much sleeker, so much more powerful. "This is something like three stories," Philip said. "We only want to publish one of them." Yes, I said. Sure. I kept my voice calm even as I bit a hole in the inside of my cheek. This is when I began my graveyard. I recommend it to every writer. I created a folder titled *graveyard* and within it stored a separate file for each of the lost scenes and images. You know how it is to cut something from a story: phantom limb pain sets in. Having a graveyard makes it easier to let go, to move on. Because you know the character with the harelip or the metaphor about the butter knife or the image of the cat yakking all over the carpet is waiting patiently for you in a velvet-lined casket—and it is only a matter of time before you resurrect them. In the original draft of "Refresh, Refresh," the grandfather played a central role—a disabled vet who kept his excised foot in a bucket of formaldehyde. Aside from a line of dialogue, he is almost absent from the final version of the story. I stuck him in the graveyard, did a voodoo dance, and then cannibalized his remains, which became "The Killing," later published in *Salt Hill* and collected in *Refresh, Refresh*.

WRITING EXERCISE

I have a bulletin board near my desk. On it I tack articles, photographs, ideas. There is always a challenge or two waiting for me up there. When writing "Refresh, Refresh," the scrap of paper I pulled down read, "First-person plural." I had recently picked up Stephen Millhauser's "The Knife Thrower"—and though I liked the idea of a collective consciousness, the story felt a bit gimmicky, perhaps because the "we" spanned the entire narrative.

I always tell my students that when you read, you should experience fits of jealousy and contempt. This was one of those moments. I liked Millhauser's trick, but I thought I could pull it off better. So I wrote "Refresh, Refresh" as a first-person singular narrative that occasionally lapsed into first-person plural—a "we" that sometimes captures the voice of Josh and Gordon, other times the voice of the entire community. Do this. Write a first-person singular story that now and then swells into first-person plural. Think carefully about when and why you do this. Make it more than a gimmick. Make it a meaningful rhetorical decision.

And a bonus exercise: Write about a hot-button subject, but don't let your politics interfere with the story. Put your characters first.

ANDREW PORTER

Departure

That spring we were sixteen Tanner and I started dating the Amish girls out on the rural highway—sometimes two or three at the same time, because it wasn't really dating. There was no way of getting serious.

This was in 1992, over ten years ago, and things had not yet begun to change in our part of Pennsylvania. I think of that year as a significant one now, a turning point in our county, the first year the town of Leola started growing and becoming a city and also the first year the Amish started leaving, selling their property and heading west toward Indiana and Iowa.

There had been several cases of runaways among the Amish that year—mostly young men, barely in their twenties, tempted by the shopping malls and bars popping up along the highways near their farms. Leola was expanding quickly then, it was becoming more common, and it worried the elders in the Amish community. And I think it explains why that spring some of the Amish teenagers were given permission to leave their farms for a few hours on Friday nights.

Out on the other side of town there was an intersection on the rural highway where they would go to hang out. It was a remote area. A strip mall with a K-Mart sat on one side of the intersection and across the road there was a twenty-four-hour diner. You would sometimes see them on Friday evenings traveling in a long line like a funeral procession, their buggies hugging the shoulder of the road as tractor-trailers rubbered by. They would park out of sight behind the K-Mart, tie their horses to lampposts or the sides of dumpsters, and then the younger ones would go into the K-Mart to play video games and the older and more adventurous would cross the street to the diner.

The diner was a family-style place, frequented only by local farming families and truckers, and it was usually empty. Inside, the Amish kids would immediately disappear into the bathrooms and change into blue jeans and T-shirts that they had bought at K-Mart, clothes which never seemed to fit their bodies right. Then they would come out, their black wool clothes stuffed into paper bags, and order large platters of fried food and play country songs on the jukeboxes, and try to pretend they weren't Amish.

That spring Tanner and I had begun stopping by just to see them. We never bothered them, just watched. And it never occurred to us that there might be something unnatural about what we were doing, or even wrong. We were simply curious. We wanted to know if the rumors we had heard in school were true: that there were spectacular deformities to be found among the Amish, that few of the children possessed the correct number of fingers, the results of extensive inbreeding.

We would sit in a booth at the far end of the diner and glance at them from behind our menus. We were amazed to hear them curse and see them smoke cigarettes. Some of them even held hands and kissed. Sometimes other people, people from town like us, would stop by, just to watch—and you could tell that it worried them. People were still scared of the Amish then, they were still a mystery and a threat because of their wealth and the tremendous amount of land they owned—and so naturally they were disliked, treated as outsiders and freaks.

At eleven o'clock, they'd change back into their clothes and very politely pay their checks. Then they'd cross the street in a big group, climb back into their buggies and leave. And Tanner and I would stand out in the diner parking lot and watch them, still not believing what we had seen, but also somehow sad to see them go.

★★★

Once the other kids at school found out about the diner, they started coming regularly in their jeeps and BMWs—not to watch like Tanner and I—but to mock and torment. It was cruel and it saddened us to see, though we never once tried to stop it. Instead we sat back in the corner and watched, angry, but also privately relieved that for once it was not us who were being teased or beat up. In the midst of targets so uncool and vulnerable as Amish teenagers, the popular kids seemed to have practically forgotten us.

There was one Amish kid who looked older than the rest. He could have been in his twenties. Tanner and I had noticed him the very first night because of his size and because of his face, which always looked angry. He came every week with the rest of them, but always sat off by himself in a separate booth, smoking cigarettes and punching heavy-metal songs into the juke box at his table.

His anger scared us more than the others. That and his size. He had the body of a full-grown man, a laborer—his shoulders broad, forearms solid and bulging out near his elbows.

When the fights started he was always involved. They usually happened out by the dumpsters in back of the diner. The odds were never even: always five or six against one. Having been raised strict pacifists, almost none of the Amish would fight. But he would. And despite his size he would, of course, always lose—though he'd last longer than anyone would believe, moving with the grace of a young boxer, gliding, ducking. His style was to stay low and bring his punches up from way down under. He was quick, had a powerful jab, and knew how to protect himself. But the beauty of his moves never lasted long. Inevitably he'd lose his focus, turn his back or look away for a second, and there would be a pile-on.

A few minutes later, his face cut up and swollen, he'd retreat across the street to K-Mart, followed by the rest of the Amish teenagers. And the next week, to everyone's surprise, he'd be back again—not even bitter about it, just sitting there at the edge of the booth, waiting.

★★★

It wasn't until late April that Tanner and I started dating the girls, but like I said, it wasn't really dating. They were all extremely shy and there wasn't a whole lot of common ground. Mostly we would ask them questions about their lives, and they would nod or shake their heads and giggle, and then we would sit and watch as they nervously stuffed their faces with cheeseburgers.

Later, we would walk them back across the street to K-Mart, and then sometimes, if no one else was around, they would kiss us in the shadows. And then—almost like it never happened—they'd be gone again and we'd have to wait a whole week. Sometimes they'd never come back, and we wouldn't know why. We couldn't exactly call them up. Usually we didn't even know their names. So if they didn't show the next week, we'd try to meet two new ones.

Back at our school, pretty girls wouldn't look at us. We were unexceptional—failures at sports and our fathers didn't manage banks or practice orthopedic medicine. But out on the rural highway we dated the most beautiful of the Amish girls. They were attracted to our foreignness; and we, to theirs.

At school, there were jokes about us naturally. Mainly inbreeding jokes. Someone had heard that our girlfriends had two heads, three nostrils, tails coming out of their backbones. It was almost summer and so we tried to ignore it, ride it out, though it made us think about what we were doing.

And it was not right, what we were doing. We were aware of that. And in a way we were still scared of the Amish. Even the girls. There was something unnatural about them. It's hard to explain: they would only let you so close—and it was always in private where no one could see. Sometimes they would kiss you and then run away, or else you would be thinking about making a move, not even doing anything, and they would start to cry for no reason, like they knew.

I wonder now if it was not worse to let them leave the farms only once a week—if giving them only a small taste of freedom did not make

187

the temptation stronger. Perhaps that's why so many never came back: it was simply too hard.

★★★

Tanner came from country people, though he had grown up in town like me. It didn't seem to make a difference. The wealthy kids still called him a hick and made fun of the way he talked and dressed. And you did not want to have the stigma of being from the country in our high school. Tanner and I both lived on the edge of the wealthy area, just across the street from it really. We were in the seventh grade when the school zone switched and the school district agreed to let us finish out our education at Ceder Crest High where all the beautiful and wealthy kids went, the only decent school in the county.

I had grown up with them, the wealthy kids, and even sometimes felt aligned with them when I'd see some of the dirty and disreputable country kids raising hell at our dances. But among them, sitting in class or walking in the hall, I was aware of our differences. Up until the ninth grade I had lied about my father's occupation, told people that he did a lot of work overseas, that his job was sort of secretive and I was not at liberty to discuss it. College wrestling coach didn't sound that great next to heart surgeon or judge. But I don't think anyone believed me anyway. They knew where I lived and knew that I was not a member of the country club, and that I was friends with Tanner. We were not one of them, Tanner and I, though we were not as low as country people either.

★★★

There was one girl I saw consistently that summer. Her name was Rachel. She wasn't shy or afraid of the outside world. And her hair smelled like tall field grass, a sweet smell. She was beautiful, too. She did not look like the other Amish girls; she lacked the full-bodied German figure, the solid thighs, the broad shoulders, the round doughy face. She was thin, small-framed and with different clothes could have easily passed for one of the popular girls at Cedar Crest.

She was curious, too. Some nights she would want to leave the diner and ride around in Tanner's truck. She would beg Tanner and me to

188

take her into town. Or else she would want to drive out to the Leisure Lanes bowling alley to shoot pool and smoke cigarettes. She was always excited, anxious, wanting to do and see as much as possible in the few hours she had.

When we were alone, Rachel wanted to know everything about me. She wanted to know what my school was like, what my house was like, what it was like to go to Ocean City. She wanted it all described to her in detail, almost like she was saving it up, collecting it.

Only once when we were parked outside the diner did she tell me about her family. It was an enormous family, she said. More than twenty of them lived in one house. Her father was seventy years old, the patriarch of the entire household, and he had set up rules and standards based on the very first order of Amish, now three hundred years old. These were standards that she was expected to uphold and pass down to her children. She had an obligation, she said, being one of the chosen very, very few. But she seemed upset as she told me these things. I could tell it made her feel guilty to think about her family, especially when we were together. And after that one night we never talked about them again.

★★★

All summer the heat was getting worse. It had not rained for a record six weeks. Out in the deep country the crops were drying up and in town the grass on people's lawns, even in the wealthy areas, was turning into a yellow thatch. There was no escaping it. Even at night the air was thick with humidity and stuck to your skin like wet towels.

One thing Rachel liked to do was go down to the river valley where there was an old railroad track that had been out of service for more than fifty years. In all that time no one had ever thought to take down the tracks. They were rusted now, covered with weeds, and you could follow them for a mile or so to where they crossed over the river on an old wooden bridge, more than thirty feet high.

Rachel liked to have barefooted races across the planks of the bridge. The planks were evenly spaced, about two feet apart from each other. With a full moon it was easy, you could see where you were stepping, but other nights it would be pitch black and you would have to do it blind. It came down to faith. That and timing. If you slipped once, if your timing was just slightly off, your foot would slide into an empty space and you might snap a shin bone, or worse, if you were unfortunate and slipped through, you might fall thirty feet into the water. And of course we were young and confident and so we never once slipped, or fell, or even stumbled. The trick was always to get a rhythm in your head and to concentrate on it. But like I said, it mainly came down to faith, an almost blind trust that the wooden plank would be right there when you put your foot down. And it always was.

Tanner would sometimes come along with a girl he had met that night and we would all take a blanket and some iced tea down by the river and sit out underneath the stars. Some nights it was so hot Tanner and I would take all our clothes off and jump in the water, and the girls would watch us and giggle, never once thinking to join us; and we, of course, never asked. We knew the limits. We knew how far to push things and the truth was we never wanted to push, being inexperienced in those matters ourselves, and also not wanting to ruin what we had. We were young and somehow sex seemed intricately entwined with those other things—responsibility and growing up— and we were not interested in anything like that.

By then we had stopped hanging out at the diner altogether. It was no longer exciting to watch the fights and Rachel said it depressed her. More and more people had started coming out to watch and he was becoming somewhat of a local celebrity. Rachel told me one night that she knew him. She said his name was Isaac King and that she'd gone to school with him up until the third grade when his parents pulled him out to work. She said that that past winter he had watched his brother die in an ice-skating accident and that everyone thought he had gone a little crazy from it. He had stopped going to church, she said, and it was only a matter of time before he left the community altogether.

★★★

Some Fridays we'd just drive, the three of us, with Rachel sitting between Tanner and me. Tanner liked to take his father's truck onto the back country roads that were all dirt and race it with the headlights off. It was terrifying and more fun than almost anything I've ever done—coming around those narrow curves at a high speed, not knowing what to expect, sometimes not knowing even if we were on the road or not, and then flying a little, catching some air when there was a bump or a small hill. Rachel loved it the most, I think. She'd close her eyes and laugh and sometimes even scream—she was not afraid to show her fear like Tanner and me—and finally, when she was on the verge of tears, she would beg Tanner to stop.

"No more!" she would scream." Pull over!" And he would.

By July everything was changing quickly. Many of the Amish were already leaving, selling their farms to the contractors who had harassed them for years. Rachel never talked about it much, though I know that it was on her mind. People she had known her whole life were being driven off their land. Corporations even wealthier than the Amish themselves had moved in, offered sums of money that seemed impossible to refuse, and then, when that didn't work, had threatened them.

Rachel was beginning to change too. I knew she had strong feelings about leaving the Amish community by then, vanishing like the others had, though she never came out and said it to me, only hinted at it. For the first time, she had begun to complain about the tediousness of her life. Once she had even tried to leave, she said. She had packed up a bag with clothes and food but had stopped when she got to the highway near her farm, realizing she had no money and did not even know which direction led to town. With each Friday our time together seemed to go by quicker, and each time it got harder for her to go back home.

I think now that she wanted me to do something. It was not unusual for Amish women to marry at fifteen or sixteen, and I know that she was under a lot of pressure that summer to get married. Sometimes I tried to imagine what my parents would say if I brought her home with me, explained to them that she would be moving in. I imagined her coming to

191

college with me and taking classes. I would get carried away sometimes, ignoring the absurdity of it, wanting to believe it could work.

***

It was a good summer for Tanner and me, our best, I think. Though we did very little until Friday nights. Days we stayed inside because of the heat and watched horror movies and drank iced tea by the gallon and nights we drove around by ourselves in Tanner's truck planning what we'd do the next Friday. We were wasting time, wasting our lives our parents said, and it felt good. That next year would be our last in high school and I think we were aware, even then, that we were nearing a pinnacle of sorts: the last summer we would still be young enough to collect allowance and get away without working jobs.

Our parents were never home that summer. There were cocktail parties and barbecues five or six times a week on our street and it seemed that almost every night the parents in the neighborhood got trashed, never stumbling home before one or two in the morning. Sometimes Tanner and I would show up at a party just to steal beer. We would stick ten or twelve cans into a duffle bag and then go back to my house and drink them on the back porch, and sometimes end up falling asleep in the backyard by accident.

In late July we started driving the truck out into the deep country during the days. The roads were all dirt out there and illegal to drive on. Occasionally we'd go out on a Saturday afternoon, hoping maybe to see Rachel or one of the girls Tanner had met the night before.

It was different out there. Aside from the humidity and the bugs, it was somehow depressing to watch all the young Amish kids working in the fields in such heat, fully dressed in their black wool suits, struggling with their ancient and inefficient tools, horse-drawn plows, steel-wheeled wagons. It seemed cruel.

One Friday night I borrowed Tanner's truck and took Rachel to the other side of town to see my house. We parked outside, just looking at it, not even talking. That night my parents were having a party and inside we could hear people laughing and the record player going. I could imagine my father slumped in his big leather recliner, surrounded by a circle of drunk guests, telling stories, and my mother carrying around trays of pierced olives and glasses of cold gin. Later on I knew my father would step outside and begin wrestling people, and everyone would yell "Go coach! Pin 'em!" My father had been a wrestling star in college and whenever he drank, he'd start challenging his guests.

The thought of my father rolling around on the lawn with another grown man depressed me and I suddenly wanted to go back to the diner. But Rachel seemed happy listening to the music and laughter from inside.

After a few minutes she said, "Let's go inside."

I looked at her then and suddenly thought of what my father would do if I brought my Amish girlfriend into his house while he was throwing a party. My father, like most, did not like the Amish.

"Let's go," she said. "I want to try a beer."

I told her that it would be easier if I went inside and snuck the beer out to the truck myself.

A few minutes later I emerged with a couple of six packs and we drove down to the river and drank all twelve beers. Afterwards we lay down in a patch of grass near the water and acted silly. We felt loose and we were affectionate with each other. It was Rachel's first time being drunk and she was being funny about it, kissing me in strange places: my elbow, my eyelid, my pinky.

Then at one point—I can't remember exactly—I started to understand that she was trying to tell me something: that it was okay. We could. That is, she would, if I wanted to. She was gripping my body tightly then, and it surprised me. And it scared me, too—because it did not feel tender anymore, but angry almost—and I know now that whatever she was trying to do, whatever she wanted that night, did not have anything to do with me.

And even though we never did, she still cried for a long time that night, and I held her. And later, when I drove her back to the diner and we said goodnight, I was scared that I would never see her again.

★★★

In late August Tanner and I drove out into the deep country for the last time. Rachel had not showed up at the diner for two weeks and I had hopes of seeing her. I needed to talk to her. And Tanner, my best friend, drove me around all day.

We never did see her. Though we did see Isaac King as we were driving out toward the highway. It surprised us to see him and we stopped for a while and watched him working in the field. He was the equivalent of a foreman, in charge of the younger boys, probably his brothers and cousins. It was strange to watch him at work. He was a different person out in the fields, not quiet like he was at the diner, but loud, animated. He moved around the fields swiftly, like an animal, and the young boys listened to him and even seemed a little scared of him.

We parked up on a hill, out of sight. We were still scared of him ourselves, even from a distance. I can tell you now that I did not really hate him. But those nights I had watched him take on four or five kids at once, I believed that I hated him. I hated him for never acknowledging the futility of the situation, for not bowing his head like the others and going home. For not accepting his place like the rest of us—like my parents did, like Tanner did, and like I did.

He must have spotted us before, because he came up slowly from behind the truck and surprised us. He might have thought we were two of the kids from the diner who beat him up every week, looking for some more action. But if he did, he didn't say anything. It was illegal for us to be on that land, even illegal to be driving a car on those back roads, but he never asked us to leave. He just stared at us until he realized we were not there to fight him and then he turned around and went back to the field.

★★★

Rachel finally showed up at the diner the last Friday in August. She was shy with me and distant. She told me that a lot of families in the community, including hers, were moving to Indiana at the end of November, after the harvest. The town was growing quickly, she said. It was just a matter of time before they would be forced to leave. She looked at me very solemnly as she said this.

"So what does that mean?" I said. "You're leaving for good?"

She nodded. "I think so."

I took her hand. "That's terrible," I said.

"I know," she said. "I know."

I've sometimes wondered what would have happened had I asked her that night to leave her community—to marry me and come live with me and my family. I thought of asking her even then, that night, but it would have been a cruel thing to suggest. My parents would have never agreed. It was an absurd thought, when you got right down to it. I was a pretty good student, after all, college bound.

Rachel had been begging me to take her to a movie all summer. She had never seen one before. So instead of spending our last night talking as we usually did, I took her to a rerun of an old Boris Karloff film playing at a place called the Skinny-Mini.

After the movie we drove around for a long time, just talking, though neither of us ever brought up that last night we had been together. I am certain now that she had been thinking about something else as we had watched the movie, and then later as we drove around. And somehow I could tell, even before she said the words, that she wasn't going to miss it.

We drove through town without talking. Rachel seemed disinterested, not even looking out the window. And the town seemed sad now, in the way every town looks sad right at the end of summer. It seemed cold already and empty, as if all the possibility Rachel had seen in it that summer had disappeared and now it contained only the same dismal potential it had every year.

It's strange, but I was not angry at her for leaving like this. I could tell she was not happy about it. And as we drove back to the diner I suddenly wanted to tell her how much I had enjoyed the time we had spent together, how much it had meant to me. I wanted to assure her that I would not forget her. But I never did.

When we got back to the diner, there was a crowd in the back lot, as usual. We walked over and saw Tanner watching. He was alone.

"Ten minutes," he said. "Fucking unbelievable."

Isaac King had been up for ten minutes. It was a record.

Kids were gathered around the circle, shouting, some of them jockeying for position. I moved in closer to the group and found a spot near the edge. I could see that Isaac King was still up on his feet, his arms flailing.

What I never understood was why he never gave up. It shows that he was not right. Because even if he had been able to do the impossible—defeat five at once—there would be five more waiting on the sidelines. And then five more after that. And so on.

But that night it was clear that something was different. He wasn't going to let himself go down. In fact, he lasted a record twenty minutes. In the end, it took six or seven guys to finally get him off his feet and even after he'd been pinned down on his back he was still trying to move his arms and legs. Someone finally used a two-by-four to knock him out. It was an unnecessarily hard blow and even today I do not know which of the kids delivered it. His head split open near the hairline. And when the blood started, everyone scattered.

I walked over to Tanner. "Hey," I said. "What the fuck just happened?"

"I don't know," he said. "I have no fucking idea."

It took a half hour to get him across the street and into a buggy. He was losing a lot of blood by then and had passed out. I suggested calling an ambulance, but Rachel said they never used the hospital. I tried to insist but she was stubborn about it.

"No," she said. "They wouldn't like it."

"Who's they?" I said.

But she turned away.

I never got a chance to say goodbye to her. When she left she was crying, though I knew it was not because she would never see me again.

Tanner and I went home after that and never went back to that part of town or talked about that night again. Instead we went into our senior year of high school and took the SATs, and then off to college like everyone else. I never saw Rachel again. But a few months later I found out from Tanner that Isaac King had died of a brain clot six weeks after that night. It was a small article in the paper and no allegations were made.

★★★

These days almost all of the Amish have left. Most have sold their land off cheap to real estate agencies and contractors and gone west to Indiana and Iowa. We have new malls and outlet stores where their farms were, and out where Rachel used to live actors dressed in Amish costumes and fake beards stand along the thruway, chewing on corn-cob pipes and beckoning carloads of tourists to have their picture taken with them.

I am twenty-nine years old now and not married. I am not yet old but some days I am aware of it closing in on me. Tanner lives in California now with a woman who will one day be his wife. But I can remember when he still lived in Leola, just a few blocks away. And when I think about Rachel now, I think mostly about those races we used to have out across the railroad bridge, thirty feet above the water, and I still shudder at our carelessness, our blind motions, not watching where we were stepping, not even considering what was below us.

Inside "Departure": Mining a Setting for Emotion

When I first started writing "Departure," I didn't know that I was even thinking about it as a story. I simply wanted to write about this little strip mall on the outskirts of the small rural town in Pennsylvania where I'd grown up. Much like the strip mall in "Departure," the strip mall I remembered had a K-mart attached to it and a twenty-four-hour diner across the street. It was a place where my friends and I used to go to hang out and play video games in the late afternoons after school, and much like the strip mall in "Departure," it was a place where a small group of Amish teenagers would occasionally show up on Friday nights. Usually, they'd hide their buggies out behind the dumpsters at the far end of the strip mall, and then they'd wander over to the arcade in their street clothes and begin playing video games. It was a strange sight to see.

I'd grown up with the Amish, but I'd never seen them in street clothes before. I'd never seen them smoking cigarettes or playing *Donkey Kong*. Later, I'd learn that this strange little ritual was part of an experiment designed by their parents to prevent them from leaving the Amish community and to strengthen their convictions about the Amish way of life. But at the time I didn't know any of these things. I simply thought it was strange. I'd look at my friends, they'd look at me; then we'd shake our heads in disbelief and go back to our video games.

It wasn't until many years later that I actually began to think about any of this stuff in terms of fiction. I was in my early twenties then, living in Houston, Texas, and trying to write what I hoped would be the very first stories in my collection. I hadn't written a lot of stories at that point. I'd written a few Raymond Carver rip-offs in college, and a few beginnings of stories that never quite got off the ground, but I hadn't ever written anything that I felt proud of, anything that I felt I could show to my friends without feeling embarrassed.

At the same time, I'd been thinking a lot about those Amish teenagers and that strip mall I used to go to back in high school. For some reason, the image of that place had always haunted me. There seemed to be something intrinsically sad about it, the setting itself, but also the image of these kids trying to fit in when they so clearly couldn't. I felt that there was something there that I wanted to express, something I wanted to write about. I just couldn't put my finger on it. I didn't know how to access the story inside the memory.

Finally, I decided that I'd just start by writing about the setting itself. I'd write about the setting and the things that I remembered in hopes that these images might eventually lead me somewhere else. In my very first attempts, I think I wrote almost exclusively about the arcade. This is where I had spent most of my time, after all, and I also thought that there might be something interesting I could do with the juxtaposition of the video games and the Amish teenagers trying to play them. The problem was every time I read over these drafts, they seemed inaccurate to me—false. There seemed to be something about the flashiness of the arcade itself, and also the comic nature of these descriptions, that was working against the basic sense of isolation and loneliness I wanted to convey.

I decided to put the story away for a while, and the next time I approached it, I started somewhere else: the diner across the street. What seems strange to me now is that I don't think I ever actually stepped inside that diner in my life. I certainly never ate there, and I definitely didn't remember what it looked like. But then again, maybe that's what freed me up to write about it, allowed me to veer the story away from my own memories and into the realm of fiction. All I know is that once I set the story there, once I had an image of that place in my mind, everything else seemed to fall into place. I probably wrote about five or six pages about the diner alone, most of which never made its way into the story, but somewhere in these descriptions were certain images, certain lines, that I held on to: the Amish kids disappearing into the bathrooms to change clothes, the buggies traveling along the highway like a funeral procession, the one angry kid who never spoke and listened to heavy metal. There was something about these particular images that seemed to resonate with me, that seemed to speak to some sort of emotional truth in my own experience.

In any event, after I'd written about five or six pages of description, I started looking for story elements, things I might bring out and develop. There was the one Amish girl the narrator liked, the angry kid in the booth, the people from the town, and so on, but I felt like I needed something else. At the time, I was writing all of these descriptions from the perspective of a single teenage boy, sitting alone in a booth. I imagined him to be a loner, an outcast, but somehow his alienation combined with their alienation was taking the story too far in another direction. It was becoming too sad. So

I decided to give him a friend, Tanner, and once I had an image of Tanner in my mind, things started to roll.

In fact, shortly after I had created the character of Tanner, I wrote the two sentences that would later become the opening paragraph of the story:

That spring we were sixteen Tanner and I started dating the Amish girls out on the rural highway—sometimes two or three at the same time, because it wasn't really dating. There was no way of getting serious.

I don't know where those two sentences first appeared—probably in the middle of a longer section—but as soon as I had written them, I felt fairly certain I had my opening. I cut and pasted them at the top of a new document, and then went forward from there. What happened after that is a blur. I wrote the rest of the story in a matter of days, probably two or three, and when I'd finally finished, I didn't know what to make of what I'd written. It was so unlike anything else I'd ever written before that I just couldn't tell if it was any good or not. I ended up deciding to submit it as part of my application to the University of Iowa Writers' Workshop, and when they later accepted me, I took this as a sign that the story probably wasn't as bad as I had originally feared.

Still, the story disappeared after that. I put it away in a folder and didn't look at it again until I was almost thirty-four (more than ten years after I'd written it). I think once I got into grad school, I decided that everything I'd written before grad school was amateur stuff, juvenilia. So I forgot about it for a long time, and it wasn't until many years later that I rediscovered it in a small folder along with a bunch of other old stories. At the time, I was putting together a packet of new work for my girlfriend to look over, and I decided to slip "Departure" in among the other stories just to see what she would say. When she got back to me a few days later, she said that the other stories were good, but that "Departure" was her favorite. I told her I'd written it when I was twenty-two and that she must be kidding. She said that she didn't care when I'd written it. It was still her favorite. Since then, "Departure" has received a number of accolades and awards (all of which she takes credit for), but I still can't get past the fact that it sat in a folder for so many years, that it just sat there, collecting dust. And I can't help wondering why I never believed in it back then, why I dismissed it so quickly, why I felt certain that something I had written when I was twenty-two couldn't possibly be good.

WRITING EXERCISE

Pick a setting from your past that you associate with a certain feeling or emotion. This feeling or emotion shouldn't be something that's immediately obvious to you (e.g., jealousy, anger, fear), but rather something that you can't quite express. Then take a few minutes and write about this setting with the goal of trying to describe it in such a way that the emotion you associate with it comes through. You should try to avoid abstract language (thoughts, feelings) and focus instead on concrete, specific details. Your goal here is to capture a certain mood, a certain feeling, through the details themselves. After you've finished, go back and see if you can locate any story elements in what you've written, any images or characters that you might want to bring out and develop. If you can, go forward from there. Keep writing, trust your instincts, and see where the story leads you.

Especially Roosevelt

aiden's morning sickness was bad, and she told me to get the boy out of the house, take him anywhere. She stood in the doorway of our downstairs bathroom, just off the kitchen, her frizzy black hair bound into a ponytail that pointed toward the ceiling like a squat exclamation point. "Please," she said.

It was Saturday, the day I usually played racquetball with friends. I twirled my racket in her direction and arched my eyebrows. "Can't you wait? I'll only be gone an hour," I said, teasing. "No more than two."

From the living room, the boy, DeMarckus, mimicked the sounds of Haiden's dry heaving. I imagined him kneeling over the coffee table, his chin scrunched into his neck. The coffee table was one of our projects from before DeMarckus had become our foster child six months earlier. Haiden and I had found the table at a garage sale, then stripped, varnished, and sandpapered the finish in spots, to give it the appearance of age. Beneath the table's beveled-glass top, we had placed a tea-stained map of the world. Listening to DeMarckus's fake heaving, I pictured the six-year-old's face hovering over the bottom half of Africa.

Haiden rolled her eyes and mouthed the words, "Take him, Rick." And then, out loud, she added, "Now. Like, any minute." When I hesitated, she threatened me with the back of her hand, its cinnamon skin dry and ashy.

DeMarckus's vomiting noises stopped, and he entered the kitchen and put a fist on his hip, considering Haiden. He was dressed in only a pair of backward underwear—his usual morning attire—and he tapped a bare foot on the linoleum floor and closed one eye.

"Mama," he said, shaking his head, "you look like you been stepped on."

I tried to contain a laugh, wondering where the boy had gotten the line.

Looking ill, Haiden reentered the bathroom and shut the door. De-Marckus stared at the spot where she had been, stretching out his neck as if to gag.

"Go get dressed, Marcky," I told him. "You and me are going to the pet store."

He eyed the racket I still had in my hand. "For real?" he said. We had been to the pet store on a couple of Saturdays, but usually in the afternoon, after racquetball.

"Totally." I set the racket on the counter. "And if you hurry, we can go get pancakes."

In seconds DeMarckus was ascending the stairs two at a time, imitating Haiden, his pretend heaves interspersed with her words, "Please. Now. Like. Any. Minute."

★★★

On Saturdays the animal shelter brought abandoned cats to the pet store in hopes of finding them homes. Just like every other time we'd been, Marcky headed straight for the back corner of the store and began naming the cats after dead presidents. He probably thought he was naming them after the local elementary schools. The cages were tagged with the cats' real names and a short explanation for their sorry situation, but Marcky couldn't read, and even if he could, I doubt he'd have called the cats by names someone else had given them.

Hardware & Pets no longer sold hardware. The aisles that used to smell like fresh-cut lumber now had only that dirty-hamster-cage odor. Gurgling fish tanks lined every wall. I watched the boy poke his fingers through the cats' cage doors. Most of the cats were unresponsive, still sleeping off breakfast, their tails curled at the tips like genie shoes. Marcky stopped at a cage labeled, SLIM: OWNERS HAD TO MOVE, and said, "Eisenhower. Eisey, Eisey, Eisey. Wake up!" The fat tabby opened one eye and then must have farted, because Marcky pinched his nose and turned to me in disgust. I plugged my nose in sympathy and made a face that said, *Ewww*.

"*That* was uncalled for, Eisenhower," Marcky said, scolding the cat with his free index finger. Though his voice was nasal from the pinched nose, his tone perfectly mimicked Haiden's. In six months of fostering DeMarckus, Haiden and I had rarely heard what the boy's real voice sounded like. He was always imitating people—their inflections and cadences, long strings of their exact words. Some of his imitations were funny. He could do the bubbly clerk from the video store: "I absolutely *love* this movie. Really. It's, like, my all-time favorite." Or my mother, while we were watching a movie: "Isn't there something more … I don't know, *useful* we could all be doing?" Other times DeMarckus's mimicry unsettled Haiden and me. Once, when I turned out the light after tucking him into bed, he said, "Oh, no. We don't cut the fucking lights out in this house. We leave the lights *on*." His voice was so cool and detached I thought there might be someone else in the room, but when I flipped on the light, I found only Marcky, angled across his bed.

I asked, "What was that?" in a voice that was equal parts anger and confusion. Instead of answering me, Marcky said, "Thank you. That's better." He pulled the sheet over his shoulder and smushed his cheek into the pillow.

One night, before she became pregnant with Ben, Haiden had just dropped hot dogs in a pan to boil when she heard a snide voice from the bathroom say, "DeMarckus? What kind of name's DeMarckus?" A feminine voice answered, "Maybe it's a black-boy name. Because he's a *black boy*." Then an unchildlike voice said, "I'll show you a fucking black-boy name, bitch."

Haiden opened the bathroom door and found Marcky staring into the mirror, his backward drawers around his knees. He quickly hoisted his drawers and jeans, ran water over his hands, and left without flushing the small turd floating in the toilet.

Later that night, during dinner, Haiden asked Marcky how school had been that day.

"Cheese pizza," he said.

Marcky often answered questions with non-sequiturs about food. His favorite was "Applesauce." Haiden assumed his peculiarities were caused by two things: one, his attention-deficit disorder, for which we fed him fifteen milligrams of Ritalin each morning; and two, the defense mechanisms he'd acquired during the years he'd spent with a negligent birth mother and in and out of questionable foster homes. At first she'd felt we should ignore it and give him time to adjust. But that night at dinner Haiden persisted.

"What about the other kids at school?" she asked. "How are you getting along with them?"

Marcky, his hot-dog bun covering his mouth, whispered, "Green beans." Then he rolled his eyes in feigned exasperation—an expression we found endearing—and added, "Applesauce."

Unaware of what Haiden had witnessed earlier that afternoon, I raised my hot dog high, like a scepter, and said, "Applesauce, indeed." I had expected the table to shake with laughter, but Haiden didn't laugh; instead she opened her eyes wide, as if to keep from crying. Confused but still smiling, I turned to Marcky, whose expression perfectly mirrored Haiden's.

In bed that night Haiden told me why she had been so upset. "And then you—you go and encourage him, saying 'Applesauce, indeed.'" She made a face and raised an invisible hot dog. "Do you think that's wise, Rick?" she said. "Encouraging this?"

I had no idea. I wondered if she was worried about living in Woodhull. We'd bought a big two-story house there two years earlier and were one of about six black couples in the neighborhood. A few black children went to the elementary school, and before we'd brought Marcky home, we'd talked to their parents, who told us things were fine, really. Not bad, anyway.

"The kids will adjust to Marcky," I told Haiden. "And he'll adjust to them."

Haiden sighed and rolled onto her side, facing away from me. It wasn't just finding him talking to the bathroom mirror, she said. It was more than that. There was something going on. "All that's happened to that boy," Haiden said. "The life he's lived ..."

"He's with us now," I said. "We're the life he's living." My words hung over us for a moment, but Haiden never responded. When I leaned over her to look at her face, her eyes were shut.

★★★

After Eisenhower passed gas, Marcky tapped the door of the next cage over, marked, EL NIÑO: HE WAS BREAKING HIS OWNER'S HEART. A scrawny Siamese at the back of the cage sat up and began pulling himself forward using only his front paws, his lifeless hind legs dragging behind him. "Roosevelt," Marcky said, "what's wrong, boy?"

It seemed prescient of Marcky to name a cat that couldn't walk "Roosevelt." Another time he'd named an unneutered male with an erection "Kennedy." Sometimes the boy seemed to just know things.

Roosevelt collapsed with the top of his head against the cage door. "Atta boy," Marcky said. He scratched behind the cat's ears with two fingers. "You like that, don't you?" Roosevelt's front legs stiffened. "Just don't fart, OK, Mr. Roosevelt? Could you do that for me?" Marcky put his nose close to the cage and cooed, "I think you can. 'Cause you a good, no-fart kitty."

Sometimes part of me forgot that he was a boy, a six-year-old boy, with a capacity for empathy—for love, even.

A pretty, college-age white girl in a tight T-shirt approached and stared at Marcky, admiring the way he interacted with Roosevelt.

"Do you want to get El Niño out of his cage?" she asked, a little too eager.

Under his breath, Marcky whispered, "Pancakes."

"He's a very sweet cat," the girl said. "I think we should get him out."

Marcky turned to me, his eyes wide, and made a face like, *Can you believe this girl is talking to me?* A few months ago he would have scampered over to me and pressed his face into my leg. I was glad to see him hanging in there for a change, trying.

The girl placed a hand on Marcky's shoulder. "Do you have any pets at home?" she asked.

"Hydrangea," Marcky said.

The girl's brow furrowed, and she looked at me. Haiden and I had a cat named Hydrangea, a fluffy white ball of fur we'd owned for almost our entire marriage. "Our cat's name is Hydrangea," I said.

The girl knelt so she was eye-level with Marcky, her palms on her thighs. "Let's get El Niño out of his cage, hmm?"

Marcky tilted his head to the side and screwed up his face as if he smelled a dirty litter pan. Then he put *his* hand on *her* shoulder while she knelt before him, as if he were knighting or blessing her. "His name's Roosevelt," Marcky said, "and I don't think that will be necessary."

The girl stood, and Marcky's hand fell to his side. "Well, wouldn't you like to take Roosevelt home," she asked, "so Hydrangea can have a brother?"

Marcky stuck his finger in his ear, twisted it, and whispered, "Butterscotch," so low I almost had to read his lips. Then he added, out loud, in a voice that was all his, "Goodbye, Roosevelt. Goodbye, pretty girl. I love you." And he walked past me into another part of the store.

"He's a cutie," the girl said. "How old is he?"

"That kid?" I said. "I've never seen him before in my life." I chuckled, to let her in on the joke, but the girl's brow furrowed the way it had when Marcky had mentioned Hydrangea. I followed Marcky to find out where he'd gone.

★★★

About six weeks after Ben was conceived, Haiden and I sat Marcky down and explained to him that she was pregnant. I was worried about his reaction, but it turned out OK, about what I'd expect from a six-year-old: He walked over to Haiden, pointed a finger at her belly, and said, "You mean you have a baby in *there*?"

"Do you want to put your hand on my belly," Haiden asked, "to say hello to the baby?"

Marcky looked at Haiden as if a horn was protruding from her forehead, and he began backing up. "No, thank you," he said. "I don't think so."

A few weeks later, though, Marcky was talking to Haiden's belly in the voice we were beginning to recognize as his, saying, "Remember, little brother or sister: Pancakes are the perfect breakfast." Or, "Don't get mad when I get to stay up later than you. You'll get to stay up late too when you're older." He was also calling Haiden "Mama" and sometimes, after I read to him from the *National Audubon Society Field Guide to North American Birds*—the kid loved birds—Marcky would call me "Dad," and I would wonder at the strange sound of it.

But there was still the problem of those voices the boy remembered from his past—the years he'd spent in foster care and being raised by a mother who'd eventually lost custody of him and his two older siblings. Until we signed adoption papers, the caseworker couldn't tell us where he'd been and what he might have seen before coming to us. We worried there was something predetermined about the boy's fate, no matter how much love we gave him. Even Marcky's innocent reactions—asking me, in his six-year-old voice, "For real?" or pointing at Haiden's belly and saying, "You mean you have a baby in *there*?"—sometimes seemed like an act, as if he was merely behaving the way he thought we expected him to.

★★★

I found Marcky perusing the dog toys not far from the cats' cages. Seeing me walking toward him, he pulled a five-dollar bill from his pocket, pinched the money at both ends, and snapped it twice in the air.

"Where did you get that?" I asked.

"Where do you think?" Marcky said. He huffed, and his eyes drifted toward the ceiling. "Mama gave it to me," he said. Then he held the bill out to me and asked, "How much is it?"

I pointed at one of the bill's corners. "You tell me," I said. "What number does it have on the front?" The boy couldn't read, but he knew most of his letters and all of his numbers. I guessed this was what parents did—they quizzed kids, to teach them.

Marcky disregarded my question and picked up a rubber pork chop. "Could I buy this?" he asked. "For Hydrangea. I think he deserves a treat. He's a good—"

I took the toy from him. "I asked you a question."

Marcky's lips trembled, and he started to cry. "I was just trying to do something *nice* for the kitty," he said.

The boy's tears and attempt to play innocent annoyed me. Marcky would try this at bedtime, too, or when he wanted candy, and it was simultaneously artificial and sincere, the way it is, I imagine, when most six-year-olds cry. I grabbed Marcky under his arm, and the five-dollar bill fell from his hand and floated to the floor.

"I asked you what number was on the front of your money," I said, "and I would like for you to answer me."

My grip on Marcky's arm tightened, and I noticed the boy was on his tiptoes, real tears collecting in the corners of his eyes. I spread my fingers wide, and Marcky shrugged away from my grip and looked at the floor. In the kindest voice I could manage, I asked him to pick up the money.

Marcky bent to retrieve the bill, and when he righted himself, his tears were gone. "It's a five," he said. "OK?"

I wasn't surprised by how quickly the boy had stopped crying, but I was caught off guard by the strange assurance in his voice.

"I want to buy Hydrangea something," he said. "I want to spend all *five* dollars Mama gave me on Hydrangea."

"That's very generous of you," I said, "but this is the dog-toy aisle. Let's go look at the cat toys." I put my arm around Marcky's shoulder, and he pressed his head into my side.

"Yeah, yeah," he said, "very generous of me."

★★★

Haiden's getting pregnant with Ben after Marcky came to live with us wasn't something we planned. We had tried for three years to have a child—three years without doctors. Then, rather than seek a medical explanation for our difficulties, we registered to become foster parents.

Before Marcky came to live with us, his caseworker told us the boy was "SACY," an acronym that stood for "sexually aggressive children and youth," which we were told didn't mean that the boy was a preschool sex offender; he just knew more than most kids his age about sex. We had to notify the school when we registered him for first grade, and the principal said they'd handled SACY kids before. They just had to keep an eye on him around the other students. Nothing out of the ordinary.

Haiden and I knew there had to be reasons for this designation, but those reasons were locked inside Marcky's six-year-old head, and in a file his caseworker kept, which we would be allowed to access only after the adoption took place—if it took place. Haiden and I tried to find out what the boy had been exposed to, so we could know what we were dealing with, but the caseworker said the information was "sensitive." It included police and psychiatric reports and the names of other foster parents and what had happened in their homes. There was no way, the caseworker said, that she could present that kind of information to people who might choose to maintain custody of the boy for only a day or so.

Haiden and I were OK with this at first; we didn't think there was anything we could find out that would make us not want to take Marcky into our home.

And then Haiden got pregnant.

When we told the caseworker, she seemed almost alarmed. "OK," she said. "There are ways to handle this. It isn't anything to get worked up about."

We hadn't known that it might be, and all this secrecy was beginning to get to us. We asked just what was in that file. "Just tell us," I said. "Let us know."

Without giving any details, the woman said that Marcky might be better off in a home without any other children around. She said it could work out all right, though, that often there are no problems at all.

But that wall of doubts the caseworker had erected around Marcky was enough. If it had just been the three of us—Haiden, Marcky, and me—I think we could have made it work. But it wasn't going to be just us three.

We told DeMarckus's caseworker we would keep the boy for now, until she found another suitable foster home, but that, after thinking it through, we weren't going to adopt him.

★★★

For Hydrangea, Marcky picked out two realistic-looking brown mice filled with catnip and handed them to me along with his five-dollar bill. "You pay," he said.

While the store owner rang up the mice, Marcky stood by my side and drummed his fingers on the counter. "Excuse me, lady," he said. I thought maybe he wanted to tell her about Hydrangea or let her know he was paying for these gifts with his own money. But Marcky looked concerned, his eyebrows close together.

"Yes, young man?" the store owner asked.

"Those cats back there," Marcky said. He pointed toward the back of the store. "Where do they live when it isn't Saturday?"

The woman smiled and said, "Well, their real house is the animal shelter."

"Then what?" Marcky said.

The store owner turned to me, and I shrugged, as if to say, *Are six-year-olds supposed to know about the mechanics of animal shelters?*

"Well—"

Marcky stopped her. "I don't want the mice," he said. "I want to give all my money to the kitties."

"Oh, honey," the woman said. "I don't think—"

"To the kitties," he said. "All five dollars."

I reached out to put my arm around Marcky, but he pulled his shoulder away from my hand. I had never seen the boy so serious-looking. "All I want is to give the money to the cats," he said. "Maybe especially Roosevelt."

On previous trips to the store, I had entertained the idea that Marcky had an intuition about the animals' plight, but the boy's interest in the cats had always seemed uncomplicated, as if he liked them more for their cat-ness than anything else, the way any kid would.

But this, this felt different.

"All right," I told him. "It's your money."

The store owner asked us to wait, and she snagged the college girl, who brought out a marker and a donation sheet shaped like a cat's paw. Marcky placed the paw on the store's counter, and I spelled out his name for him, one letter at a time. Meanwhile, the store owner produced a Polaroid camera to take our picture.

In the photos Haiden and I have of Marcky, he is only half-smiling, as if he has just asked a question and received an answer he doesn't understand. When I look at those pictures now, I smell the boy's bad morning breath; I see the streaks of toothpaste he used to leave in the sink.

The college girl stood behind Marcky, bent at the waist, and placed both her hands on his shoulders. I tried to slink out of the shot while the store owner looked through the camera's viewfinder.

"Oh, no," she said. "Get back there, you."

I stood behind them and off to the side, just barely caught by the camera's flash. The store owner took two pictures, one to attach to the cat's paw Marcky had signed, and one for us to have as a keepsake.

★★★

On the drive home from the pet store, Marcky fiddled with the window button and asked his typical six-year-old questions, like "Do flowers have feelings?" or "Superman isn't *really* a man, right?" His mind had already moved on to something else. I tried to answer his questions as best I could but my head was filled with *All I want is to give the money to the cats. Maybe especially Roosevelt.*

When we made it home, Haiden was in the kitchen making a salad, and all signs of sickness had left her face. Marcky bounded through the kitchen on his way to the television. The Polaroid, I would find out later, was still in the car, where Marcky had dropped it.

"How was your trip to the pet store?" Haiden asked as she halved a handful of grape tomatoes and tossed them in a bowl.

"Well," I said, "it looks like we have a hero down at Hardware & Pets."

Haiden, of course, had no way of knowing what I meant, but she placed her knife on the counter, smiled, and said, "Come here."

And I held her there in the kitchen, with the bump of Ben between us. We were so isolated, yet so together right then. We held one another and didn't let go, and it felt like we were waiting: For Marcky to gag over the coffee table. For him to say, "Applesauce."

For anything from him at all.

Inside "Especially Roosevelt": Uncovering Meaning in an Anecdote

Not long after this story was published in *The Sun*, I received a letter from a woman who had read it. The woman said she was certain the story I had written was autobiographical, and she wanted to know if I ever learned what had become of DeMarckus. Had he found someone to adopt him? Did I finally discover what had made him "damaged goods"? The woman said, too, that the story was heartbreaking, and that the only other writer she'd ever been inclined to contact was Jamaica Kincaid.

My initial reaction was conflicted.

On the one hand, I'd never been contacted by a reader in this particular manner. And I'd never received anything from a reader who wanted to know "more" about a story I'd written. I was touched that the woman had taken the time to find my campus address, type out a letter on her personal letterhead, and hand-address the envelope. The fact that this was only the second time she had done such a thing—and that the other writer she'd written was Jamaica Kincaid—certainly made me feel, to some extent, for perhaps the first time, like a writer. And I wanted to "reward" this woman for her efforts by providing her with all of the information she was looking for.

On the other hand, this woman's reaction was exactly the kind of thing that I was hoping for. And I was hoping to achieve that kind of reaction by writing a story, a fiction, which, hopefully, wouldn't require any kind of explanation or elaboration. Fiction, instead, offers an experience, and the woman who'd been moved to write had bought, so to speak, the experience I'd sold her.

I still haven't contacted her, though I feel bad about it. The reason I haven't is because I kind of want to protect the integrity of the fiction, to allow the reader to access only the art itself. When it is really working, there is a kind of magic to fiction, and to reveal the magician's methods is to spoil the trick forever.

However, since this is a craft essay about the story, I am going to allow you, reader, a peek behind the curtain. It is my hope, though, that you will not "care" about the story-behind-the-story, but that you might find the "tricks" I employed educational, and that you might use them to create your own magic.

Though this story isn't, as the woman who wrote me assumed, autobiographical, it did begin with a real-life incident. My brother- and sister-in-law took a foster child into their home about seven years ago, and not long after they began fostering the boy, Devontae, my sister-in-law, Jil, became pregnant. While she was pregnant, my brother-in-law, Scott, took Devontae to a pet store, where he donated five dollars to the orphaned cats the pet store had on display.

So, there's the incident, the anecdote, on which the story is based. When Jil told me about the pet store incident, my wife and I agreed that it was pretty cute, pretty prescient in some way, but I didn't plan to write a story about it. I'd worked from real life in the past and always had a hard time negotiating "what really happened" with the fictional world I was putting on the page, and so I'd begun to enjoy simply "inventing" everything in my stories, so that I didn't feel bound to their "real world" counterparts.

At some point, though, I sat down and started writing a scene that took place at a pet store. Devontae had become DeMarckus, and Scott had become Rick, the story's narrator. Though the "real world" pet store where the incident took place was probably a PetSmart, or some other chain, I set it at a little pet store in Murphysboro, Illinois, where I was living, called Hardware & Pets.

I kind of liked the scene I got on the page. DeMarckus had a little bit of personality, and I felt like I was doing a pretty good job of moving the characters around. I worked on the scene for a few weeks, however, and realized that all I really had was an anecdote about a foster kid who donates his money to some cats.

I set it aside for a while and eventually felt compelled to come back to it. When I did, my writing process led me to take two "leaps" that helped me to make this anecdote an honest-to-goodness story.

The first leap: I imagined a troubled past for DeMarckus. I had him not speak directly to other characters as a kind of defense mechanism, and I gave him this kind of weird ability to imitate people, which was a little frightening for Rick and Haiden. This leap helped me, I think, to make DeMarckus's character a little more complex, and it also added something to the tone of the story, a sense of mystery, in that Rick seemed to be trying to figure the boy out.

After I began writing about DeMarckus's troubled past, I still wasn't sure exactly where the story was going, even if I did feel like things were improving. In real life, Jil and Scott, while Jil was pregnant, decided to adopt Devontae before their child was born, and I was, in some way, beholden to this real-world development of events. So, my story was mostly about the narrator's worry about what was going to happen—in the lives of both DeMarckus and his unborn son, as they eventually grew up—in light of the events that took place at the pet store.

I was still in grad school when I was writing this story, and, under the pressure of a deadline to turn it in, I was trying to figure out what I could do to "Especially Roosevelt" to make it a story worth showing to my classmates. I was in my office, bouncing a tennis ball off the wall and catching it, when I realized that Rick and Haiden, unlike Jil and Scott, decided not to adopt the boy.

Once I realized this, the story took shape pretty quickly. It took me about six months of writing to make this discovery, and the story still wasn't anywhere near the state in which it ended up being published.

The final two stages of revisions took place very slowly, over the course of about two years.

The first thing I did was work on simplifying the story's style. In the story's initial incarnations, the narrator was filled with quirks. He was a very reluctant narrator, and this reluctance manifested itself in strange verb-tense shifts, the use of ellipses, and in a disorienting use of em-dashes. He also, in an attempt to mimic DeMarckus's ADHD, moved around in time and place without orienting the reader. Over time, I decided to just have Rick narrate the story in simple past tense, and I got rid of many of his quirks, though he still summarizes a lot of dialogue, which was my attempt at having him "appropriate" the voices of others, the way DeMarckus does.

The second thing I did was change Haiden and Rick's race. In my early drafts, I didn't really mention race at all, other than to let the reader know that DeMarckus was African American. When a teacher of mine read the story, she said that she assumed the narrator was African American as well, since race was never really brought up. And I thought to myself, "Sure. That makes sense to me."

The way I saw it, Rick and Haiden were relatively affluent people. They had the resources to provide for both DeMarckus and their un-born son, but chose not to, because of their fears. And I thought that if these two were African American, then the gravitas of their situa-tion might be heightened just a little, that it all might be just a little more heartbreaking.

The problem, then, was figuring out how to get this across. Early on, I did it in a very simple way—by calling the girl at the pet store a "white" girl. I figured that pointing this out would show that she is "different," race-wise, from the narrator. Once the story was accepted by *The Sun*, however, they wanted me to make the narrator's race a little more obvious, and I agreed that this was necessary, so I made a few changes.

I didn't think much of the fact that I was appropriating the voice of an African American until I workshopped a late draft of this story at the Sewanee Writers' Conference. One of the first comments made in the workshop was from a class member who was uncomfortable with a white person—and she knew I was white because I was sitting in the room with her and had been all week—writing from the point of view of an African American. Other class members agreed with her—it wasn't something they would do.

One of the workshop's leaders, Richard Bausch, said that while he agreed it was a valid concern, he also felt that appropriation, in general, is all we writers have. If we can't do that, then what can we do?

While I think that there should be a certain type of thoughtfulness that goes into any type of appropriation—whether a writer is choosing to write from the point of view of a different gender, race, ethnicity, or whatever—I also agree with Bausch that some type of appropriation is pretty much always necessary, if we want to investigate in any way the human condition on the page.

It was ultimately that impulse—the one that causes me to think and write about what it means to be human—that helped me to take an anecdote about my nephew and present it as something that might be understood more universally. I am not a parent, but if I were, I would certainly, I think, worry about what was going to happen to my child when he or she grows up. I might ask myself: What might this person end up being capable of? What am I doing right now to influence who this person will become? When Rick and Haiden asked themselves such questions about how DeMarckus and his troubled past might affect their unborn son, they decided not to adopt him.

It was my hope that readers might be moved by the decision that these two characters made. And, as I noted above, their decision did move at least one reader, though I still don't think I'm going to contact her and let her know how things turned out. She would doubtlessly be as happy as I am that things didn't end as tragically in "real life" as they did in my story. Just this week, in fact, Devontae was making fun of my new haircut and begging me to take him fishing. But I don't want to let her in on that happiness. I want her to stay just where she ended up after reading the story, the fiction—heartbroken, longing the same way Rick does to know what ever happened to the boy.

WRITING EXERCISE

What I hoped to show in my craft essay was how a writer can take an anecdote and make it into something a little more meaningful. The anecdotes we often tell about ourselves make sense only because the people to whom we are telling them know us. So, what I often do as a writer is get hold of an anecdote—whether it's funny, quirky, or heartbreaking—and then figure out the character or characters for whom that anecdote might be most meaningful.

If I were to reduce the story I wrote to a headline, it would be this: FOSTER CHILD GIVES MONEY TO ORPHANED CATS. What I spent about three years figuring out, then, was who that child was, who his foster parents were, and what the significance of it all was.

With *Tabloid Dreams*, Robert Olen Butler wrote an entire collection of stories based on headlines gleaned from the tabloids. He managed to take bizarre "surfaces"—JEALOUS HUSBAND RETURNS IN FORM OF PARROT, TITANIC VICTIM SPEAKS THROUGH WATERBED—and look much more deeply into them, in order to find the funny, tragic, heartbreaking stories hidden there.

As an exercise, collect some newspaper headlines. They can be strange or mundane, but look for stories that appeal to your sensibility—stories that maybe have embedded in them some kind of image or narrative that you want to explore. Then, ask yourself: For whom might this anecdote be most meaningful? Where is it taking place? Who all is there? How did things wind up here?

You can do this alone or with a group of people. What makes it interesting in a group—whether the people are writers or not—is that you will begin to see the lens through which others view the world. Do certain people want to always make things ironic? Do others want to always make things sensational? Happy? Sad?

The stories that take shape, you will see, can go in hundreds of directions, but you will most often realize that there is only one way that *you* can really see the story taking shape, and that is the direction you should take it.

To get you started, consider the following headlines, which I've seen in the news lately:

COUPLE FINDS WOMAN ASLEEP ON THEIR COUCH

MAN COVERED WITH BARBECUE SAUCE ARRESTED FOR BURGLARY

LOCAL COUPLE TRAVELS COUNTRY TO WELCOME BACK SOLDIERS

GEORGE SINGLETON

Voted Most Likely

After the obstetrician set the date of my Caesarian delivery, my mother visited a number of grocery store chains and bought up everything with "Expires 7-3-73" printed somewhere on the package. I understood the implication later, maybe by the age of six, when my father bought me a set of Hardy Boys adventures, and we needed to clear away a half-dozen deep Rubbermaid bins that held loaves of Sunbeam bread and unopened cartons of milk. The bins had been duct taped heavily to keep me from prying, but I spent some hours as a child looking through the opaque walls at what my mother said, "Expired, so you could be here, Stet Looper." She was some kind of believer in cycles. She leaned toward fatalism. And she always called me by my first and last name, for some reason, in the same way a mechanic might chastise a customer for forgetting to add antifreeze in the radiator. Not that I kept a running log, but I don't believe my father ever pronounced my name again after what I secretly tabbed the St. Valentine's Day Mascara.

"I believe that I've made it clear as to how many times you can play with rocks," my father said often over the six years after having moved the expired food items into one of his outbuildings. "The very first time I catch you playing with my rocks, Stet, I'm going to make you drink that milk. What expired at your birth will make you expire right now."

All rocks on our property, and below the surface of the Unknown Branch of the Saluda River, were *his* rocks. I was not allowed to pick one up, except while working. I was not allowed to skip them across the river during calm periods. Somehow my father knew the exact spots of where his rocks held. He could look out across the way, point, and say, "There's a nice inch-thick piece of granite, big as a TV dinner tray, over there a hundred yards downstream that'll make a good paver on someone's back porch one day, but right now I'll let it hide that trout," et cetera. My father—and his father—were consumed and obsessed, which ultimately made Carolina Rocks probably the most successful landscape rocks operation in western North and South Carolina.

I said, "I'll buy a rock from you, Dad. I'll trade off some dredging work." The thought of drinking sour, twelve-year-old milk stood right about in the same spot as sliding down a hundred-foot razor blade naked, or eating French fries boiled with a fat man's sweat, on the continuum of things that made me sick to my stomach.

After I explained it all—and it only took until the afternoon of Valentine's Day to understand why my father compromised—I spent the entire week before February 14 dredging the Unknown Branch of the Saluda River, which divided my father's property for a good half-mile, at least, and served him, and my grandfather before, so they could sell to rustic chimney builders, and the occasional weekend fool who wanted to build a path, a fence, or a family room floor out of smooth flat rocks. It's not like I didn't know how to use a variety of his handmade pulley buckets to dredge. I'd been setting off dynamite up river since the age of ten to loosen rocks during particularly slow stretches.

After dredging that first day, I fingered through the pile of smaller rocks—ones used for decoration, ones sold to various fish tank salesmen, ones sold to people who preferred rocks below their azaleas instead of bark mulch. I daydreamed. To be honest, I had a new interest in hanging out on the edge of the river seeing as a girl my age I'd never seen at school came down the steep slope on the other side about once a week for a month, wearing what may or may not have once been a seed sack, and just stared at me. I waved at her the first time. She didn't respond. The next time—my father happened to be out on deliveries—I skipped rocks the girl's way, hoping to nail her shins. No response to that, either, and then she climbed on back up the embankment, then the slope, and disappeared. Maybe it was my imagination, but I don't think she wore underwear.

My father said, "You're wasting your time. Tell me again what you're looking for? There are rocks that look like lungs and liver and maybe kidneys. Fingers. Spleen. In all my years I ain't seen no heart-shaped rocks come out of the river, without they being chiseled."

I didn't tell my father I'd seen one, that I'd used it to skip toward the girl across the way, and that now I wanted to retrieve and give it to her. I said, "I thought I'd give it to Mom for Valentine's Day. She's always saying how bought things don't mean as much to her as handmade things."

He looked at me hard. I could tell from his eyes that he knew I'd found one, that I'd tossed it back, and so on. "Like a real human heart with ventricles? That might be tough. I've seen knobs on oak trees that looked such, but not rocks." He pointed at an oak tree behind us, behind the house, up on a bluff.

"No. Like a Valentine's Day heart, you know." I held my index fingers in the air and made the sign of the heart.

"The water's cold, so put on some waders. And don't tell your mother about this little project."

My father looked like a science classroom's poster that details a man's sinews, tendons, ligaments, and muscles. He mostly kept a blank expression. He gave off a pinkish hue. All the years of pulling rocks out of a river, inspecting them, then stacking rocks into their appropriate chicken wire enclosures atop pallets—as a child he, too, worked for his father at Carolina Rocks—pretty much never gave him reason to join a gym. I said, "Why would I tell Mom? It's going to be a surprise."

I looked up at our long log house on the hill. I imagined my mother inside, thumbing through another book on reincarnation that she special ordered. My father said, "Find as many as you can, Stet. I won't charge you. Just make sure to stack them apart from all the other rocks." He smiled. I should've understood that he formulated tricks, ulterior motives, flat-out mean-spirited plans. He wiped his hands on my shoulders. "I know! Set aside what you find in the shed next to your expired milk and bread."

I said, "Okay." I said, "Thank you, sir."

My father shook his head and laughed. "Why'd you throw the first one you ever found right back into the river?"

I'm not sure why my only answer came out, "Catch and release."

***

My grandfather had installed makeshift spotlights back in the 1960s, when Carolina Rocks ran two shifts. He had sunk telephone poles on down the river in fifty-yard intervals, each with its own lamp and switch. My father came back from Vietnam, married my mother before he found out that she'd spent two years reading up on reincarnation while he hunkered down in rice paddies, and slowly watched the family business dwindle in regards to supply. I'm not sure if I spontaneously formed the power of logical and rational thought, but something told me to go downstream, turn on one of the lights, and scoop for heart-shaped rocks farthest from my house. This was on a flat piece of bottomland where my grandfather once tried to raise pigs: He had built a three-sided pen that led straight into the river, not knowing that pigs swam. They escaped soon thereafter, turned feral, evidently mated often, and roamed these southernmost regions of what people mistook for the Blue Ridge Mountains. My father said often if he leased the land off to boar hunters it would make up financially for a lack of available flat rocks, but he couldn't in good conscience because of what he learned in Vietnam. He never explained the connection, and I knew better than to ask.

I came home from school at newly constructed Andrew Jackson Prep—home of the fighting Jacks, whatever that meant—threw my books down on my desk, said hello to my mother if she didn't seem in a trance, and made my way down to the river. Andrew Jackson Prep, by the way, wasn't a white-flight school. The student population ran fifty-fifty in terms of blacks and whites. There weren't any Cherokees, though, I guess because of a certain collective unconsciousness that ran deep in the Native American community in regards to the man who herded a slew of them off to Oklahoma. Anyway, I got down there and threw a special chicken wire box out into the water, let it settle down, then pulled it back with a rope. On my first throw ever I culled two black rocks, both perfect Valentine's hearts the size of a rubber coin purse. I looked across the river, then upstream, spying for my first-ever girlfriend. I dumped the river silt and pebbles onto the bank, then cast again.

Was her name something like Rosemary? I wondered. She looked like a Rosemary to me. Or maybe a Heidi. I imagined a slew of names, and knew that the girl with no underwear wasn't named something like Gertrude—there was an Aunt Gertrude I'd read about once in one of those Hardy Boys books. She exclaimed a lot of things *excitedly* and *eagerly*, just like Frank and Joe, their friend Chet, and every other goddamn character.

I pulled out a few more heart-shaped stones on the first day, washed them off nicely, and carried them up to where the dead milk and bread thrived. My arms hurt. I imagined handing over these stones to Rosemary or Heidi or Emma-Marie, and her commenting on the size of my biceps from drawing the rock-trap ashore like some kind of river marlin.

On that first night I came inside late for supper. My father looked at me and raised his eyebrows. I nodded. He said, "Good."

My mother—who had contacted a number of antique dealers throughout the South and bought high-school yearbooks from them because she felt as though, sooner or later, someone would either become famous or infamous and then she could resell the things—looked up from her chair. "Clean up," she said. "That little girl you're looking for only gets to come out on Fridays, if you're wondering. I've kept track."

I looked at her and squinted. "What?" How could she know? I thought.

"She'll be out again on Valentine's Day. Her name's Cecilene."

Cecilene! That was close enough to Rosemary or Heidi, I thought.

When my mother looked down again I jerked my head for my father to follow me into the kitchen. I turned on the tap and washed my hands. "Did you tell her what I was doing? Does she know I'm trying to find her some rocks for Valentine's Day?" My father shook his head. He said, "I didn't tell her. What's all this talk about a girl? Are you getting rocks for this girl, or for your mother?"

I said, "I found five the first day. Go out to the shed and tell me they don't look exactly like cut-out paper hearts."

My father put his finger to his lips. Loudly he said, "Now sit down at the table and eat every bean and pea on your plate." In the den he said to my mother, "I need to go work on a motor."

While I ate supper my mother said, "This 1942 Forty-Five High School yearbook has nothing in it. I guess the boys went off to war and either got killed, or too shell shocked to become either talented or wicked. One thing that you can count on, Stet Looper—if you want to make a mark on this planet in any of your lives, you need to be talented or wicked, one or the other."

I daydreamed about inventing a personal jet pack, skipping over the river to meet Cecilene, then pulling her dress all the way off.

★★★

Maybe we had not paid enough attention to the smaller rocks over the years, for I ended up with three dozen smooth heart-shaped river rocks, all ranging in size from a half-dollar to the palm of my hand. They also, in an odd way, looked like miniature versions of the state of South Carolina when turned slightly one way or the other. On Valentine's Day morning I took off for the outbuilding early and set them across the top of Mom's expired foodstuffs. I arranged them from smallest to largest, from lightest to darkest, from first to last found. I placed them in a flat box that once housed the 1955 Louisville Male High School yearbook that my mother felt certain would include probable maniacs and/or politicians. I retrieved them one by one and replaced them in a velvety purple Crown Royal pouch, then pulled the drawstrings tightly. Perfect, I thought. I looked around the outbuilding and noticed how there must've been a hundred such bags stacked around the place, and thought about putting one stone heart in each, but didn't.

I made my way to the end of our clay-rutted drive. I waited for the bus, which showed up about 6:30 because the students of Andrew Jackson Prep lived scattered around a forty-mile stretch of scenic Highway 11.

I don't remember if my classmates handed out cards, or if the cafeteria women baked red cakes, or if the biology teacher made a big point out of teaching us the various nodes of the heart and the importance of cardiovascular exercise. I sat staring out the window, imagining what Cecilene's voice sounded like, and how she'd squeal out, "This is the nicest thing anyone's ever done for me!" I envisioned her living in a giant house the next ridge over, and that she didn't attend my school because her father employed a host of experts to come in daily and offer the latest in lectures. Or, I envisioned her poor as a bucket of chicken livers, and having to work in her father's one-man sawmill. But at least her daddy didn't beat her, I talked myself into believing, since he had no fingers left. And then I jumped forward ten years and saw Cecilene and me graduating from college, and coming back home to merge our family businesses together, and building state-of-the-art solar powered mountain retreats, half rock, half lumber.

I got home from school long before four o'clock and took off running down our drive, straight for the outbuilding. I hoped that I wasn't too late, and tried to remember when I'd seen Cecilene on the other side of the river those few times. Over the entire week I had it all planned out: I would go down to the most shallow part of the river near where I found my stones, cross over holding my shoes

226

and socks in one hand and the rocks in the other, then follow a deer trail that meandered more or less on the opposite side until I reached her. That's the point where she'd tell me it was the nicest thing ever, and so on.

But the rocks weren't atop the bin of expired milk and bread where I'd left them.

My Crown Royal pouch wasn't anywhere to be found.

I think I said, "Fuck *me*," in a way that might've sounded menacing and realistic for the first time, at least coming out of my mouth. And right afterwards I heard my mother up on the hill inside our house. She screamed and cried out in between the unmistakable sound of shattering glasses and plates. There were dull thuds emanating from up there, too—which ended up being her yearbooks hitting my father's torso, I found out soon thereafter.

When I reached the porch my father ran out past me. He didn't make eye contact, but said, "You owe me, boy." He made it to his truck, and I swear I saw it move in a wide reverse arc before I even heard the engine start. He took off driving away, red dust hanging in the dry, abnormally warm February air.

My mother pelted the tailgate with a handful of my heart-shaped stones and yelled, "That's what you think? You think I need more hearts of *stone* to go with the one you've already given me over these years?"

I said, "Hey, those are my rocks."

My mother looked down at me, breathing hard. Her heavy mascara—I'd not seen her wear make-up before, and learned later that she wanted to look sexy, or partake in some kind of role-playing game best known to married couples in a rut—ran down both sides of her face and met at the tip of her chin. She said, "Was this your idea, Stet Looper? Did you put your father up to handing me a *sack* full of *rocks* for goddamn Valentine's Day?"

I said, "They kind of look like the state of South Carolina, too," and went down the steps to retrieve what had bounced off my father's truck bed.

My mother said, "That's even worse, reminding me where we're stuck forever."

★★★

I gathered the rocks that I could find. A couple had chipped in my mother's tirade. One was stuck more than halfway in the den's sheet-rock. There were those few outside. The Crown Royal pouch was half on fire in the kitchen sink. My mother had made some cookies, which were now broken on a cooling rack atop the stove. She said, "I made some gingerbread cookies for you to give Cecilene. They were shaped like Airstream trailers, you know, because I think she lives in one over at the RV park, Stet Looper. Tell her the goddamn things got hit by a tornado. Maybe y'all can treat them like puzzle pieces and put the trailers back together."

I didn't know if my mother had ESP, if my father told on me, or what. I do know that he, at this point in his life, didn't have enough imagination to think up his own romantic gifts and that it backfired in his face. For about a minute I thought, Maybe I shouldn't offer the stones. But then I remembered what my mother once told me: True love relies on percentages. She said that all newlyweds should buy their wedding bands at pawn shops, for the rings couldn't be tainted bad luck forever. She had told me that she wished that she and my father hadn't spent so much money on brand new bands bought from one of those mall jewelry outlets.

Without waders I crossed the Unknown Branch of the Saluda River, hearts in my pockets and cookies in a bag, too determined to care about the most shallow stretch of water. I trudged in at the closest point from our house, kept my head lifted, and pretended that I never slipped on flat rocks my father would one day dredge up and sell to people who read gardening magazines and how-to books. On the other side I whisked my wet pants from the knees on down. I walked up the embankment where I'd viewed Cecilene's underside, found the cleared deer run, and followed it parallel and upwards from the river.

Did I expect to reach the ridge top, look down, and see a spar-kling vibrant village with Cecilene standing front and center? Yes. I'd seen something similar in a movie. Was I disappointed when I got to the apex and only saw more woods—though it looked as if the treetops had been lopped off ten to twenty feet up their trunks, probably from past wind storms—stretching down to a valley? May-be. Did it occur to me that most twelve-year-old boys would've had the curiosity to cross the river at least once when his parents weren't home, just to see what was on the other side? Not until years later, after I'd finished off a few bachelor's degrees and embarked on a low residency master's in Southern Culture Studies did I realize that maybe I feared my father's vengeance in an abnormal way, which hampered my sense of adventure.

I got scared and dropped my mother's Airstream trailer cookie parts about every ten steps, should I need to find my way back home.

And then there sat Cecilene, in the branches of an unaffected oak tree. I will always remember her first words she spoke down to me: "You *pee* on yourself?"

I am not too proud to say that I jumped about four feet off the ground. I had not seen her at first, seeing as I paid more attention to the ground. I looked up and, sure enough, she didn't know how to cross her legs in any kind of manner outlined in an etiquette book. She wore a faded cotton dress the color of the tree bark, and what I had thought was her naked nether regions ended up being a seam in her pantyhose. What girl my age wore pantyhose in the woods? Cecilene.

I said, "No. I crossed the river."

From in the tree she said, "You feeding squirrels?"

I couldn't think of a lie. I said, "With spring coming I thought maybe they'd be hungry."

I watched her eyes follow my trail of trailer park cookies. She said, "What's your name?"

"Stet."

"Oh, yeah, that's right. Stet Looper. Sometimes I hear your moth-er calling you. Sometimes I hear your mother yelling out for you.

She always uses both names." Cecilene climbed down the tree. As I inspected her legs I thought she had a skin condition until I realized that her hose had a number of runs.

I said, "And you're Cecilene."

Cecilene didn't seem surprised that I knew her name. She turned to face me, looked down, and said, "You got something in your pocket?"

I thought she talked about something else, of course. I stood there like a helpless freak, staring at her. Up close she was prettier than I imagined. Her eyes and hair matched in an unnatural way—a deep brown that made me think of chocolate. I said, "Uh-huh." I said, "Where are you from? Do you go to school? Where are you from? Do you go to school?" and I would've continued looping these two questions had she not interrupted.

"My daddy's a zoologist. We live mostly up and down the Appalachian Trail, and sometimes on some islands off the coast of Georgia. My father studies wild boar and feral domesticated pigs. He promises that this might be the last year, though. If he gets a grant to study the armadillos and fire ants, we'll have to move between Texas and Alabama. Right now we're waiting for sows to have their litters. I helped my daddy tag them, last year."

I tried to figure out a logical marriage of businesses between a river rock tycoon and a pig watcher's daughter, but couldn't. In a way I was disappointed that her father wasn't the gruff sawmill operator I had imagined. I said, "Oh, in my pockets, yeah!" and reached in to pull out the heart-shaped stones I'd recovered. I said, "Happy Valentine's Day."

Cecilene inspected them one by one, held them to the sunlight, traced their edges. She said, "They look like hearts. Did you make these?"

I shook my head. "They were in the river. I got them out of the river."

Cecilene—and it would take me another twenty years before I understood this—dropped one rock into a front pocket on her dress. She said, "I'll take *one*. Give me another next year, if we come back this way. But go put the rest back in a spot on the river so they'll be easy to find. You can see how much smaller they get as the years go by. You can see how much the friction diminishes these different hearts of yours. And if I don't ever see you again, you can give them to other girls. I'll understand."

I stared at her a little too long trying to figure out what she was saying. I said, "So you just get home schooled?" For the first time in my life I felt as though I had been sheltered, that my parents had shaded me from some of the secrets of life. Understand that this was 1985, and I had only heard about things like video games, or cable television, or drugs.

Cecilene leaned over and kissed me on the lips. She said, "Happy Valentine's Day back at you." She pulled her head way back and said, "That little scar on your cheek—were you born Caesarian and the forceps got you?"

I shrugged. Like most things, no one ever told me. Cecilene said, "I was born breech. I'll show you my scar another time, maybe."

And then she skipped away through the woods, in a manner, I imagined, that girls skipped away from the Hardy Boys. On my way back home I picked up the pieces of my mother's trailer cookies, but they'd already gone bad, turned hard as rocks, expired.

★★★

I stomped onto the porch, shivering at this point for a variety of reasons. I needed to shake excess water from my pants, but I also wanted to announce my presence should my parents be mid-knife fight. When I entered the front room and looked over at the dining room table, I found my parents seated, a vase of red roses between them. Both smiled at me. My mother said, "Oh, Lord, Stet Looper, how'd you get your pants so wet and dirty?"

"Go change your clothes, son, and get on back here," my father said. He patted the table top.

I said, "I went across the river to look for that Cecilene girl, and then I buried the rest of the stones in case we ever want to see them again."

"Good for you!" my mother squealed out. She seemed ecstatic. Was there a fight not three hours earlier? I wondered. She said, "In one of my high-school yearbooks I noticed they had a geology club. They dug things up. You bury them. You're kind of like the anti-geology club."

My father slapped his knee and pulled his head back, laughing. "He's like the anti-Looper—we've been digging up river rocks for fifty years, and he goes and hides them." My parents tried to high-five each other across the table. Both of them accidentally brushed the roses.

For some reason I felt like I might cry. Was this some kind of Valentine's Day ruse? Had they play-fought to see how I would re-act? And was my reaction—to go traipsing off across the river and get scared and dole out cookie crumbs in case I got lost on what ended up being, I learned years later, about a three-hundred-yard trek—the one they expected? Maybe they thought it was time I quit moping alone forever, and it was the only way they knew how to get me across the river toward the only girl—phantom as she may have been—within a five-mile radius.

I said, "Are y'all drunk?" and went in my room to change my wet pants. When I came back my parents still sat there. Neither parent had brought dishes to the table, and the scents of supper didn't fill the room. The light failed from outside. No one got up to turn on a lamp. Even the television wasn't turned to the one channel we received without static.

My mother said, "I have an idea," and got up. She returned from the pantry with a variety of half-burned candles arranged on a cookie sheet. My father pulled a matchbook from his front pocket and began to light them. My mother went back to what my parents called "the office," and came back with a stack of high-school yearbooks. She also brought along two photo albums that contained off-centered Po-laroids of my birth.

My father said, "I hate to be a baby, but I don't know if I can stomach some of the pictures. They're grisly."

My mother said, "Luckily I couldn't see the incision from my vantage point. Or the blood." To me she said, "Tell me the truth: Were those rock hearts supposed to be for me, or for your secret girlfriend?"

My father said, "I'm not talking about the pictures of the boy's birth. I'm talking about the mug shots of all those kids with acne, back in the day."

I opened a high-school yearbook right to a group shot of the Forty-Five High School's Home Ec Club. There was one male in a group of two dozen women. I flipped some pages and found the same guy in the Future Farmers of America, the Glee Club, and the French Club. There he was again in chorus, in the band, and as one of the office aides. He received Most Likely to do something, but it had been scratched over completely. I thought, How pathetic: This will be the high point in this fool's life, unless he goes on a killing spree in need of notoriety.

I opened up the photo album—which I realized would be my yearbook should I be homeschooled like Cecilene—and turned to a picture of my mother in a hospital bed pre-delivery. She gave my father the finger, but smiled.

I wanted to vote myself Most Likely to Discover Something.

I could smell the roses from where I sat. Peripherally I noticed that my parents, in the candlelight, breathed deeper than usual.

Inside "Voted Most Likely": Our Never-Dry Well

It took me until I was forty years old before I realized that there was a never-dry well in regard to adult characters looking back at bizarre conflicts they underwent as children. Although we probably don't realize it while growing up, each day presents something scary, awe-inspiring, enigmatic, or comedic. Old dogs might stretch out on the back porch and barely watch a toad hop by, but a puppy will go

YOU MUST BE THIS TALL TO RIDE

berserk at the promise of a new experience, and so it is with adult narrators coming to terms with all the rites of passage they have, somehow, endured.

I had been writing a series of stories about Stet Looper as an adult, after he made the decision to turn his back on the landscape rock business that had been in his family for three generations, and right at the point where he decided to get a master's degree from a low-residency outfit called Ole Miss-Taylor. Sometimes the stories came right into my head, and sometimes they didn't. When I felt as though I'd become brain dead—or more brain dead, I suppose—I dropped my bucket into that never-dry well and tried to find out how this Stet Looper fellow grew up on the rock farm in order to become the kind of character he seemed to be.

So for "Voted Most Likely," I intended only to have a little girl on the other side of the river, existing as a siren of sorts. That was it. I wanted Stet to find a heart-shaped rock, and I wanted him to offer it to Cecilene. I had found a heart-shaped rock at Wrightsville Beach in North Carolina a year earlier, and kept it on my writing desk alongside about a hundred other oddities that range from rat skull to the mouthpiece of a tuba that I found, also, on the beach. (Who is playing tuba on the beach? What person attacked the tuba player, thus causing him to run away, dropping his silver-plated Clements Ensemble mouthpiece? That's another story, I imagine.)

When, for some reason, it cropped up that the father would steal his own son's heart-shaped rocks, I probably said, "Yes!," to myself, but I had not planned on that little juke step in the story. Likewise, I had no clue that the mother would get angry at receiving rocks from a rock farmer for Valentine's Day.

Also, in the original story I portrayed Cecilene as the daughter of sharecroppers, or hermits, or ne'er-do-wells. How in the world did her father become a zoologist tracking down wild boar in the southernmost part of the Blue Ridge chain? Easy: As I wrote the story, I read a local news article about how there are wild boar, and there are feral pigs. I thought, *Hey, I bet I can jam that idea into the story I'm working on.* Plus, some kind of animal had been rooting around in my front yard—I live out in the country, across from a tree farm—and I became slightly obsessed with thinking that it might be a wild pig escaped. Or one of the supposedly extinct dinosaurs that still roams these parts.

Originally, I saw bins of grocery items in an outbuilding with Stet Looper's birthday stamped on them for expiration dates. Not that I was thinking, *Hey, that might be symbolic!*, for sitting around trying to think up "symbolic" moments or images is about as useful to the writer as three thumbs might be for the visual artist. This expiration-date idea came from my buying a pack of Goody's Headache Powders with my birthday stamped on the cardboard box. But I had no clue that the mother would be a collector of high-school yearbooks. In a way, it adds to her sadness—she spends her time poring over the lives of eighteen-year-olds, and imagines how their lives turned out, not living with a man who dredges rocks out of a river, then steals from his son in order to give his wife rocks. As my own little joke, I included the 1955 Louisville Male High School yearbook, because gonzo journalist Dr. Hunter S. Thompson's picture is in that particular edition. I put in the thing about Forty-Five High School because I've published some collections of stories that take place in imaginary Forty-Five, where no one ever got famous or infamous.

I don't think I've ever had a notion about how a story will—or should—end, so that scene with Stet and his parents sitting quietly at the table came as a surprise to me. I had no clue that he would look at a yearbook, or look at the family album of his own birth. Some editors like for stories' endings to come back and hold hands with the beginning of the story. I guess that's what I did, seeing as the story starts with a mention of his birth.

So to summarize, I began "Voted Most Likely" with the image of a rock. One sentence led to another. One image led to the next. A bunch of happenstance occurred along the way.

WRITING EXERCISE

If a story can be reduced down to its basic elements, a protagonist wants or needs something and the antagonist(s) stands in the way. Writing from a first-person point of view, start off a story with the narrator being a hundred feet away from a person he or she wants to meet or talk to. In between, have obstacles. If the two characters are in, say, a high-school cafeteria, the narrator must think about getting out of his seat, passing through a bunch of jocks and cheerleaders and the geeks who will never be brave enough to act thusly, a mean teacher-monitor, and so on. When the protagonist gets there, see what happens.

In the first sentence, make sure there's an obvious conflict. "I needed to ask Lois if she'd let me copy her homework," or "... go with me to the dance," whatever. In the opening paragraph or four, explain the situation and be descriptive. When the narrator finally approaches the antagonist, begin dialogue, for that automatically causes some action.

Other places to set this scene might be a mall, church, restaurant, party, park, and so on. You can pick and choose about a thousand of these scenarios, I promise.

Otis Is Resurrected

It was three days after our old man died that my brother Donald accomplished the most spectacular deed of his life. I wish I could have been there to see it: Donald taking the Greyhound down to Nogales all by himself, buying the baby armadillo for eight hundred pesos from a pie-faced Indian woman at the Santa Acuna market, tucking the little thing under his arm like a football and running the length of the pedestrian border station, past the heat-struck tourists in their sombreros and loud socks and the guards with their sidearms and walkie-talkies, pushing through the last steel-toothed turnstile and sprinting like a madman into the heart of the Nogales slums.

It was his proudest moment, though it did take him the rest of the day and half the night of wandering among the hookers and street corner punks to find a bus that would bring him back to Ajo. I don't know how he managed not to get robbed or killed or at the very least his teeth kicked in, but there he was after I came home from hours of frantic searching, sitting stiff-backed on the couch, beaming. The little armadillo was rooting at the crotch of his pants and Donald's pink sweating face had screwed itself up with such a grin of utter self-satisfaction you might have thought he was right in the middle of an orgasm.

Donald ended up giving the armadillo to me. A present, he said, something to make me feel better. I thanked him, took the armadillo,

237

which clawed at my t-shirt like a cat, and gave it a little squeeze. What else could I do?

My father had worked as a janitor for twenty-one years, but he was also a reader of books, a scholar—if it is possible to be a both a scholar and a sixth-grade dropout—and one of his favorite subjects was zoology. He could bore you into a coma with what he knew about the great horned owl or the common mealworm or the laughing hyenas of Africa. But of all the beasts of the animal kingdom, he loved and admired the humble armadillo most.

"Nope, not the smartest or prettiest," he would say when one of them scatted across the highway in front of our old Le Mans, "but the hardiest, you see what I'm saying, the most resourceful."

He often promised he would get us an armadillo for a pet, but he died before he could come through: an end-all heart attack standing in line at the grocery store. His heart pretty much exploded inside him and he went down so fast, dropped with such a suddenness, that the other customers thought he'd been shot, victim of a drive-by or some such, and hit the deck themselves to avoid the gunfire.

I was seventeen, Donald nineteen. Our mother, a Guatemalan migrant worker who had married my father under the impression he would one day be a rich man who could buy her a Cadillac and a house with a swimming pool, had run off when we were babies, so it was just the two of us now. It took me about a week to get over the shock and then I did what I had to: I dropped out of school, started working full time pouring concrete for Hassenpheffer's and moved Donald and me to a cheaper apartment near the McComb and Sons wrecking yard, where Donald could watch the cars getting pulverized from our bedroom. We got money from the state that paid for Donald's medication, but the rest was up to me. I toyed with the idea of finding a job for Donald—maybe Burger King or Goodwill could find something for him to do—but in the end decided against it. A few years back our father had tried to help Donald get a job— he thought it would do wonders for Donald's self-esteem. Donald worked for one day at a taco shop (fired for handing out the tacos

free of charge) and lasted about twenty minutes as a restroom atten-
dant at the English Acres Country Club (peering over the tops of
toilet stalls).

Donald was really something else. What could be done with a
guy who ate his own earwax? Who carried a maroon mini-Bible in
the band of his underpants and read random scriptures out loud at
inappropriate times? Who could be sashaying about the room one
minute, doing a dead-on impression of Sammy Davis Jr. and the next
be downstairs in the closet grunting like a pig and trying to tear his
hair out?

My father wanted to believe that Donald was some kind of eccen-
tric genius, or at least a savant who had an amazing but as-of-yet un-
discovered mathematical or musical skill. By the time Donald turned
twelve, my father finally gave in and took him to see a series of doctors, who confirmed for us what we had suspected all along: Donald
was seriously fucked up. Manic depression, schizophrenia, obsessive-
compulsive disorder—a whole list of diagnoses, none of which solved
anything except to keep Donald where everybody but my father
agreed he belonged: finger-painting and making crafts out of maca-
roni and popsicle sticks with the other Special Ed nitwits at school.

From a distance, you wouldn't have been able to tell him from any
other teenager. He had relatively good hygiene, did not usually talk to
himself in public, and was something of a handsome devil with his dark
hair hanging down over pale green eyes. Sometimes, I would take
him to a party or a dance with me and the girls would flock around us.
He could be as charming as Hugh Hefner in short bursts, quoting his
scriptures or doing a dead-ringer for Perry Como, before he'd have to
run off and hide in the bathroom.

I remember once when I was nine or ten and we were playing in
the backyard. He kept pestering me, saying, "I am the Indian, you are
the cowboy, okay?" I told him to shut his trap, I was busy building a
cave for my army men. He wouldn't give up, "Me Indian, you cowboy, okey-dokey?" Over and over. "Damnit, Donald, you freak!" I
hollered. "Do whatever you want, but just shut up for a second!"

"I'm not a freak," he said, sticking his chin out.

"Alright, then," I said. "You're a retard extraordinaire."

The next time I looked up Donald was on top of the doghouse with the bow and arrow set my father had bought for him at a garage sale. He had the arrow notched and pulled back to his ear, just like the Indians we saw on TV. I hadn't noticed before, but now I saw that he had taken off his shirt and tucked it in the elastic of his shorts so it looked like he was wearing a loincloth and had used a little blood from the scab on his elbow to make fiendish red streaks across his face. He was doing it perfect, really, just like a TV Indian, an honest-to-God savage. I didn't believe he would really shoot me, so I just sat there like a jackass, my hands full of dirt. I didn't see him let go of the bowstring but I certainly did hear the *thop!* the arrow made when it hit me in the chest, dead-center. More from the surprise than anything, I fell flat on my back. It was a target arrow, with a rounded, dull point, but it pierced my sternum just enough to stand upright from my chest, waving around sluggishly like a reed in a river.

I lay in the grass and stared up at the neon yellow fletching of the arrow. My hands were still full of dirt. Donald jumped down from the doghouse and stood over me. He was smiling an odd, satisfied smile, as if he was expecting to be congratulated on his marksmanship. He looked down at me for a long time before he gently put his hand around the shaft of the arrow without pulling it out.

He said, "Right smack-dab in the heart, white man."

★★★

I told Donald I wanted him to name the armadillo. After several days of deliberation he decided to name it after Otis, the happy drunk on *The Andy Griffith Show*, who our father had resembled in almost eerie detail.

The first time we saw *The Andy Griffith Show* was the day we got our first TV, a little black-and-white Zenith with a twelve-inch screen. When Otis, unshaven and blubbering drunk, walked in to the courthouse to allow himself to be incarcerated for the weekend, Donald grabbed both his ears and screeched "Oh no, it's Pop!" half terrified, half overjoyed at this development: our own daddy showing up on television. Donald might have been fucked up in all kinds of ways, but he wasn't an out-and-out idiot; it wasn't long before he understood that it wasn't our dad at all, just somebody who could have passed for his identical twin. Still, he never missed an episode of Opie and Aunt Bee and Barney Fife and all their many hijinks, and he would whistle that peppy goddamn theme song until I had to lock myself out of the house just to keep from throttling him.

I got used to taking care of Donald alone—I had no choice—but Otis was a different story. First of all, Otis *smelled*. He gave off a musky odor that intensified whenever he was nervous or hungry and no matter if we scrubbed him raw with industrial soap and water, the smell would come back in a hour or so. And then there was the furniture. Armadillos are burrowing animals—this is something I learned from my father—and in the confines of our small apartment Otis didn't have many opportunities to burrow. Instead, he would march through the house like a tiny gray tank and move the furniture around. One of his favorite tricks consisted of wedging his body between the wall and refrigerator and puffing his sides out, moving the whole refrigerator inches at a time. Once bored with that, he'd waddle into the living room, put his blunt forehead against one of the legs of the coffee table and bear down, inching it around the room, his little squirrel-claws scrabbling on the wood floor. At least once a week, without fail, he would crawl between the mattress and box springs of my bed and take a dump. My father was right about armadillos: They are hardy, they are resourceful, and if Otis is typical, are as dumb as donkey shit. Sometimes, in the course of his incessant apartment wandering, Otis would find himself trapped in a corner and would spend the rest of the evening attempting to claw his way out.

I never considered getting rid of him, even though it was like living with a large, dim-witted rat. Otis was technically my pet, but Donald cared for him, worried over him, tormented him, teased him, then made up with tearful professions of regret and affection. While I was away at work they would do things together. Donald would carry Otis around outside, conversing with him, rooting in the weeds in the vacant lot, searching for earthworms or crickets for Otis's dinner. He also liked to build obstacle courses in the apartment with pillows and end tables and couch cushions, all of which Otis could bulldoze in a matter of seconds. Sometimes, while Otis was going about his business, oblivious to everything else, Donald would hide behind the recliner and when Otis passed by, would jump out and shout in a high soprano wail, "LOOK OUT, OTIS!" Poor Otis would spring two feet into the air, like a startled cat, his leathery body twisting, his claws clutching at nothing and once he'd landed he'd scurry into the hallway, looking back over his shoulder, embarrassment in those little piggy eyes.

This kind of living arrangement was no boost to my social life, I can tell you. If I ever wanted to bring a girl home, I figured I'd have some difficulty explaining why the apartment smelled like a bear's den, why the furniture was strewn around as if a hurricane had blown through, why my brother was naked and hiding behind the couch waiting to scare the daylights out of an armadillo.

It took five years before I found someone I loved enough to bring home. Allison was good about everything, told me I was a saint and a Christian to be taking care of Donald, off in the head as he was. She was so wonderful and beautiful and good-smelling I could barely stand it, and we made love that first night on the floor of our apartment, while Donald snored happily under his bed and Otis watched us like a little night-devil from his special spot behind the refrigerator.

About a week later I proposed to her, after which I went home to talk to Donald. It was springtime in the desert, the smell of cactus blossoms everywhere, and I was so full of love and desire I could barely see straight. Allison and I had decided that we would get an apartment nearby, that with my new promotion at Hassenpheffer's and Allison's job at the county courthouse, we could afford our own place and, with the help of the government, support Donald. Donald would be all right as long as we checked on him daily, made sure he was taking his medication, occasionally washed the place down with ammonia so the smell wouldn't bother the neighbors.

I have to admit the thought of escaping from Donald and Otis and that cave of an apartment was almost as enticing as the thought of being together with Allison. I loved my brother, but that night I felt a weight lifting; I had caught a whiff of the sweet scent of freedom, like a prisoner on the verge of escape.

At home, when I sat Donald down to explain things to him, I could barely get a word out; I stuttered and stammered, kept wiping my mouth. When I finally made things clear, Donald whipped out his mini-Bible and frantically paged through it but couldn't seem to come up with anything—the first time I had ever seen him at a loss for a scripture. He yanked at his hair and ground his teeth together until they squeaked. Finally, without saying anything, he snatched up Otis, who had been napping under one of the couch cushions, went into the laundry room, and slammed the door behind him.

I felt like kicking that door down and wringing his neck—couldn't he at least try to be happy for me, to think of somebody other than himself for one minute? I went outside by the stairwell to cool off a little, settle my mind. There was a fat moon out and down in the junkyard a coyote, white and gliding like a ghost, passed between the tangled mountains of ruined cars. No, I did not want to be here anymore. I wanted only to be with Allison, and I hated Donald for making it so difficult, hated him for the years of responsibility and obligation and lost opportunities, hated him in the way only a brother can hate a brother.

I took a few steps toward the stairwell to leave—I didn't care, I was going to stay at Allison's, my first night ever away from Donald—when I heard a splashing noise from inside the apartment. The laundry room door was locked and I shouted Donald's name, but got no response. I tried to kick in the door, which was made of something like cardboard; my foot went right through it. Once I had my leg free, I looked through the splintered hole and could see Donald hunched over the overflowing utility sink, both arms submerged up to his biceps. The back of his neck was purple and pulsing, full of angry blood, and it took me only a moment to understand he was trying to drown Otis.

I unlocked the door and grabbed him from behind, but he resisted me, grunting and plunging Otis deeper into the water. I wrestled him out into the living room, where we fell sideways against the couch. Donald twisted away from me and stood up, the water dripping off his elbows, forming a puddle around his shoes. Otis was curled up in a ball, just like when he slept, and Donald began to shiver so badly that he lost his grip and let Otis's body slide out of his hands and hit the floor with a wet slap.

Donald's face twisted into a mask of concentrated, unabashed grief. "See?" he wept. "See what I did?"

Looking at my brother, I felt all the parts of me that had been opening up since I had met Allison collapse on each other like so many empty rooms. It would have to be me and Donald, brothers, inseparable, no one else allowed.

I don't remember if I looked away, or if it was as sudden as it seemed, but one moment Otis was a sad, wet corpse, as dead as an armadillo could be, and the next he was huffing and twitching and scrabbling to his feet.

Donald let out an arching shriek, which sent Otis zig-zagging into the kitchen where a mad chase ensued, Donald slipping and flailing, knocking over chairs and pulling down the drapes, still choking and sobbing, now with relief. He finally herded Otis under the table and once he had pulled him out, he held him up, his fingers locked in a death-grip around his little body and cried, "Otis is resurrected! Otis is resurrected!"

★★★

A fair trade: Donald got his armadillo back and I got to marry Allison. Never again did Donald show any sign of jealousy or resentment; he was the best man at our wedding, read a long section from Zephaniah at the reception, even bought us a gift: a book called *Hot Sex for Cold Fish.*

Things went well those first few years. We saved up enough to buy the concrete business from old Hassenpheffer, who retired to ride his Harley around the continent, and Donald and Otis seemed to thrive together. We stopped in to visit as often as we could—Allison cooked dinner for them on Tuesdays and Thursdays—and we paid a house-cleaning service to scrub the apartment down every week, put the furniture back in place, and steam the carpets.

Donald had his first episode one night while I was in Phoenix at a heavy equipment auction. They found him digging up the lawn in front of the City First Bank, blabbering about how difficult it was to find high-grade earthworms on the south end of town. When the cops tried to approach him, he pelted them with dirt clods and threatened to eat a fistful of worms if they got any closer. He spent most of the night in the holding tank before Sheriff Brasky figured out who he was and gave me a call.

We took him to a doctor in Tucson who told us there was nothing to worry about as long as Donald took his medication faithfully. A few months later, Donald climbed an old elm at the city park, which branched out over a sidewalk. He managed to pee on a few passersby before the groundskeeper knocked him off his branch with a well-thrown rake. "Habakuk two-eleven!" he read from his Bible as two deputies wrestled him into their cruiser. "Woe to him that buildeth a town with blood and establisheth a city by iniquity!"

We tried a different doctor, who adjusted his medication and suggested that Donald be put in a home, where he could get the care and attention he needed, where he could socialize with somebody besides an armadillo. I brought up the subject with Donald, but he told me he would rather die than give up Otis to live in a house with a bunch half-wits and knuckleheads. The only other option, we knew, was taking in Donald and Otis ourselves. Allison was eight months pregnant with our second baby, the business was really starting to take off—it just wasn't a good time, we told ourselves, we might be able to work something out in a few months when things had settled down. By the end of the summer, Donald was dead.

The call came in the middle of the night, like they always do. Sheriff Brasky told me that Donald had been hit by a car on 70 near the refinery, where all the construction was. He had run through traffic completely naked, dodging cars and sprinting down the median, until and old couple in a minivan clipped him with their bumper, knocking him over a temporary steel divider and on to a concrete platform where he was partially impaled on a jutting piece of rebar. He bled to death before the ambulance could arrive.

After I went to the hospital to identify his body, I drove out to the accident site. For half an hour I combed both sides of the highway without a flashlight until I found Otis, cowering under a piece of discarded plywood. His left foreleg was mangled, nearly torn from his body, and he was bleeding from the soft flesh of his belly. I could tell by the distant, cloudy look in his eyes that he was in shock. I drove him over to the only veterinarian in town, Larry Oleander, and pounded on the door until he answered. Larry was an old retired cowboy with a glass eyeball and a dent in his head where a mule had kicked him.

"Jesus Geronimo Christ," he said. It was four o'clock in the morning.

I held Otis out to him and he said, "What you have there is an armadillo."

"Fix him up," I said.

"Son," he said, "I don't know what you think ..."

"Save him."

Larry Oleander peered up at me. He wasn't wearing his glasses, but I guess he could see the look on my face, even with only one good eyeball. He sighed and held the screen door open. "Come the fuck on in."

Larry amputated Otis's leg, stitched up the wound on his underside, bandaged him up until he looked like one big wad of gauze. When I tried to pay him he waved his hand in front of my face, took a slug off a bottle of vodka he kept under the operating table. "Jesus, Richard. Just promise me you'll never make a peep about this to anybody."

I took Otis home and he has been a part of our family ever since. Over the last few years, I have added on a wing to the house just for him. He has room with a skylight and two bay windows, his own pillowbed to sleep under and a bunch of old furniture to push around. I put in a little doggy door in the wall and now he can go out and tear up the backyard any time he wants. As far as I am aware, he is the only three-legged armadillo on Earth with his own personal wading pool.

Allison is not thrilled about having an armadillo in her home, never has been, but she knows it's important to me. The kids—we have four of them now—can't stand Otis either. They want another pet: some kind of happy, slobbering dog or an albino snake to impress their friends. Otis is not only *real, real* dumb, they argue, but also *handicapped*, they're not sure which is worse. And his unique stench doesn't get past them, either. The little ones hold their noses and squeal, *He smells like doo-doo!* I tell them they are correct, they'll get no disagreement from me, but Otis is our pet, and we're going to love him no matter what.

I try not to let myself forget how blessed I am: my beautiful family, my dream house up in the hills, a successful business that pretty much runs without me. I am happy and satisfied most of the time, but every so often, maybe once or twice each year, something will come over me, a dark mood that I can't shake, usually at night when everyone is asleep and the house is quiet as a tomb, and I'll get Otis out from under his pillowbed and take him upstairs. I run a bath, sitting on the lip of the tub, holding him close to my chest the way he likes it. When the tub is almost overflowing I take him firmly in both hands and plunge him into the water. There is not a clock in the bathroom, so I count. *One alligator-two alligator-three alligator*—this is how I count off the seconds. Otis struggles like a tiny lion for the first minute or two, writhing and spasming wildly, sending up a boiling foam of bubbles, fighting and scratching with everything he's got, and I hate myself for what I'm doing to him, for what I have to do. Usually between the third and fourth minute is when he starts to lose his will and his thrashing weakens as he gradually curls up in on himself and goes utterly still.

This is always the hardest part for me—the urge to pull him out is almost unbearable—but I go ten or fifteen seconds longer than the last time, until I can't stand it any more. I lift him out and he lies there in my hands, like a deflated soccer ball, and I'm sick with dread, knowing that this time I've taken it too far, I've killed him. I stare down at him and wait, hardly blinking, wait for that first twitch or jerk, for his nostrils to flare with life, and usually there's an almost imperceptible shudder from under his hard shell, a stirring, and his tail will begin to vibrate like a piano wire and he slowly, hesitantly, opens up, stretches himself, clawing the air and coughing like a newborn.

It's at this point that I'm always overcome by the same vision: Donald clutching a newly revived Otis, his face slick with tears, transformed from a man twisted inside out with grief to someone awestruck at the realization that our worst mistakes can be retrieved, that death can be traded in for life, that what has been destroyed can be made whole again.

With a sudden surge Otis struggles to get out of my lap—he is alive and he is an armadillo and there is exploring to do. I let him down and watch him slide around on the linoleum and try to push the toilet off its base and I feel a small, bitter joy lodge in my heart. "Otis is resurrected," I announce, careful not to wake anybody up. I carry him to his room and make sure he is comfortable under his pillowbed and only then will I be able to walk peacefully through the dark, quiet halls of my home, kiss each of my children goodnight, and lie down next to my wife to sleep.

Inside "Otis Is Resurrected": The Core of Longing

As a kid, I was, to put it mildly, obsessed with armadillos. Before I turned eight, I had only a passing interest in the curious little beasts; I'd seen pictures of them, had marveled at their strange habits and alien physiques, but I didn't have any feelings for them beyond the idle curiosity I harbored for, say, the duck-billed platypus or the proboscis monkey of southeast Asia. But then we moved to Texas, and on our drive from New Orleans to Waco, I began to notice what looked like deflated gray footballs scattered among the weeds at the side of the road. I asked my father what they were.

"Armadillos," he said. "Dumbest animal that's ever walked the Earth. Besides maybe the domesticated turkey."

As we drove through the piney woods of western Louisiana, I began to spot more and more of them. A few were flattened into bloody pancakes, and occasionally we passed a dismembered or partial armadillo but, uncharacteristically, I was not too interested in those. I had eyes only for the whole ones, the perfectly intact ones, lying on their sides or backs looking like they were taking a peaceful nap and waiting for someone—a kid like me, say—to pick them up and take them home. I can't say why this feeling overtook me so strongly, but suddenly I couldn't bear the thought of going on in life without an armadillo. I imagined keeping one in my sock drawer or hauling it to school to impress my new hillbilly schoolmates. I considered how striking it might look displayed on the mantle above the fireplace of our new house. Dead or alive, it didn't matter to me in the slightest: I had to have an armadillo.

But how was I going to acquire one? Any number of them were whizzing past my window, tantalizingly close, but I could only assume that my father would have no interest in stopping the car so I could get out and retrieve a dead armadillo from the side of the road. There had to be better way, and I quickly settled on a plan. For a child, claiming the need to use the bathroom is one of the few power plays that has any chance of success, and I made the play for all it was worth. I moaned, I grabbed my stomach and held my breath until my face turned red. When my mother asked what was wrong, I told her I was having a "number two emergency," as we referred to it in my family. My father asked if I couldn't wait until we made it to Beaumont, which was only an hour and a half away, and I moaned louder and writhed on my seat in such a way as to make it clear that if he didn't stop the car soon, he would regret it for the rest of his days.

When I got out of the car, I scanned the highway for armadillos and spotted a promising candidate about a hundred yards away, on the other side of the road. I started across and my mother called out the window to ask what I thought I was doing. I told her I needed my privacy, and the weeds on this side of the road were much too short to provide it. I hustled down the white line and, trying to look natural, picked up the dead armadillo by its skinny tail, which felt solid and potent in my grasp, like the handle of a bullwhip. The body of the armadillo had a good bit of dried blood along its soft underbelly, and a yellow substance that may have been vomit crusted around its mouth, but nothing that wouldn't come off with a good scrubbing.

Just then, my mother began to screech and my father laid on the horn. My brothers and sisters were hanging out the windows of the station wagon laughing and pointing. Instead of immediately stuffing the armadillo under my shirt and hustling back to the car, as I had planned, I had been caught admiring the object of my desire. Certain that I had just ruined my only chance at happiness in life, I gently laid the armadillo back in its resting place next to a flattened Coors can and made a solemn promise to return and retrieve it at the first opportunity.

Life being what it is, such an opportunity never showed itself, and though there were armadillos in the countryside around Waco, they didn't often venture into the part of the city where our house was located. I hunted empty lots, poked around junk heaps and alleyways, but couldn't seem to scare one up. Disappointed by the real world, I turned, as I always have, to books. I read everything I could about the armadillo. I learned, for example, that the armadillo has been around for more than fifty million years and though (as my father pointed out) it is notable for its stupidity, it is also one of the most successfully adaptive species on the planet. If threatened, it can run faster than a human over short distances or burrow itself completely underground in less than a minute. It is as fastidious as a cat, is the only vertebrate in existence capable of natural cloning, and amazingly, has the ability to hold its breath for more than ten minutes, which allows it to cross streams and ponds by simply walking along the bottom until it gets to the other side.

It wasn't long before I was a certified armadillo authority, a connoisseur, a treasure-trove of armadillo-related facts. But all this vital information had no outlet—nobody, not even my ring of nerdy friends, seemed to share my interest in what was obviously the most fascinating creature on God's green Earth.

As I grew older and gradually came to the conclusion that I wanted to be a writer, I decided that I could work out my armadillo obsession in stories and poems and possibly the occasional heavy-metal ballad. But the poems turned out to be nothing more than lists of armadillo facts, the stories bad knockoffs of *Charlotte's Web*, and why don't we just forget about the heavy-metal ballads. I came to realize a few things. One was that a lot of interesting facts do not a good poem or story make. Another was that animals tend not to make good fictional characters because what interests us is people, and to make an animal compelling, it must be turned into a person. And finally: The easiest way to ruin a heavy-metal ballad is by putting an armadillo in it.

I graduated from college, got married, published my first book and still had not fulfilled my ambition of creating the greatest armadillo-related work of literary art known to humankind (along the same lines, I had also failed in my campaign to get my wife to agree to let me keep a pet armadillo in the house). I tried to shoehorn armadillos into nearly every story I wrote, even considered writing a children's book in which a plucky young armadillo named Tom walks across the bottom of the Atlantic Ocean in search of his addled grandmother, but nothing seemed to work. And then one day at a family reunion, I mentioned my interest in armadillos to my Uncle Tim, who told me the story of how, as a young man in his early twenties, he had smuggled a baby armadillo across the Mexican border and kept it as a pet for more than a year before it ran away, never to be seen again. He said that he had bought it from an Indian woman in a Nogales market, and that if he had been caught crossing the border with it, he could have been detained or thrown in jail.

I was floored. Until this moment, I was the only person I knew of who had any interest in armadillos—much less in obtaining one for a pet—and here was someone, my own blood relative, no less, who had managed to pull it off.

I asked him why he would go through so much trouble, put himself at such risk to acquire an animal that Audubon had once described as "a small pig saddled with the shell of a turtle."

"I don't know," he said. "I just wanted one."

It occurred to me then that my armadillo obsession started out in the same way: I just wanted one. And I began to see that the interesting part of my story, and of my Uncle Tim's, was not necessarily the armadillo itself, but in the desire for one. Good stories, I had been taught, are principally about longing. They are about loving something and not being able to have it, or about having something you love and losing it forever. I realized that I could write about an armadillo, but for the story to be compelling, to connect with readers who didn't share my obsession with the strange little creatures, it would also have to be about those most human of emotions: desire and longing and regret. And that is how I came to write "Otis Is Resurrected." I sat down and pounded it out in a few days; it turned out to be one of the easiest stories I've ever written.

The heavy-metal ballad I'm still working on.

WRITING EXERCISE

Think back to your childhood. This is easier for some of us than others, but I can say with reasonable certainty that if you think hard enough, you will remember more than a few obsessions. Make a list of them, and remember that the object of an obsession can be anything: a toy, a person, an event, a television show, an idea. Once you've got yourself a good list, don't dwell on it too much; simply choose one of these obsessions and use it as a springboard for a story or scene. It doesn't need to be central to the plot, necessarily, but it should drive at least one of the characters, who can be a child or an adult (we are all former children, right?). Because this obsession once belonged to you, the writer, it should compel you as well as your characters. This should help you invest your story or scene with an emotional resonance you otherwise may not have been able to achieve.

LAURA VAN DEN BERG

To the Good People of Mars

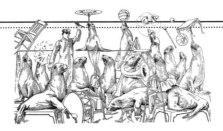

Amelia, my daughter, became obsessed with outer space the summer my husband and I separated. Three nights after I moved out of our house and into a co-worker's spare bedroom, my husband called to tell me that Amelia was building herself a space suit from aluminum foil and that she would only speak to him if their conversations revolved around astronauts. *How do astronauts breathe in outer space?* she wanted to know. *How do they become weightless? How do they learn to float? Once they leave for a space mission, how long do they get to stay away?* When my husband was unable to answer her questions, Amelia started spending all her free time reading books about space travel, and requested her after-school snack and supper be left outside her bedroom door. *This wouldn't be happening if you hadn't left*, my husband told me during one of our conversations (we had agreed to talk on the phone every other night, to try and work things out). I was sitting on my co-worker's living room sofa, staring at the fishbowl on her coffee table. Its sole occupant, a fat, orange goldfish, kept bumping against the glass and then drifting back into the water, as though stunned by the impact. I could hear my co-worker putting away clean dishes in the kitchen, and wondered how hard she was trying to not listen. I reminded my husband of the time he dreamed of being a racecar driver, or when I wanted to become a world famous figure skater. *This is just a phase, one*

of those things that kids do, I said. *You're not seeing what I am*, he replied, then hung up the phone.

Amelia's fascination with space didn't end when my husband and I got back together just after Labor Day, when we tore up the divorce papers and I promised to ignore his moods and he agreed to forget my fling with the man who delivered office supplies to the interior design firm where I worked, helping people chose between granite and marble for their kitchen counters, between sand dollar and silver sage for their bathroom walls. *This goes beyond the imaginings of a normal nine-year-old*, my husband said a few months after we'd reconciled, and by the time the slate-gray skies of winter had come and gone, I was forced to agree. Wandering the house in an aluminum foil space suit and refusing to take off her father's old motorcycle helmet at dinner, the face shield pulled down and gleaming like obsidian, was strange enough, but I didn't start worrying until she lost her appetite for anything but freeze-dried foods, like the astronauts ate, until bricks of dehydrated Neapolitan ice cream, ordered in bulk from a space center in Florida, replaced chicken fingers and meatloaf. She grew paler and smaller; darkness shaded the delicate skin beneath her green eyes. In the night, I would wake to rustling noises coming from her bedroom, and worried she wasn't getting enough sleep. We were called to her elementary school for a conference, during which the principal informed us that Amelia was failing to thrive, and when her report card arrived, it showed her failing every subject except math and science. That evening, my husband shouted—a clear violation of our reconciliation terms—that he'd been right all along, waving the report card over my head. I resisted telling him that I didn't object at first because I didn't want our daughter to inherit his lack of imagination, that I wanted her to keep growing her big, bold dreams.

Each time a billionaire or schoolteacher declared their plans to travel to space, Amelia tried to track them down. When Charles Simonyi, a Microsoft executive, paid the twenty-five-million-dollar orbiting fee and started training at a space center in Kazakhstan, she prepared a letter addressed to his office, asking him to consider her for adoption. I accompanied her to the mailbox, under the guise of helping her send the letter, but returned after she'd left for school and tore open the envelope. I was pained to read that she not only demonstrated her extensive knowledge of planets and moon rocks and told him about keeping photographs of Roberta Bondar and Shannon Lucid tucked underneath her helmet for inspiration, but also wrote about her parents—our bickering about who forgot to refill the salt and pepper shakers, the stacks of files and folders from our offices that competed for room on the kitchen table, the books with titles like *Building the Affair-Proof Marriage* and *The Path to Healing* that cluttered our bedroom floor. *Help me*, I whispered to no one in particular, standing in the driveway, pressing my daughter's letter to my chest. In the end, I threw the letter away and said nothing when Amelia became distraught by Mr. Simonyi's failure to reply. *You'll be ten soon*, I told her. *Don't you think it's time to grow up?* She didn't answer, and when I lifted the black shield of the motorcycle helmet, her head was bowed and tears were streaming down her freckled cheeks.

Just when my husband and I thought we couldn't take it anymore, our midnight fights about Amelia wearing our marriage down faster than any black mood or affair, she gave us this test after dinner. *Knowledge of space*, she told us, *was essential if we wanted to keep being her parents.* Amelia had always been an advanced reader, which pleased us until we saw her test, the questions, both short-answer and multiple choice, listed neatly on college-rule paper, and realized, thanks to the tower of space books in her room, how much more about the solar system—and probably many other things—she knew. Right away, we were flummoxed by questions about the most volcanically active planet in the solar system and how long it takes a space shuttle to reach its orbital speed and the length of Mars's largest valley. Of course, we did not admit defeat, but dutifully wrote a paragraph for each short-answer and circled random letters for the multiple choice, figuring we had a twenty-five percent chance of picking the right one. We consulted each other for some questions, but could never agree on what to select, and I almost always picked a different answer than my husband, just to show him that I wasn't going to be bossed around. *Parents are supposed to know more than you do*, our daughter said after reviewing our test results and announcing she would clearly have to build the space machine on her own, since none of the billionaires or schoolteachers or NASA personnel had replied to her letters—I said nothing about my interceptions, which had not stopped with the letter to Mr. Simonyi—and her own parents didn't know enough to be of any use. *Quite right*, my husband said, then went into the kitchen, opened the bottle of champagne we had been saving for my birthday, and started drinking straight from the bottle.

One weekend in early spring, we decided something had to be done. Since dawn, we'd been listening to Amelia hammer away in the basement, even though neither of us had any idea when she, at nine years of age, had learned to use tools. I argued that telling her to stop thinking about space, that nothing beyond earthly travel is possible, would be a terrible thing, but the astronaut ice cream was getting expensive and I knew I couldn't endure another one of her tests, so I followed my husband down the basement stairs and didn't protest when he threatened to stop her allowance if she didn't curtail her interest in the cosmos. The lights were out in the basement. I heard Amelia working with what sounded like cardboard and wood and maybe a small saw, saw the fleeting beam of her flashlight. *Maybe we need to have an X-ray taken of her brain*, my husband whispered, but before I could reply, Amelia raised the flashlight to her face. Her aluminum foil spacesuit and motorcycle helmet gleamed silver and black; she looked as foreign as a deep-sea creature, and I tried hard to picture the child underneath—pale, frightened, desperate to leave. *You don't understand*, I told her, *your father and I are here to help.* I moved towards her, my arms outstretched like a sleepwalker. My husband trailed behind me, swearing when he stepped on a sharp piece of wood. It was then Amelia shrieked and started waving the flashlight back and forth, as though she was trying to signal a rescue plane, her tin-man arms flapping. It was only after I grabbed her shoulders in the dark and my husband scrambled to hit the lights, only after we pushed aside the lop-sided mass of plywood she'd erected in the center of the basement and took off her helmet and saw a flutter of white paper, that we found the next letter, this one addressed to the good people of Mars, caught in her hair.

Inside "To the Good People of Mars": Experimenting With Language

---

"To the Good People of Mars" emerged from a writing exercise given during a short-short fiction workshop, taught by Pamela Painter, at Emerson College. The exercise Pam gave us was called the "ABC Story." Each sentence of the story had to start with a letter of the alphabet, moving sequentially, so the first sentence began with an "A" word, the next with a "B" word, and so on. The story also had to be written in the first person, but a limited number of sentences could begin with "I." Additionally, we had to have one sentence fragment, one sentence that was exactly one hundred words, and one sentence that was only one word. *And* the story was supposed to be good.

To be frank, this exercise kicked my ass. I remember sitting at my desk and banging my head against the proverbial wall as I struggled to conjure a sentence that would take the story where it needed to go and—as if that wasn't difficult enough—start with the letter "K." Or "O." Or "Q." And we won't even talk about "X" and "Y." Between the assignment of the exercise and the due date, I gathered at the usual MFA watering hole (home of the cheapest drinks and the dirtiest bathrooms in downtown Boston) with my workshop comrades and complained about the exercise. *What's the point of all these rules?* we whined. *Why can't we just write a story?* But we soldiered on and when it came time to read our exercises aloud in class, I was struck by several things. An unusual amount of stories contained the word *Xanadu*, and more than one narrator was a fan of the Xylophone, but that wasn't all! The writing I heard, from myself and from my peers, sounded different. We were trying new sentence structures, new rhythms. Our prose had gotten more ambitious. We were experimenting. Simply put, our linguistic horizons had been broadened. And, of course, this had been the point of the exercise. To make us beat our heads against the wall over language, the very thing we build our fictional worlds and characters from, to push us toward greater invention on the sentence level. In my own draft, I had gotten rather carried away, with a number of hopelessly overstuffed sentences to show for it, but, despite all the kvetching at the bar, I had enjoyed the challenge and was happy to have gotten something on the page that I wanted to keep working with.

In revision, I broke away from the "ABC" format, but the exercise was nevertheless an illuminating experience. As someone who frequently writes in the first person, I hadn't realized how entrenched I had become in the habit of beginning most sentences with "I." The exercise caused me to question old habits, to utilize the same level of imagination with the shaping of my lines as I would with my characters and plot. It made me think harder about every word, the construction and purpose of each sentence. Unlike most of my drafting, during which I usually resist the impulse to line edit, subscribing instead to the "plow through" approach, I wrote "To the Good People of Mars" line by line; I trusted the language to lead me to the story.

But, of course, there were other challenges. Since Amelia's antics build steadily throughout the story, I was somewhat flummoxed by how to end the thing. When a character keeps outdoing herself, how do you bring that momentum to a successful conclusion? How do you not let the story spin out of control, or create an ending that closes things down too much, causing the narrative energy to drop off in an unsatisfying way? Ultimately, I decided to end when things are still really on the brink, and with some ambiguity, as opposed to reaching for a more definite resolution. I just did my best to follow the story, line by line, into a place that I hoped was vibrant and true.

There was, however, one thing I did know from the start: I wanted to write about childhood, about growing up. I wanted to capture the unfettered imaginative powers that children tend to possess and, because of their creative prowess, how their meltdowns are often acted out in more interesting fashions than adult freak-outs—which typically just lead to people getting drunk or gambling or having inappropriate sexual encounters. Bo-ring. There's also often a hopefulness in young children that can be very poignant and, in Amelia's case, that hopefulness comes in the belief that she can, at nine years of age, create a plausible means of escape from these nutty adults in her life. Naturally, her parents are at a total loss of what to say or do or think, because, presumably through the process of growing up and dealing with adult disappointments, they've lost their sense of imagination and optimism—though, at the same time, they still somehow manage to be pretty immature. I've read that Marilynne Robinson once called plausibility "purely a matter of aesthetics." I love that quote, and I think it also speaks to the essential difference between Amelia and her parents in "To the Good People of Mars." They have different life aesthetics, if you will, different ideas about what is possible.

Perhaps hanging on to a more elastic sense of plausibility is part of what makes writing so appealing to us grown-ups. While most of the writers I know have "grown up" in the sense that they are gainfully employed, pay their taxes promptly, and do their own laundry, the act of writing, of imaginative creation, preserves the part of ourselves that "adult living" can all too often kill off—the unbridled imagination, the reckless hope. And while some elements of our childhood selves might be prone to getting lost as we tread the path of adulthood and at a certain point we're supposed to put whatever happened in our youth behind us, I'm not at all convinced we, for better or for worse, ever fully extricate ourselves from the people we were as children; rather, I think those people remain fundamental parts of our human fabric. We sculpt and adapt and finesse our childhood selves, but they never really disappear; they just become muted, like shadows, a persistent reminder of our origins. And, of course, this comes up in writing, or at least it does for me. Flannery O'Connor said (I'm paraphrasing) that anyone who survives childhood has plenty to write about. This has always felt true to me, and not because we go through so much in childhood, but because of the ferocity with which those early years linger. The notion of "resolving one's issues," particularly the maladies that date back to the days when we didn't pay taxes or do our own laundry, seems, to me, like an absurd joke. Sure, we can resolve our issues enough so they don't actively interfere with our adult lives, but can we ever really be rid of them? Do we enter the adult world already saddled with unshakable baggage, whether it be satchel-sized or more like a steamer trunk? Fifteen years from now, will Amelia still be hatching elaborate escape plans? I don't know. But, if all goes according to plan, I have plenty of time to find out. And, if I'm lucky, to write it down.

WRITING EXERCISE

Write a story in the first person, aiming for about a thousand to fifteen hundred words, with the following stipulations:

1. Begin only three sentences with "I."
2. Have a single-word sentence.
3. Have one sentence that is a hundred words long (no semicolons).
4. Have one sentence that is twenty-five words long.
5. Have one sentence that is three words long.
6. Use two sentence fragments.
7. Have one sentence that comes in the form of a list.
8. Think about what grammatical configurations you tend to avoid and use them. Dashes, colons, semicolons (except in the hundred-word sentence!), et cetera.

Youth Group

I'm sleeping against the van window when they all start gasping at the sight of the Rockies and wake me up. I squint in the sudden bright afternoon, looking for these mountains, but all I can see is a distant dark bulk. I'm in the last row of seats, crammed against the side of the passenger van because I'm sitting next to Aaron. He's sprawled out like always, legs and giant sneakers spread across our row. And I know sitting anywhere else would be more comfortable but I always sit next to Aaron. In fact, I *have* to sit next to him because I'm in love with him. Though none of us has figured that out yet.

I'm fourteen years old and there are twelve of us in the van—besides Aaron and me, seven other high-school kids and three adult chaperones. This is our church youth group summer trip, and we've almost made it from Missouri to the campsite in Colorado where we'll stay the week. I'm yawning as Aaron notices my nap is finished, and then punches my shoulder. The hit makes my arm feel dead for a few seconds until the throbbing begins—my pulse flaring right where a bruise will emerge tomorrow. "Mountains," he says, pointing to the front of the van.

"Thank you so much." I say it deadpan and rub my arm.

Aaron is a year older than me. He's tall and solid, a sophomore player on our school's varsity football team. He's going to be in the Army so he's always wearing camouflage. The sun reaching into the van lights up the clear bristly hair that covers his chin, arms and legs. He smiles and scratches his shin near the spot where a spider almost killed him. A rare pleasure of mine is asking him to stab this spider scar with a knife; the tissue is so damaged and desiccated that even a blade can't split it open. It's his invincible spot, as though he's Achilles in reverse. I love the story of the spider bite and when I've heard it and watched him press a knife into the scar, I've imagined his hospital stay, the deadly fevers, a doctor's needle squirting antidote into his veins at the very last second. That Aaron, the weak, helpless one, is so different from this one next to me, it's almost as if part of him did die from the spider's bite, leaving an Aaron I can marvel at, and be a little afraid of.

"Here," Gina says from the seat in front of us, handing me her paperback book. "I'm done with chapter six." We're sharing the same novel because I didn't bring one. She reads a couple of chapters, then I catch up. It's a book about married geneticists—the husband is sterile so he and his wife create a test tube baby who mutates into an amazingly intelligent but psychotic toddler; the kid ages too quickly though and eventually tries to murder them. Sex *and* violence. It's the best book I've ever read.

I say thanks, and fan out the pages to find my chapter. Gina is the oldest of us. She'll be a senior in high school this fall. Whenever I'm with her, I somehow feel younger than I actually am. She turns around in her seat and rests her chin on the back of it. "Aaron, come here," she says. He leans his ear close to her mouth, she whispers something, and then he cups his hand around his mouth and whispers something back to her. I watch and strain to hear their secret but everyone is still talking about the stupid mountains. Almost touching her dark straight hair, Aaron's large hand is tightly strung with fleshy wires and knobs; the tiny twitches moving under his skin remind me of a machine, of what I see when I peek under the cover of my piano at home while I'm pressing on the keys.

Miles go by. The nearest huge mountain slowly rises above our van and glares down like a bully. I've tried ignoring their secret but can't. Silently, I elbow Aaron, point to Gina's back and mouth *What?*

He shrugs and says loudly, "Just something about your book. Mind your own business." Gina turns around. She eyes him, then looks at me, looks at him again, and this time, she smiles. He licks his fingertips and wipes them on my face.

★★★

The campsite, for church groups and Christian families, is called "Sermon on the Mount," and it features huge vinyl tents that look like white hay bales, a cafeteria and fellowship center, showers and indoor toilets, picnic tables and a swimming pool. The boys are in one tent with the male chaperones, and the girls are in the one next door. I follow Aaron, the other boys in our group, and our youth leader into the tent where we flump our sleeping bags into a heap on the floor.

After that, all of us stand in the shade between the tents trading dazed expressions. Brad, one of the other boys, sneaks behind Aaron and tries to clamp him in a headlock. Aaron easily tosses him off and then presses him down into some gravel and pine needles. Brad begs for mercy, then mutters he'll get even later. When our youth group goes on trips like this, whether we stay in tents, cabins or hotel rooms, the boys organize epic pillow fights. Sometimes I think pillow fighting is the real reason Aaron is in youth group. He's impossible to knock down and he's strong enough to land his feather pillow on your cheek like a sack of flour. He delivers instant headaches with a single tooth-loosening blow. In previous summers when we've spent weeks at a camp with cabins in the Missouri woods, each night, the bunk beds were stripped and the mattresses were all piled in the middle of the room. All of the boys would sock each other until only one was left standing: Aaron, on the uneven mass of mattresses, the boys with weaker arms and fluffier pillows whimpering at his feet.

Because I weigh about ninety pounds, I'm a watcher of pillow fights instead of an actual fighter—although I am usually pulled into the ring at least once, most often when Aaron grips my ankles and yanks me in for a pummeling. I'm the whipping boy of youth group. It's just so easy for them to hold me upside down or wad me up and shove me in a kitchen cupboard. And, like the bruise that's rising up on my arm from Aaron's punch in the van, there is some pain. But as much as I make a big show when they wring my arms with Indian sunburns or twist wet fingers in my ears, as much as I squeal in protest and flail around, silently and secretly, I do crave the attention—especially Aaron's.

He lets go of Brad just as our guides tromp up the gravel path. Blake and Cindy, fit and muscled, blonde and pink-cheeked, both wearing gold crosses on chains and expensive sunglasses. Their smiles are identical. This week they'll take us white water rafting, rock climbing, rappelling and even hiking—several miles out where we'll pitch tents on a mountain, cook over a fire and drink from a perfectly clear stream. Blake sweeps his arm across the wide sky and points to a short mountain on the other side of the interstate. A glacier slid down its face and dug out the straight scar we see now. Then, a road was cut across the mountain, clearing out a line of pines about two-thirds of the way up. With my eyes, I follow his tanned arm drawing a cross in the air and then I see it carved there into the mountain. "God's mark on God's mountain," he says. Blake tells our circle to join hands for a short prayer before dinner. I knew this was coming so I'm already standing next to Aaron though I pretend some reluctance, putting on my *Can you believe this guy?* look.

Church is just like school—we go because we have to. The worst part is waking up early on Sundays and getting dressed up. Once we get to church, and slide down a pew to sit in the sanctuary, I'm fine because I only have to pretend to listen. I'm free to daydream, to make up stories in my head. As long as I keep my eyes pointed up front, nobody knows how I'm not really getting it when the pastor says *salvation*, *grace* or *sin*—words that sound important but don't mean much. I imagine that for everybody else those words have a physical sensation, a feeling like your belly is full of warm water or the lightheadedness after spinning in one spot over and over, and I guess that because I never feel anything in church or when I pray, I must be doing it wrong. Like now, holding hands with Aaron in the circle of kids, the only thing I feel is his hand. Blake says, "Amen."

Time to eat. As Blake and Cindy lead the group to the cafeteria, I try matching Aaron's huge stride. A few paces ahead of us, Gina turns to another girl, and points at Blake's tiny blue shorts. "He's hot," she whispers.

★★★

The next day, we cram ourselves into wetsuits and go rafting on the Arkansas River. There's a guide in each raft to steer our inflatable vessel with long wooden oars, point out rock formations and tell us when to bail the inches of water pooling at our feet. Almost every stretch of the river has a name—Gunbarrel Rush, the Widowmaker, Sledgehammer Falls, Big Drop. For six hours, the water jerks us down its course and I can't stop thinking how easily my face could be scoured off by each jutting boulder we pass. My wetsuit is three sizes too big, and between dangerous spots on the river, I concentrate on trying to flatten the spongy wrinkles around my middle and crotch. Aaron looks like a superhero in his wetsuit—as dark, hulking and polished as Batman.

When we return to camp that evening, we're all sunburnt and soggy. After I wrench off my wetsuit in a bathroom stall, and change into a T-shirt and shorts, I limp into the big tent and collapse on my sleeping bag. With the late afternoon sun slanting over the mountains, the air is warm and still, and after the daylong turbulence, I don't mind it. One by one, the others climb into the tent, including Aaron, to change clothes and rest before dinner.

His army duffel bag is unzipped next to me. I nod to him as he unlaces his sneakers and brushes sand grit off his feet and shins. I'm lying on my back, my damp hair grinding into my pillow, and I throw my right arm over my face like it's too bright. In the blurry margin of my vision, I see Aaron lift his chin and pull down the zipper of the wetsuit at the root of his neck. The teeth unlock in a long high note like a sigh, and from the noise and movement beside me, I know he's stripped off the suit, and he's down to his camouflage trunks. He steps out of the suit and flings it into a wriggling pile near my feet; drops of water hit my petrified legs. More digging in the duffel bag, then a T-shirt is unfolded and shaken out, snapping like a flag.

My eyes still point at the crossbars holding up the tent's ceiling but they want to peek at Aaron. I want to see him, the hidden parts of his body I've tried so hard never to think about. If I turned my head just a bit, if I only glanced, I could probably catch a quick flash and he wouldn't notice. And if he did notice, couldn't I pass it off as just looking around? My tired eyes wandering without *really* looking? Would it have to mean something?

There's the sudden soft shushing of his swimming trunks as he pushes them down his legs. Now, he's naked beside me, no more than a few feet away. Right there. I'm frozen in fear, afraid of what I want to see, afraid of what I want to do, afraid of what he'll do if I look. In my head, with my eyes staring hard at the black X above me, I try picturing what he looks like, and I can see all the parts of Aaron I've already seen, with a murky gray nothing floating over the rest.

In a few seconds, he's pulled on fresh clothes; it's over. He drops his heavy body to the platform to put on socks and shoes. With his right leg, the spider leg, he reaches over and rubs his bare foot on my face.

"You going to dinner or what?" he says.

"Knock it off," I say, pushing him off, pretending to be crabby.

★★★

We're ready early in the morning for the hike—through a forest and up a mountain to an expanse of grass where we'll spend the night. Blake warns us how tough it's going to be. "It's June," he says. "And today, you're going to touch snow. That's how far we're going." I'm not impressed, I can see the snow from here. We're all strapped down under enormous backpacks, full of gear we have to carry though most of it isn't actually ours. Because I'm so short, my pack stretches over my head and something rough rubs my neck left then right then left again as I waddle under its weight. "You all right?" Aaron asks.

"Oh yeah."

The hike takes all day, and there are several moments when the cramp in my side almost forces me to toss my body down the scrubby flank of the mountain. At one point, Blake doubles back to encourage me; I'm the last of the group, behind all the girls, which isn't necessarily surprising to me but is strange to him. I've already drunk all the water in my canteen. We've gone about a quarter of a mile.

"Hey, big guy," he says. "You've got to pick it up if we want to reach the peak by dark." I want to say something but I've lost the ability so I just nod and squeeze my cramp and continue daydreaming that I'm not really there.

When we reach the grassy flatness that will be our campsite, we pitch our tents and then gather in a circle around Blake as he bows his head and thanks God for our safe journey and for this majesty. But the view is so gorgeous it's fake, as if we're standing in front of giant postcards. Wide sky, thick pines, the snowy peak reaching up and sparkling, an actual babbling brook—I recognize the beauty but that doesn't mean I feel anything. With Blake's hushed voice praying, his words droning like a hum, I can't keep my eyes on anything besides Aaron's sweaty forearms. And when I look, there is real feeling—something physical that runs through me with a sudden thrill like fear.

At the moment, I don't know what staring at Aaron really means. I've tricked myself into thinking that I like looking at his body because mine is so small and shapeless, as if this is Mrs. Kline's second-hour biology class and Aaron is one of the rubbery frog specimens we have to examine and touch and report on precisely. At the moment, I've also never kissed anyone and don't really understand what kissing is, or what you do with your body once you start kissing someone. So I don't think about that either when I stare at him. I don't think about what his body could do to mine. What I do think about is all the strength working inside him, the force when he collides with players on the football field, how this hike was nothing for him, not even hard. And sometimes I do wonder what it would be like to take on that force, to be crushed by him and squeezed from the inside out—like the cramp in my side except over my whole body.

After the prayer, Blake says it's time to keep hiking to that snowy peak, and he points to it looming above the trees. General excitement among the group—the tying of shoes, the chewing of GORP, the rubbing of sunscreen on noses. I nudge Aaron's arm. "He really thinks we want to hike again?" I ask, smirking.

"I'm going," he says. "But you probably don't have to go if you don't want to." He rolls his sleeves over the humps of each shoulder.

"Aaron," Gina shouts. She's standing with Blake. She says, "Let's go," and he heads after her.

For a second or two I consider following him, but decide instead to throw myself across a boulder, to just lie in the sun and pout.

An hour later, I shake out of a daze when I hear distant laughter, screams. I open my eyes and squint at the mountain peak. They made it. The group stands at the edge of the snow, straddling the line between white and green, cupping out snowballs, propping their flat hands over their eyes to look at everything below. Blake points at things. They nod. And then I see Aaron, charging through the snow in his shorts, Gina on him, piggyback. Her arms are locked around his neck, they're both squealing and laughing in the sun.

That night, after the campfire dinner, after tiptoeing in the crickety darkness to pee, I sleep in a small three-person tent with Aaron and Brad. Between Aaron and Brad. They each unroll their sleeping bags along the tent's sides so I'm in the middle. Which is scarier than white water rafting, scarier even than hanging from my fingertips off the smooth face of a rock when we went climbing. Because it's exactly what I wanted and now I don't want it. I'm scared most of the defenselessness of sleep, of this pull towards Aaron forcing me to reach out to him in the night or say something weird in a dream. As we settle down on the tent floor, bodies stuffed and sweating against the flannel linings of sleeping bags, I lie stiff and pray that I won't accidentally touch Aaron.

With the steady wind outside rippling the fabric walls, and Aaron and Brad breathing low and slow on either side of me, I feel like I'm sealed inside a lung. Lying on my side, I can't stop listening to the eerie quiet, all the sounds I don't normally notice, like my heartbeat tapping on my eardrums or my eyelashes scraping my pillow as I blink in the dark. But then I have to flip over so I'm on my back; I can't sleep facing him because what if he wakes up? What if these feelings are visible on my face like pillowmarks? As I wriggle around, my shoulder brushes his but he doesn't stir.

So there are only inches between us. Our shoulders—mine white and thin with the dark smudge of a new bruise, his firm and knotted. I imagine my shoulder reaching out like a fingertip to touch his, just pressing against it and staying there. Listening to the mountain, I fall asleep while pushing my finger against my bruise, and each time there's comfort in the certainty of the pain.

★★★

We return to "Sermon on the Mount" the next day, our last one before going home. We wander around with zombie faces, all of us dazzled by the exhaustion of walking up and down mountains. It's the part of the trip where we're getting sick of each other—when I can guess what someone will say before they say it. Even Aaron starts bugging me. Something about how he won't stay in one spot and how I keep losing track of him.

Later on, we say goodnight to the adults and hang out in the swimming pool under the too-bright stars with the mountains huddled around us. I'm wearing my T-shirt in the water. We splash each other. When that gets boring, we try some stunts—Brad attempts some tricky dives, cannonballs, belly flops. Gina suggests trying to stand and balance on Aaron's shoulders. And of course, she goes first. He hoists her up and grips her ankles as she wiggles with her arms straight out to either side. Pitching back, she collapses into the pool and comes up spurting water and laughing. They try again and again, and she keeps falling.

"Let Ryan try," someone says. Maybe it will be easier for Aaron to hoist me, instead of her. I *am* the smallest one. In slow motion through the water, I walk to him, and he crouches down, neck-deep in the pool. I steady myself with my hands on his slippery back and then press my feet into the rubbery divots of muscle in his shoulders. He counts, one two three, and then pushes us up and out of the water. Once he's braced, I stand too, balancing perfectly.

As we stand above the water, I fight the urge to pull on my clinging T-shirt. My shirtsleeve is hiked up, I know that Aaron's bruise is probably showing, I don't want anyone to see it—they're all looking up at us with hushed faces. But to fix it might set us off-balance, might force me to wiggle too much and fall, splayed onto Aaron. Everything sits still for several seconds. But before I can move, Aaron tips himself forward while holding my feet, and his weight pulls me toward the pool.

We crash into the surface. I twist under the water, and his hands surround my shoulders and push down. I can't open my eyes because I can't stand the chlorine so there's only the dark and the swoosh of legs thrashing and bubbles tickling my face. My arms stretch out for something, and as Aaron holds me under, one of my hands presses full against the warmth of his chest while the other wraps around his hard arm. His body feels like the slick stones we lifted from the river when we rafted. I brace myself against him and we float for a second or two with me feeling the sensation of feeling him. Suddenly he wrenches me up, back to the air. When I open my eyes, he's several feet ahead of me, swimming away.

He joins the rest of them in the shallow end, sitting on the stairs submerged at the entrance of the pool. I swim to them too, and we lounge in the warm water under the floodlights on telephone poles, while hunched over in the distance the outline of the mountains is almost as dark as the sky. Everyone is talking about penises.

Gina can't imagine what it's like to have one, so she's asking. What does it feel like to be kicked there? In the morning, why do guys always wake up with erections? Aaron and Brad and the other boys laugh and joke and answer. Gina's swimsuit is yellow and black plaid, and it looks like it doesn't fit her, as if it's too tight around her breasts, which she covers by crossing her arms in front of them. I'm staying

quiet, grinning and smirking according to how the other boys react to
Gina. She stands with her back against the turquoise tiles of the pool
wall, stroking her fingers across the top of the water; the other girls beside her are quiet too, and continuously shifting—adjusting swimsuit
straps, fixing ponytails.

What about sex, she asks. "Why do some guys finish before you
even get started?" she says, coyly. This silences the other boys. Brad
says, "Oh my God," and Aaron says, "Wow." Gina smiles again. "I'm
just asking. I'm just asking. Why can't I ask that question?"

Brad starts to answer. Then blushes. Then continues and gets embarrassed again. Aaron takes over. "Sometimes you're just too, you
know, excited? You just can't stop." His shoulders shrug. His big
beautiful wet shoulders.

"What are blue balls?" Gina asks. "They don't really turn blue, do
they?"

"No," Aaron snorts.

"So what are they then?" she presses.

"They just hurt," he says, his eyes focusing on hers, like they're
opponents in a staring contest. "You get them when you're hard for a
long time without—"

"Oh," she says. "So what hurts?"

"Your *balls*," Aaron says, grinning again.

"But why does it hurt?" she asks, skeptically.

I decide to answer this one. "It just hurts because you're excited,
and then it's over, and you're like 'okay, what now?'" I stand with my
arms up, palms to the sky, in the cartoon pose of a question. I know
the answer because I remember it from health class. It's something
about blood flow—who doesn't know that? Everyone in the pool
nods, waiting for the next question. Gina quickly turns to face me.

"And how would *you* know?" she says. Her forehead crinkles in
disbelief, and she shakes her head and snickers. I feel a sting in her look
and her words—how she knows I've never had sex because she knows
why. Brad starts laughing, and he flicks his hand against the water and
splashes me. The girls laugh, and the other boys laugh, and then Aaron

laughs. I stand there, heat rushing up and drying out my throat like I'm on the mountain hike again.

I thought we were all just pretending, I didn't think any of the kids in the pool have actually had sex. In youth group, we talk about waiting for marriage, about love and men and women, and most often, about temptation. And because I never feel tempted by girls, I assume not giving in is easy for everybody else. I don't know yet that my desires live inside a tiny spot too tough to open. In the pool, under the white lights, even though my face is pink, I laugh too. I splash Brad back and keep laughing because I want it all to be a joke.

★★★

Somehow, since the last time we drove over it a week ago, Kansas has stretched out three or four times its actual size. In my seat, my body begins to feel stunted, like I'm compressing myself by being stuck in here. The sun shines in on our faces and arms but our legs are freezing from the full-blast AC. I'm sitting next to Aaron who is sitting next to Gina. A long flannel blanket that's covered in potato chip crumbs is pulled over all three of us.

Gina finishes our novel. "Here," she says, reaching over Aaron and thrusting it into my hands. "The ending is stupid. You don't have to read it if you don't want to." Thanks, I say, and flip to the third-to-last chapter where I left off. I don't see how it could end badly when everything that's come before has been so good. Aaron is sleeping, mouth wide open, and now Gina yanks on the blanket to cover her chest and arms and she tilts her head back and closes her eyes too.

The bump bump bump of the tires on the highway, the whine of the stereo, the soft murmur of conversations. I try to stay focused on the killer test-tube toddler, but I can't stop yawning and my eyes close suddenly, like the darkness is something I need. Quickly, I enter a dream. In an hour, I wake up when someone shouts that we're about to cross from Kansas into Missouri. I bend my stiff neck, pop my knuckles and look around in the sun-flooded van. Aaron still sits beside me, now staring at the road ahead of us like he's got to know exactly where he's going. I'm lucky enough to have skipped about eighty flat Kansas miles and I stretch, smiling as I yawn again.

What I've also skipped, what I won't know until about a year later, is what happened under the blanket while I was sleeping. I'll be in our high school's library with my English class, all of us supposed to be researching our term papers. Mine is on whale poaching. And because my teacher is down the hall smoking in the janitor's closet, when I see Aaron for the first time in a long time, he'll sit down at my table. It will be a long time because neither of us will go to youth group anymore. We'll talk in whispers about what's been going on and then we'll talk about this trip. And he'll tell me that when I slept beside him in the van, Gina pretended to sleep too, but crept her hand under the blanket and slid it into his shorts. And the night before, the night all of us stood in the swimming pool and talked about blue balls, after everyone else went to sleep, Aaron and Gina had sex. And as he leans in close to whisper the details—how they searched for a wide enough shadow, how she laid her beach towel over gravel and pulled him down—I'll finally understand I feel something real for Aaron, some kind of love, because I'll feel betrayed. But I'll confuse the feeling with disappointment, thinking they shouldn't have given into temptation, not during youth group, not at a religious campsite, not ever, because they didn't even like each other, not really, but most of all, because it's a *sin*, a word that also finally feels real. And I'll hate Gina for it, for making him do it, and for what she said in the pool, confusing that feeling too because it won't be hatred I feel for her—it will be jealousy.

Before we left Colorado to drive home, I decided to start collecting rocks. It seemed like something I should want to do, especially with so many rocks around, and I was immediately thrilled by my new hobby. I couldn't find anybody to walk around with so I set off alone, searching the campsite for something worth keeping forever. I didn't know exactly what kind of rock I was looking for—craggy, fossilized, smooth, or the kind where shapes emerge if you stare long enough and then suddenly recognize a lumpy apple, a man's fist, a curled fish. Near the bottom of the slope that reached up to the interstate, I found one. About as big as my head, this rock must've weighed nearly ten pounds. I had trouble holding it with one hand, but as I turned it in the sun, and looked at its weird streaks of rust and yellow and glittery black, I somehow knew this was what I wanted. Even wrapped up in T-shirts, the rock felt no less heavy, and I was barely able to heave my duffel bag into the van when it was time to go.

Now, barefoot on our church parking lot in Missouri, I stand at the back of the van with the rest of the group. The thought of leaving them, all of us going to separate houses and families is awful; I've been sick of everybody but now I want to know what they're doing tonight. Aaron stands at the van doors and starts pulling apart the great mass of our luggage. He grips each suitcase from the pile, and swings it down to its weary owner. Mine's on the bottom. I watch him and know it will be days before I'll see him again—probably not until youth group next week. When he finally hands me my bag, and the weight of it tugs at my arm, I can't believe how much I struggle to carry something he doesn't even notice.

Inside "Youth Group": Surrendering to Memory

Among those who know me well, I've got a reputation for a good memory. "Good" is how we describe a memory that's accurate, and also miserly—which is to say, a memory that saves everything for a long time; though I'm not convinced a memory that works this way is necessarily always a good one. These friends of mine often depend on my good memory to verify dates or timelines of certain events. And when I go riffling, seeking their answers, I can't help but watch whole scenes pop up, and I always end up retrieving many more details than I expected to find. Weather, the song that was playing in the background, somebody's exact words and outfits. "That was in January," I'll say. "And I was wearing my maroon sweater."

Wondering about how the memory decides what to save seems a natural enough concern for a creative nonfiction writer. Especially because crowded in there beside all those timelines and sweaters are hundreds of small moments that don't seem worth keeping. Like a scene of blowing out candles. I am seven or eight, and Father's Day falls on my birthday, so the cake is for both my dad and me. And standing on the cake for Dad is a plastic figurine of a golfer. The tiny man's polo shirt is blue, he is reared back in a grand swing, his thin plastic club is cocked over his shoulder and tilts down. My mom lights the candles, they sing and I listen, watching the small flames shiver in the room's breath. As I suck in my deepest gulp of air, one of the candles catches the golfer's club—instantly, it seems, the stick blackens and curls, and a nearly invisible fire spreads over the man's arms, shoulders and face. All his color melts to white, all his features disappear. I am mesmerized until I remember to let go of my breath, and finally, I put the golfer out of his misery.

Other than maybe the fiery spectacle and the grotesque transformation of the plastic guy, there's nothing special about that memory. That's all there is. But it's as vivid and close as any so-called important memories, even if I have no idea why it's still there.

"Youth Group" began with a memory like that charred, faceless golfer. The scene in the pool, with Gina's barbed question—and all it implied—had always been utterly clear in my memory, probably because it was so cutting. But I was never sure why that small moment felt so monumental, or why it had always been the quickest of shortcuts to the larger experience of the trip, and then to those not-very-hidden feelings for Aaron. So I decided to write about that moment, if only just to figure it out. But I had to back up first, and work my slow way to it.

In my earliest drafts, I avoided digging too deeply into the religious and spiritual aspect of the piece because I was afraid of it. I suppose it felt too large, as though it might crush the smaller, softer story of my hopeless adolescent crush, which was what I thought I was writing about. Later, I saw that what I was sidestepping was the most essential part of understanding the experience. More than that, it was *the* reason for writing. Even so, in those earliest drafts, by never explicitly addressing those themes of belief or faith, I accidentally dramatized (our old favorite lesson of *show, don't tell*) how my adolescent self fell into the comfort of religious language without understanding why it was comfortable. Through writing—and probably because I didn't know I was doing it—I realized what I hope the piece now demonstrates, drafts and drafts later: that those initially hollow-feeling concepts of sin and faith were comfortable because putting into language what was *really* bothering me was impossible.

So the piece wasn't ever about the pool, but the pool was still the turning point. In revision, what stuck out to me about the pool scene was the water thing—being pulled down and wrenched back up— and all of the obvious religious symbolism. And as I went through my rough pages, I saw that references to and questions about belief and faith were suggested on nearly every one—even if I had tried steering clear. When you're finding metaphorical potential in your descriptions of real events, or when it's somehow made it to the page without your planning it, then you know you're onto something. An early reader pointed out that "mountain" is probably in every paragraph. Which made sense because we were in Colorado, *in* the mountains. But this reader also suggested that as she read, she felt as though the mountains—giants always standing around, looking down on all the action—began to represent the giant issues looming over my narrator. I took credit for this, of course, and even tried to use "mountain" a few more times. (In fact, "Aaron," which is not this guy's real name, means "mountain of strength" in Hebrew, and *that* I did on purpose.)

What I'm taking too long to say, and certainly not for the first time, is that it seems only when I surrender to the memories of an experience does any real writing happen. By *surrender*, I mean not worrying about what the memory adds up to, but just writing it—doing my best to use words to make the memory as vivid on paper as it is in my head. If I had sat down trying to make mountains stand in for adolescent sexual anxieties, I would still be waiting for the first sentence. I learned to trust myself with this piece—but to trust not just my memory, but also my imagination. We don't know why some images stick in our memories or why they are important, so allowing the imagination to make stories of those strange moments can help us get closer to the truth. I'll even admit that it's often hard to distinguish between the images handed over by memory and the ones suggested by imagination, and especially with nonfiction like "Youth Group," when I'm not sure what I'm writing about when I'm writing, I don't bother much with the difference.

Sometimes people tell me my creative nonfiction "reads like a short story," and that might be my favorite compliment. I suppose I'm drawn to the contained intensity of a short story—lots of energy in a small space. But nonfiction still needs something else besides action and tension and characters. In some way, the writer has to include his thinking on the page, the story of thought, as it's called, that runs along the story of the experience. So once I figured out what "Youth Group" was about, I needed to go back into those scenes and layer in the story of how I came to understand the experience within the experience itself. And that's the trickiest part, at least personally—making the reflection essential without it getting in the way. But I didn't make up anything. In fact, there were actual details from the trip I purposely left out because they were so metaphorically perfect, they actually became implausible. While I'm interested in how creative nonfiction deals with the complication of the truth seeming *too* true, it also felt too risky to make readers skeptical. So I cut out those details.

I think what I love most about creative nonfiction is that as much control as I think I have over the words lining up in neat rows on my pages, or as much as I read and study the work of my heroes, there's always something else going on. (This is certainly true for other genres.) I guess I enjoy thinking that my imagination is smarter than my memory, and that it's my imagination's job to make a good story from my memory's truth—to make, finally, a story that feels so vivid but also so true that the reader can recognize and share it.

WRITING EXERCISE

There's an illegal method of catching fish called "snag fishing." You take a length of weighted fishing line with a lot of hooks tied up and down it, secure it to a speedboat and sink it in the water. Then you drive your boat like hell, snagging whatever gets in the way. I have never done this, nor do I want to. Snag fishing is certainly barbaric—which is why it's against the law—but in concept, it's how I visualize a certain strategy of freewriting, one I use either for starting new projects or for working on drafts that need more development.

Without worrying about what it might mean, or where it might go, select from your memory a particularly poignant image or moment. In list form, and as rapidly as possible, write down every single tidbit that comes to mind about your selection. Put yourself back in that moment and get down the sensory details, as well as what you're doing and why, and the spoken words you can remember hearing; with the other people involved, also think about their posture, gestures, appearance, etc. But don't forget easy stuff like time of day and year, your age, basic details of place. (Sometimes writing out the easiest, most obvious detail will trigger the more elusive one.)

When you have a solid list—say, a page—take the items one by one, and try to render each as vividly as possible. Write quickly, not paying attention to language, but instead to precision. Always keep pushing yourself to write one more sentence. If you ever feel stuck in your description, ask, "How did I feel about _____ at the time?" (How you feel about it *now* will probably be close to the core of any eventual essay.) Most important, if you feel yourself drifting into imagined territory—a detail that doesn't adhere to the strictest truth—don't worry. As long as it feels *possible*, write it down. Allowing imaginative freedom is the essential part—even in nonfiction writing. (Ethical questions are a revision-stage issue.) Don't be concerned about transitioning from one item to the next, either. Just develop each one into a paragraph or so, skip a couple lines, and start on the next.

The idea here is to pit your imagination against your memory—to force yourself into the shadowy places your memory can't reach, to bump into things and snatch hold. Once you've stretched the material out as much as possible, read over it looking for story or, at least, for movement. What is the emotional problem suggested by your details? What patterns do you see? What metaphorical connections? You probably won't end up using most of the material you've generated. It's still worth the endeavor if you pull up a few good pieces because a couple of the pieces will probably speak to each other in some way. So get rid of the rest, and shove those together to see what happens. Then keep filling in as your imagination and/or memory suggests new ideas. Whatever develops, keep going without stopping, and without thinking too much.

About the Contributors

STEVE ALMOND is the author of two story collections, *My Life in Heavy Metal* and *The Evil B.B. Chow*, the novel *Which Brings Me to You* (with Julianna Baggott), and the nonfiction book *Candyfreak*. His new book is a collection of essays, *(Not That You Asked)*. He lives outside Boston with his wife and daughter Josephine, who can now make the noises of seven different farm animals. His online home is www.stevenalmond.com.

AIMEE BENDER is the author of three books: *The Girl in the Flammable Skirt*, *An Invisible Sign of My Own*, and *Willful Creatures*. Her short fiction has been published in *Granta*, *Harper's*, *Tin House*, *The Paris Review*, and more, as well as heard on *This American Life*. She lives in Los Angeles.

KATE BERNHEIMER is the author of two novels, *The Complete Tales of Ketzia Gold* and *The Complete Tales of Merry Gold*. She has published a children's book called *The Girl in The Castle Inside The Museum* and has edited two anthologies, *Mirror, Mirror on the Wall: Women Writers Explore Their Favorite Fairy Tales* and *Brothers and Beasts: An Anthology of Men on Fairy Tales*. She edits the journal *Fairy Tale Review* and teaches in the MFA program at the University of Alabama.

RYAN BOUDINOT is the author of the collection *The Littlest Hitler* and a novel forthcoming in the fall of 2009 from Grove Press. He teaches at

Goddard College's MFA program in Port Townsend, Washington, and lives in Seattle.

JUDY BUDNITZ is the author of two story collections, *Flying Leap* and *Nice Big American Baby*, and a novel, *If I Told You Once*. Her stories have appeared in *Harper's, The New Yorker, The Paris Review, McSweeney's, Prize Stories 2000: The O. Henry Awards*, and elsewhere. She has received grants from the NEA and the Lannan Foundation, and has taught creative writing at Brown, Columbia, and Princeton.

DAN CHAON is the author of the novel *You Remind Me of Me*, a national bestseller, as well as two collections of short stories: *Fitting Ends* and *Among the Missing*, which was a finalist for the 2001 National Book Award. A new novel, *Sleepwalk*, is forthcoming in 2009. Chaon's stories have appeared in many journals and anthologies, including *Best American Short Stories, The Pushcart Prize* anthology, and *Prize Stories: The O. Henry Awards*. He lives in Cleveland and teaches at Oberlin College.

BROCK CLARKE is the author of two novels, *An Arsonist's Guide to Writers' Homes in New England* and *The Ordinary White Boy*, and two short story collections, *Carrying the Torch* and *What We Won't Do*. He has twice been a finalist for the National Magazine Award in Fiction. His fiction and essays have appeared in *The Virginia Quarterly Review, The Believer, One Story, The Southern Review, Georgia Review, The New York Times*, and *New England Review*; in *The Pushcart Prize* and *New Stories From the South* annual anthologies; and on NPR's *Selected Shorts*. He is a 2008 NEA Fellow in Fiction and teaches at the University of Cincinnati.

MICHAEL CZYZNIEJEWSKI grew up in and around Chicago. He received a BA from the University of Illinois and an MFA from Bowling Green State University, where he currently teaches and serves as editor-in-chief of *Mid-American Review*. More than fifty of his stories have appeared in a variety of publications, including *The Southern Review, StoryQuarterly, American Short Fiction*, and *The Pushcart Prize XXXI: Best of the Small Presses*. His debut collection, *Elephants in Our Bedroom*, appeared earlier this year from Dzanc Books. He lives in Bowling Green with his wife and son.

STUART DYBEK is the author of three books of fiction: *I Sailed With Magellan*, *The Coast of Chicago*, and *Childhood and Other Neighborhoods*. Both *I Sailed With Magellan* and *The Coast of Chicago* were New York Times Notable Books, and *The Coast of Chicago* was a One Book One Chicago selection. His fiction, poetry, and nonfiction have appeared in *The New Yorker*, *Harper's*, *The Atlantic*, *Poetry*, *Tin House*, and many other magazines, and have been widely anthologized, including work in both *Best American Fiction* and *Best American Poetry*. Among Dybek's numerous awards are a MacArthur Prize, a Rea Award, a PEN/Malamud Award, a Lannan Award, a Whiting Writers Award, an Award from the Academy of Arts and Letters, several O. Henry Prizes, a Nelson Algren Prize, and fellowships from the NEA and the Guggenheim Foundation. He is Distinguished Writer in Residence at Northwestern University and a member of the permanent faculty for Western Michigan University's Prague Summer Program.

MICHAEL MARTONE was born in Fort Wayne, Indiana, where he learned, at a very early age, about flight. His mother, a high-school English teacher, read to him of the adventures of Daedalus and Icarus from the book *Mythology* written by Edith Hamilton, who was born in Dresden, Germany, but who also grew up in Fort Wayne, Indiana. Martone remembers being taken by his father to Baer Field, the commercial airport and Air National Guard base, to watch the air traffic there. He was blown backward on the observation deck by the prop-wash of the four-engine, aluminum-skinned Lockheed Constellation with its elegant three-tailed rudder turning away from the gates and the jungle-camouflaged Phantom F-4s doing touch and goes, the ignition of their after-burners sounding as if the sky was being torn like blue silk. As a child growing up in Fort Wayne, Indiana, Martone heard many stories about Art Smith, the Bird Boy of Fort Wayne, and his adventures as an early aviation pioneer. In the air above the city, Martone imagined the Bird Boy of Fort Wayne accomplishing for the first time the nearly impossible outside loop and then a barrel roll back into a loop-to-loop in his fragile cotton canvas and baling wire flying machine he built in his own backyard in Fort Wayne, Indiana, whose sky above was the first sky anywhere to be written on, written on by Art Smith, the Bird Boy of Fort Wayne, the letters hanging there long enough to be read but then smeared, erased by the high altitude wind, turning into a dissipating front of fogged memories.

ANTONYA NELSON is the author of nine books of fiction, including *Nothing Right* (Bloomsbury, 2009). She teaches creative writing at the University of Houston and is married to fiction writer Robert Boswell.

PETER ORNER was born in Chicago and is the author of the novel *The Second Coming of Mavala Shikongo* (Little, Brown, 2006) and the story collection *Esther Stories* (Houghton Mifflin, 2001). His fiction has been published in *The Atlantic*, *The Paris Review*, *McSweeney's*, *The Southern Review*, and various other publications.

JACK PENDARVIS has written two books of short stories and a novel, the latter of which is titled *Awesome*.

BENJAMIN PERCY is the author of a novel, *The Wilding* (Graywolf, 2009), and two books of short stories, *Refresh, Refresh* (Graywolf, 2007) and *The Language of Elk* (Carnegie Mellon, 2006). His fiction and nonfiction appear in *Esquire*, *Men's Journal*, *The Paris Review*, *Chicago Tribune*, *Glimmer Train Stories*, and *Best American Short Stories*, among other publications. His honors include a Pushcart Prize and a Plimpton Prize. He teaches in the MFA program at Iowa State University.

ANDREW PORTER is the author of the short story collection *The Theory of Light and Matter*, which won the Flannery O'Connor Award for Short Fiction. A graduate of the Iowa Writers' Workshop, he is the recipient of fellowships from the James Michener/Copernicus Society of America and the W.K. Rose Foundation. His fiction has appeared in *One Story*, *Epoch*, and *The Pushcart Prize* anthology, and on NPR's *Selected Shorts*. Currently, he teaches at Trinity University in San Antonio.

CHAD SIMPSON lives in Galesburg, Illinois, where he teaches fiction writing and literature classes at Knox College. His stories have appeared in several magazines, including *McSweeney's*, *Sycamore Review*, *The Rambler*, and *The Sun*, and has received awards from the Illinois Arts Council, *The Atlantic*, and the Sewanee and Bread Loaf writers' conferences.

GEORGE SINGLETON has published four story collections, including *The Half-Mammals of Dixie*, and two novels, *Novel* and *Work Shirts for Madmen*. His stories have appeared in *The Atlantic*, *Harper's*, *Playboy*, *Zoetrope*, and *The Georgia Review*, among other journals and magazines. He has published one book of writing advice, of sorts, titled *Pep Talks, Warnings & Screeds*.

BRADY UDALL received his MFA from the Iowa Writers' Workshop. His widely anthologized stories and nonfiction have been published in journals and magazines such as *Esquire*, *Gentleman's Quarterly*, and *The Paris Review*. He is the author of a short story collection, *Letting Loose the Hounds*, and a novel, *The Miracle Life of Edgar Mint*, which was an international bestseller and has been translated into twenty languages.

LAURA VAN DEN BERG recently completed her MFA at Emerson College. Her stories have or will soon appear in *One Story*, *StoryQuarterly*, *The Literary Review*, *American Short Fiction*, and *Best American Nonrequired Reading 2008*, among others, and has received awards from *Glimmer Train Stories*, the Bread Loaf Writers' Conference, and Press 53. The recipient of the 2007 Dzanc Prize, her first collection of stories, *What the World Will Look Like When All the Water Leaves Us*, will be published by Dzanc Books in 2009.

RYAN VAN METER's work has been published in *The Gettysburg Review*, *Indiana Review*, *The Iowa Review*, *Colorado Review*, *River Teeth*, and *Quarterly West*, among others. An essay of his was also selected for *Touchstone Anthology of Contemporary Creative Nonfiction: Work from 1970 to Present*. He is an MFA candidate in the Nonfiction Writing Program at the University of Iowa.

Index

Credits

ABOUT THE AUTHOR

B.J. Hollars of Fort Wayne, Indiana, is an MFA candidate at the University of Alabama, where he has served as non-fiction editor and assistant fiction editor for *Black Warrior Review*. His stories have appeared in *Mid-American Review, Fugue, Backwards City Review, Hobart, Memorious,* and *Bellingham Review*, among others. He lives in a small home in Alabama with his wife and his dog and their books.

WRITER'S DIGEST BOOKS

MORE GREAT RESOURCES FROM WRITER'S DIGEST BOOKS

Pep Talks, Warnings & Screeds

Indispensable Wisdom and Cautionary Advice for Writers

Toddlers—and drunks—bang around hitting walls, tables, chairs, the floor, and other people, trying to find their legs. Writing fiction is a similar process, learning to find your legs and doing your best to convince onlookers that you know what you're doing and where you're going. Acclaimed Southern story writer and novelist George Singleton serves up everything you ever need to know to become a real writer (meaning one who actually *writes*) in these laugh-out-loud funny, candid, and surprisingly useful lessons. With original illustrations by novelist Daniel Wallace.

ISBN-13 978-1-58297-565-8, hardcover, 224 pages, #Z2677

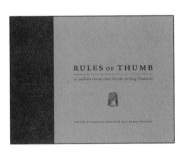

Rules of Thumb

71 Authors Reveal Their Fiction Writing Fixations

Whether it's the simplest of prohibitions (don't use too many adjectives), or a cherished writing maxim (show, don't tell), all writers have a rule of thumb that guides their work. In this book, award-winning author and teacher Michael Martone collects the best advice and pet peeves of more than 70 contemporary writers.

ISBN-13: 978-1-58297-391-3, hardcover, 256 pages, #11015

The 4 A.M. Breakthrough

Unconventional Writing Exercises That Transform Your Fiction

Writers have long turned to exercises for help with beginning—be it a new piece of fiction, a daily routine or a serious writing life. In this sequel to *The 3 A.M. Epiphany*, award-winning author and professor Brian Kiteley presents you with another 200 stimulating exercises, designed to help you expand your understanding of the problems and processes of more complex, satisfying fiction and to challenge you to produce works of which you never thought yourself capable.

ISBN-13 978-1-58297-563-4, paperback, 288 pages, #Z2615

Writing Life Stories, 2nd Edition

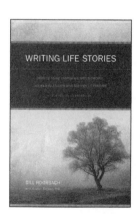

How to Make Memories Into Memoirs, Ideas Into Essays, and Life Into Literature

Whether you're creating a memoir or a personal essay, writing about your own life can be a daunting task: How much do you remember? What's important to include in your story? What about truth and artistic license? How do you even get started mining a life's worth of experience? In this fully revised and updated second edition, award-winning author and teacher Bill Roorbach offers innovative techniques for all writers of creative nonfiction that teach you to see your life more clearly and show you why real stories are often the most compelling ones.

ISBN-13: 978-1-58297-527-6, paperback, 304 pages, #Z1941

Fiction Writer's Workshop

Second Edition

The great paradox of the writing life is that to be a good writer, you must be both interested in the world around you and comfortable working in solitude for hours on end. This book is designed to help you foster a strong sense of independence—of being and thinking on your own, of becoming self-evaluative without being self-critical—in order to accomplish what others seek in classroom groups. Award-winning writer and teacher Josip Novakovich explores every aspect of the art of fiction and provides all the tools and techniques you'll need to develop day-to-day discipline as well as a personal writing style.

ISBN-13: 978-1-58297-536-8, paperback, 336 pages, #Z2054

The Mind of Your Story

Discover What Drives Your Fiction

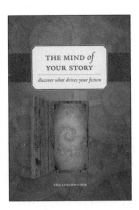

How do you create a successful story that captures readers from its first page and never lets them go until the final page is turned? The secret is a delicate balancing act between allowing a story a mind of its own and holding tightly to its reins. Combining practical advice with down-to-earth candor, award-winning novelist Lisa Lenard-Cook illuminates the often-elusive elements of fiction and helps you turn your creative obsessions into that mysterious yet undeniable connection with readers.

ISBN-13: 978-1-58297-488-0, hardcover, 272 pages, #Z0791